Roger Hood
and Richard Sparks

Key Issues
in Criminology

World University Library

McGraw-Hill Book Company
New York Toronto

Roger Hood and Richard Sparks 1970
Library of Congress Catalog Card Number: 77-90231

Photoset by BAS Printers Limited, Wallop, Hampshire, England
Manufactured by LIBREX, Italy

Contents

Introduction

This book is not intended as a textbook, in the usual sense. We hope that it will be found useful by students taking university courses in criminology, as well as by the general reader and by persons involved in the administration of criminal justice and the treatment of offenders throughout the world. But it is not intended to provide a comprehensive treatment of the subject, and is no substitute – for the student's purposes – for a book that does. Instead, we have concentrated on eight specific problems in the field of criminology: we have tried to summarise the worthwhile research which has been done to date on these problems, to draw such conclusions as can reasonably be drawn from that research, and to indicate the main questions concerning each topic which, in our opinion, future research must try to answer. Thus the range of subjects covered by the book is much narrower than that of a textbook; at the same time, we have aimed to provide a much more detailed discussion of our chosen subjects than is found in most textbooks.

The eight 'key issues' dealt with in the book are as follows. The first two chapters review the extensive evidence from two different types of research carried out in the past few years, which make use of recently developed techniques to study the problem of the so-called 'dark figure' of unrecorded crime. Chapter 1 deals with attempts to estimate the amount of this 'hidden' delinquency through victim surveys. In chapter 2 we consider the evidence from 'self-report' studies, in which persons are asked about offences which they have committed, whether or not these have resulted in arrest or conviction. These studies make it possible to compare the characteristics of all offenders with the minority who become known to the police, or appear in court. In addition we review the growing literature on the way the police use their discretion in deciding whether or not to prosecute offenders. Both these types of study shed light on the processes whereby some people are 'labelled' delinquent whereas others who have committed similar acts are not. Chapter 3 deals with the criminological issue which has undoubtedly received the most attention from sociologists in the past twenty years: the delinquent subculture. There has been a lot of theoretical controversy about the nature of one form of delinquent subculture, the adolescent gang; and after reviewing the main theories which have been advanced, we consider the empirical research which has been done on gang delinquency, to see how well the theories fit it. In chapter 4 we discuss the problems of classifying offences and offenders for the purpose of research on the causes of crime. Most criminologists are now agreed that it is unprofitable to search for a single theory which will explain all crime, delinquency or deviant behaviour. Many offender typologies and ways of classifying crimes have been suggested; we consider the merits of several of these, and the requirements of a good typology for research purposes. It will be noted that this is an especially weak area of criminological enquiry. Indeed, our review led us finally to doubt the value of most of the theoretical and empirical work in this field.

Chapter 5 deals with the decision-making process in sentencing. This is a subject which has so far received comparatively little attention from criminologists, in part (or so we argue) because the model on which research to date has been based is inadequate. We suggest a new approach to this problem, which we believe takes into account all the factors which may influence the judicial activity of sentencing. The next two chapters are devoted to research on the effectiveness of punishments and treatments. Chapter 6 summarises the evidence from many studies of the after-conduct of offenders who have been dealt with by different penal measures. The problem of offender typologies recurs in chapter 7, in which we discuss the possibility of interaction between type of treatment and type of offender: that is, the possibility that measures which are effective in preventing the recidivism of one type of offender may have just the opposite effect with another type. Finally, in chapter 8 we consider research which has been done on the sociology of the prison, and on the impact of imprisonment on the attitudes, values and behaviour of offenders of different types.

A word of explanation is needed about our choice of these eight criminological issues. What do these problems have in common, and what justifies our calling them 'key issues'? No single theme or theory underlies all eight subjects. But they are all characterised, to a greater or lesser extent, by the following three things. First, they are topics on which a considerable amount of research has been done, particularly in recent years. Indeed, if taken together they account for a very substantial share of all of the criminological research of the past twenty years; almost certainly a bigger share than could be included within any other eight topics. They are subjects which have interested many criminologists in the past two decades – in contrast to (say) the careers of adult criminals, especially of the professional and organised varieties, about which little new has been learned since the 1930s. Thus, they are subjects about which there is something to say. Secondly, in most of our eight chosen topics at least some progress has been made towards explaining the known facts. In this respect, the topics we have chosen differ markedly from a number of other equally interesting subjects, such as the ecology of crime which seems at the moment to be at rather a dead end. On the other hand there are other subjects, in particular so-called 'labelling' or 'transactional' theory, in which too little empirical research has been done. Work in this area, which examines both the processes whereby certain persons become 'labelled' as deviants, and the effects of the label, once applied, on the deviant, seems likely to develop rapidly in the future.

Thirdly, on each topic discussed in this book there still remain many interesting and important questions to be answered by future research. In other words, these eight subjects seem to us to be ones in which contemporary criminology has reached a 'take-off point': enough progress has been made in these areas of the subject in recent years that real advances are likely (or at least possible) in the next few years. They are subjects in which it is worthwhile taking stock of existing knowledge, with a view to increasing that knowledge substantially in the near future. 'Hidden' crime, subcultures, classification for the purposes of aetiological research and treatment, decision-making in sentencing, the effectiveness of penal measures, and the impact of institutional treatment – if these subjects are not exactly central to criminology as a whole, they are nonetheless central to criminology in English-speaking countries in the late 1960s, and are likely to remain so in the 1970s. Of course, our choice of topics has to some extent been influenced by our personal interests. Other criminologists, asked to list the 'key issues' (in the sense just explained) of contemporary criminology, would no doubt have produced slightly different lists.

Most of the subjects we have chosen have obvious implications for penal policy; but we would stress that this is *not* a reason for their inclusion in the book. This point needs to be especially emphasised in relation to the last four chapters of the book, which deal with what are usually regarded as penological topics. Legislators and the general public have always tended to regard criminology as the study of ways of preventing crime, and they have tended to suppose that criminologists have, or should have, a professional interest in the reformation of offenders. We do not agree with this view; criminology is not, in our opinion, a kind of social work. As the studies discussed in chapters 5 to 8 should make clear, there is plenty of scope for disinterested and purely scientific research on the operation of penal systems, and it is this kind of research with which we are concerned. The question 'What is the effect of this type of treatment on that type of offender?' is a question of fact, and it is in principle just as capable of being answered by objective empirical research as the question 'How much crime is actually committed, and who commits it?'

This is not, of course, to say that criminology cannot make any contribution to penal policy. What it cannot do is decide what the *aims* of penal policy should be. But by discovering how much crime is committed, and by showing how and why it is committed, criminologists can help to show what policy goals are reasonable; and if given certain aims, they can try to discover by research the best means of accomplishing them. It is unfortunately true, however, that at the present time much too little is known about the effects of punishments and treatments – or any of the other subjects discussed in this book – to permit us to draw definite practical conclusions concerning questions of penal policy.

This brings us to a final point. Throughout this book we have paid considerable attention to questions of methodology – that is, to questions of research design and techniques of investigation. Readers who are well versed in these matters may be bored, or insulted, or both, by our extended discussion of them. But our experience has shown us that, even with university students, one cannot take for granted an adequate knowledge of research methodology; and the general reader, with no experience of social research, is even less likely to appreciate the theoretical and practical problems involved in digging out even the simplest facts about crime. Yet the unhappy fact is that much criminological research – even in recent years – is so defective methodologically as to be virtually worthless; and many other studies are so limited in this respect that very little weight can be put on their conclusions. Moreover, as we have indicated, our concern is as much with the future as with the past. We think it is likely that real progress will be made by researchers, in the next few years, in at least some of the topics discussed in this book. It is important for the reader to understand the kinds of problem which future researchers must overcome – if only so that he can more fully appreciate what they may accomplish.

A book by two authors often turns out to be either a book by one author, or two half-books by two authors, each of whom disagrees more or less flagrantly with the other's contribution. This book is neither of those things; somewhat to our surprise, we find ourselves in substantial agreement with each other's views on the eight subjects we have chosen. Literary detectives may easily discover – by such devices as counting semicolons – which of us was responsible for the first drafts of the eight chapters. But the final drafts are all joint enterprises, in content if not in form.

Chapters 6 and 7 are both revised and up-dated versions of papers originally published by the Council of Europe in *Collected Studies in Criminological Research*, volumes 1 and 3.

We gratefully acknowledge the very extensive help given by Marvin Wolfgang in constructively criticising the draft of the whole book. Various chapters were also improved by comments from our colleagues, Tony Bottoms, Derick McClintock, Gerry Rose and Donald West. Throughout our work we were generously supported and advised by Leon Radzinowicz. None of them is, of course, responsible for our interpretation or any remaining errors.

Isobel Gawler kindly checked the proofs and prepared the index.

Institute of Criminology
University of Cambridge
December 1969

1 How much hidden crime?

Criminological textbooks nearly always open with a discussion of criminal statistics. Usually they present data on the nature and extent of criminal behaviour and the characteristics of those who are known to have committed it. Series of tables analyse crime rates over periods of time, compare the incidence of different kinds of offence, contrast the crime problems of different countries, rural and urban areas, or different localities of large cities. Similarly, a detailed statistical breakdown of those convicted of offences is usually given based on such characteristics as sex, age, race and social class. Whatever the content of the tables, they will almost certainly be surrounded with qualifications and warnings, for criminal statistics are notoriously easy to misinterpret. For example, the student will be told that an apparent 'increase in crime' may be due to more crime being *reported* rather than to more being committed. Likewise he will be warned against assuming that the persons convicted of crime are a representative sample of those committing it.

In the face of these reservations many students are likely to regard this part of criminology as unreasonably vague, difficult to comprehend and boring. They will wish to press on to the more exciting explanations of crime. Yet, it is precisely this cavalier approach to the problem of understanding the basic data of criminality that has so often led criminologists astray. A great deal of effort is often expended on the critical analysis of a theory before someone remembers to check whether the behaviour the theory is explaining actually exists! There is obviously a need to study thoroughly the phenomenon of crime before embarking on explanations of its varying incidence and the patterns of criminal behaviour.

Undoubtedly a major task of criminology is empirical – mapping the trends and patterns of criminal activity. This is not, however, only an end in itself. It provides essential data for explanations of the relationship between criminality and the social structure and culture of society. For example, without this information the study of the impact of urbanisation and economic conditions on the level of criminality would not be feasible. Furthermore, these data provide a necessary basis for law enforcement policy, for example they enable the calculation of the likelihood of persons being the victims of crime in differing social situations, such as, within different sections of a city. In other words they can be a guide to preventive action.

Theories of crime causation largely rest on the evidence about the characteristics of convicted persons contained in both officially published statistics and the case records of the police, courts, penal institutions, probation officers and others. In relying on this data the theorist is faced with two problems. First, he must estimate to what extent those convicted differ from those who have committed identical acts but have not been caught or prosecuted. Secondly, he must try to disentangle those factors which explain criminal behaviour from those which explain why a person has become officially processed as a delinquent or criminal. Walter Reckless pointed out long ago that having a broken home may be a major criterion for referring a young thief to the court, rather than a cause of thieving itself. It is essential therefore to compare the convicted with the non-convicted, and to study the process which differentiates those offenders who become 'officially' delinquent from those who are dealt with by informal means.

It is not our intention to provide a summary of the information contained in official criminal statistics – in any case this is exceptionally difficult to do on an international scale – or to review the major problems of the compilation and interpretation of these statistics. This has already been adequately covered in recent texts.[1] Instead we shall concentrate on showing how empirical research has begun to illuminate a major problem area: the 'dark figure' of crime, or what some now call 'hidden delinquency'.

All criminologists are aware of the problem of estimating the true incidence of crime from statistics of offences 'known to the police' and of the possibility that the 'known' criminal population is a biased sample of all offenders, but until very recently they have had to rely entirely on hunches about the size of the dark figure and make various more or less informed guesses about the factors affecting the reporting of crime and the decision to prosecute offenders. A major breakthrough in criminological study has been made by a recent spate of empirical investigations which shed light on both these problems. We shall see that their results do indeed have major implications for crime statistics and criminological theory. As a distinguished Finnish criminologist has said:

The investigation of unregistered criminality will, even if it does not bring about any revolution in the general outlook on crime and criminals, certainly challenge some of the established dogmas of present day criminology ... In general it is to be expected that the study of unregistered criminality will invigorate criminology by supplying a new tool of investigation and by illuminating many traditional problems of criminology from a new perspective.[2]

Two different strategies have been used in attempts to assess the dark figure. Most studies have used the method of questioning a group in the 'general population' about the delinquent acts they have committed, whether these have led to a court appearance or not. These are known as self-report or hidden delinquency studies. The other strategy, using survey research methods, has asked citizens about the acts of which they have been victims. These studies are usually referred to as victim surveys or victimisation studies.

Self-report studies are useful for the following reasons. They make possible an estimate of the number of people who commit deviant acts of various kinds, and the frequency with which they do it – so providing what Robert Dentler (in an unpublished monograph) has called a 'Kinsey-type baseline'; they allow the comparison of official with unknown delinquents; they facilitate longitudinal studies of the delinquent 'careers' of individuals over periods of time; and finally they are indispensable for any study that attempts to compare delinquents with a control group of supposedly innocent people. Studies of criminal victims serve a rather different purpose. In particular, they are better adapted to assessing the volume and nature of all criminal acts committed within some specific locality and period. Additionally they aid the study of the reporting and prosecution process. The investigator can directly ask victims why they do not report crimes to the police. He can even go further, and try to see why some crimes that are reported fail to get recorded and included in the criminal statistics.

Certainly either kind of enquiry bristles with methodological problems. Questions about criminality, like those about sexual behaviour, are especially liable to distorted and untruthful answers. We shall pay particular attention to these problems, but for purposes of clarity will deal with them separately from the major findings of the studies. It is vital not only to assess the validity of the enquiries so far carried out, but also to gauge to what extent flaws in the methods used can be overcome. Certainly, this is a contentious issue; one of the major contributors to self-report research, Robert

Dentler[3] has recently concluded that it should be discontinued because 'the method seems too shaky and the results too equivocal to deserve further effort'.

Similarly, the study of the use of discretion by the police whether or not to arrest or prosecute offenders poses major problems for empirical research. Some observers have managed to penetrate the secrecy which surrounds this activity and to look at the way the police actually process offenders, but so far most of our knowledge is only indirectly obtained from self-report studies. Most commentators have looked at the discrepancy between the characteristics of persons who admit delinquency in various studies and those who are prosecuted and convicted, and have inferred that a major intervening variable explaining this 'bias' is police discretion.

Thus there are two main empirical issues. The first – how much crime of various kinds is there, and what is the relationship between the reported or known crime and the unreported behaviour? – will be dealt with in this chapter. The second – who are the criminals and what is the difference between those officially known and those hidden in conventional society? – will be the subject of chapter 2. In addition, there is a major theoretical issue. It is precisely this 'labelling' process which distinguishes reported crime from other deviant behaviour and official delinquents from the rest, that has most interested some contemporary sociologists.[4] They point out that an essential ingredient of delinquency is the perception and definition of the deviant act as specifically criminal rather than as (say) naughty, unruly, a symptom of mental illness, or understandable adolescent rebellion. There is, they claim, a great difference between acts that are clearly defined as the rightful province of law enforcement and those which can be ignored, dealt with in other ways or excused. For this reason many sociologists would, we suspect, prefer to replace the concept of hidden delinquency or unreported crime with the more general 'hidden deviant conduct' or, better still, 'behaviour which, in some circumstances, might be defined as delinquent'. Whether one accepts this view or not, the study of hidden crime can be used to investigate not only the size of the crime problem but also the very processes through which society deals with unlawful behaviour.

Statistics of offences committed within any period or locality include only those 'known to the police'. If criminologists are to use these data to study the comparative incidence of different types of offences or changes in the level of criminality over time – through, for example, the construction of a crime index – or its relative occurrence in different social environments, they must investigate three major questions:

1 What proportion of crimes committed are known to the police, and does this ratio vary for different types of offence?

2 Is the ratio of crimes committed to crimes known constant over time and between different areas of the same country or in different countries?

3 Is the 'quality' of the crime reported constant over time and between different areas? Are, for example, 'n' cases of violence in 1927 comparable to 'n' cases in 1967 in terms of their seriousness and the circumstances in which they are committed?

Only if it can be shown that a constant ratio of certain crimes is reported will it be possible to develop an index from official statistics (like a price index) to measure fluctuations in the quantity and quality of crimes committed. Without the assumption of constancy in reporting and recording practices an uncertain amount of any fluctuations in recorded crime might be due to changes in reporting behaviour by victims and other witnesses of crime and to the actions of the police. As criminologists, notably Sellin and Wolfgang,[5] have made important progress in the technical sphere of developing methods of rating the seriousness of criminal events for index purposes, it is important that we should examine this issue in detail.

The data on the extent of the dark figure fall into four main categories – the informed guess, the study of crime from organisations such as the shop or large store, the self-report study, and the survey of victims among householders. The findings of these studies will be reviewed in turn.

Informed guesses

Leon Radzinowicz[6] has suggested that only about 15 per cent of all crimes committed in England are officially recorded: Howard Jones,[7] on the other hand, estimates 25 per cent. The German authorities Meyer and Wehner have made similar estimates for a number of different offences based on their respective experiences in research and the police.[8] It should be noted that Meyer's estimate is for the number of crimes resulting in a conviction (see figure 1:1). The Dutch police official C. N. Peijster made estimates for abortion of 0·4 per cent; shoplifting 20 and pickpocketing 33 per cent. These figures show an extremely large dark figure for all kinds of sexual

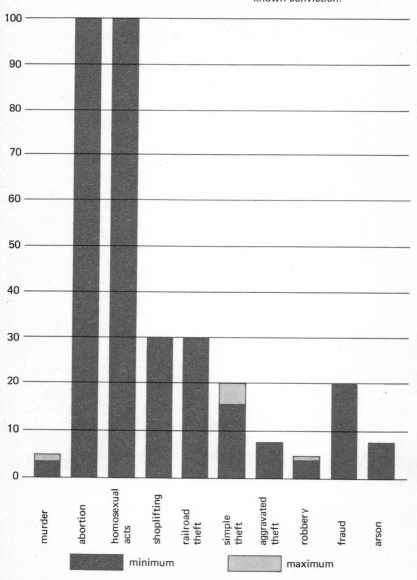

Figure 1:1a shows the number of crimes estimated to have been committed for every known *conviction*.

500

100

90

80

70

60

50

40

30

20

10

0

murder
abortion
homosexual acts
shoplifting
railroad theft
simple theft
aggravated theft
robbery
fraud
arson

minimum   maximum

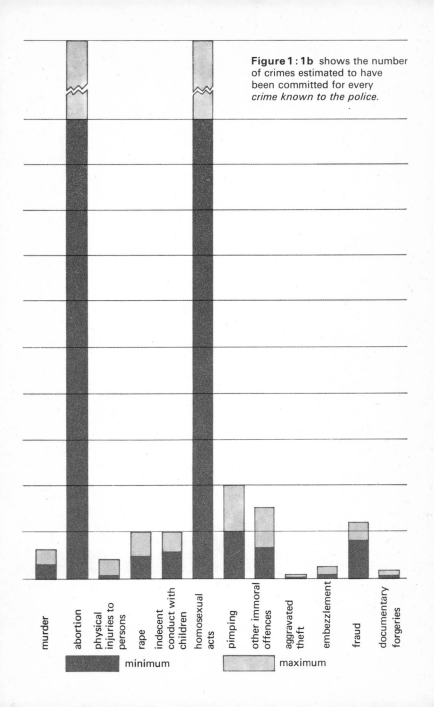

Figure 1:1b shows the number of crimes estimated to have been committed for every *crime known to the police.*

murder

abortion

physical injuries to persons

rape

indecent conduct with children

homosexual acts

pimping

other immoral offences

aggravated theft

embezzlement

fraud

documentary forgeries

minimum

maximum

offences and frauds, but they differ remarkably in relation to offences against property.

In relation to sexual offences in England, Radzinowicz has suggested that the published statistics do not make possible even a reasonably accurate estimate of the total committed in a given period: excepting very serious cases of rape he thought the amount known would never rise above five per cent of that committed.[9] Certainly, as far as 'conspiratorial offences' such as illegal abortion are concerned, commentators in all countries admit a stupendous dark figure: in England, before the law relating to abortion was liberalised in 1968, only about 250 out of an estimated 50,000 to 100,000 illegal abortions a year were known to the police.[10]

Crimes against business organisations

The only offence against business organisations which has been subject to detailed investigation is shoplifting, mainly because it is well known that retail businesses do not report all the offenders they catch. There are of course other crimes against businesses that may remain largely hidden, such as embezzlement, but there are no reliable estimates on the size of this problem.

In 1933 Sellin calculated that 5,314 thefts were known to three large Philadelphia stores. These resulted in 1,423 arrests by store detectives, who prosecuted 230 persons. Over 5,000 offences remained unknown to the police, and this is all the more startling when it is realised that the official total of thefts known to the police in Philadelphia for 1933 was 4,402.[11] In a recent study in Chicago, Mary Cameron[12] claimed that twelve department stores 'lost' $10,000,000 worth of stock in 1951. She quotes one expert's conservative figure of 100,000 thefts at an average of $15 each being committed nationally each week: $78 million a year. About two-thirds of this may be due to theft by employees: the rest to shoplifting. Cameron shows that most shoplifters are dealt with by private police and rarely enter official statistics: 'Detectives employed by a single downtown department store in Chicago arrested two-thirds as many adult women for shoplifting in that store in 1944 and again in 1945 as those shown in the official statistics on larceny as being formally charged by the police with petty larceny of all forms (including shoplifting) in the entire city of Chicago.' These detectives estimated that they apprehended only about one in ten persons shoplifting in any one day, and only ten per cent of those apprehended were charged. On this basis only one per cent of shoplifters would be known to the police. Whether store detectives are anywhere near right is of course open to doubt. Gibbens and Prince writing about English shoplifters simply stated that 'any estimate [of the amount of unreported theft] is based on the merest guesswork'.[13]

New evidence was collected in a survey for the President's Commission on Law Enforcement and Administration of Justice (hereafter the President's Commission) of businesses in Boston, Chicago and Washington DC[14] (see figure 1:2). 65 per cent of 407 owners or managers of wholesale or retail businesses claimed to be victims of shoplifting. This of course may be an under-estimate as few firms have completely accurate inventory control. Of all businesses who could estimate the amount of their loss (i.e. 38 per cent of all those surveyed), a fifth placed their loss at over four per cent of their turnover: a similar proportion lost over $1,000. As most suggested that many items taken were worth less than $10, the actual volume of thefts was large. Even when the offender was known, the stores called the police in a minority of cases; only 37 per cent usually doing so compared with 58 per cent never taking this action. The major reasons for not informing the police are shown in table 1:1. For this type of offence a considerable majority of the shopkeepers feel there is nothing to be gained from police action: informal non-legal action is preferable. In the same study there were similar findings in relation to the offence of passing bad cheques. Only 19 per cent of owners or managers said that they would automatically call the police. Over half would simply ask the offender to 'make good' the loss.

Although all these studies only give rough estimates of the extent of shoplifting, they support the conclusion that police statistics are a completely unreliable guide to the amount of this crime.

Self-report studies

Most self-report studies refer to samples of schoolchildren. The majority have been carried out in the United States, usually in relatively small towns and cities. There have been in addition a study of adults, carried out via a mailed questionnaire in New York State in the 1940s, studies of students in Texas and Scandinavia, and a survey of entrants to the Norwegian and Finnish armed forces. All these inquiries were primarily designed to get a simple count of the

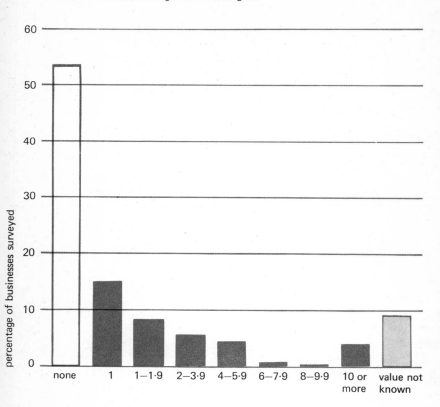

Figure 1:2 Per cent of inventory estimated by owners/managers lost from shoplifting each year for all businesses and organisations in eight police districts of Boston, Chicago and Washington.

proportion of persons admitting to the commission of certain deviant acts and to compare those who were unknown offenders with those who had been arrested or convicted. They give us only a very imprecise estimate of the size of the dark figure. Their main drawbacks, for this purpose, are that so far the investigators have never taken a representative sample of an area for which there are comparable police statistics, nor have they asked their respondents about delinquencies committed within a specific time period. If these things were done the results could be compared with the total number of offences actually reported to or discovered by the police

Table 1:1 Per cent distribution of how owners/managers of business deal with shoplifters: Eight police districts* in Boston, Chicago and Washington.

Action by owner/manager			
Calls the police			
For adults and juveniles	For adults but parents for juveniles	For adults but not children if they return goods	Only if offender refuses to pay
32·9†	2·9	0·8	5·4
Does not call the police			
Adults must pay; calls parents for juveniles	Adults and juveniles must pay	Ask offender never to return	Informal depends on circumstances
3·7	40·1	11·7	2·5

* includes only those businesses reporting shoplifting.

† the figures refer to the total for all districts.

in the same period. All that current self-report studies can show is the proportion of respondents who admit crimes who are also known to the police. We do not know how many of their offences are officially recorded. Even so, it seems that only a very small proportion are caught. For example, Kerstin Elmhorn carried out a study of a sample of about three per cent of Stockholm's schoolboys,[15] 57 per cent admitted to at least one serious offence, and of these 93 per cent were not caught. Between them, these boys claimed they had committed 1,430 serious offences but the culprit was known to the police in only 41 of them. The proportion of crimes for which an offender

Table 1:2 Estimates of numbers of boys aged 9–14 committing selected offences in Stockholm in 1961, and per cent cleared up.

Type of offence	Estimated number of boys	Per cent cleared up by police (official records)
Car theft	75	33·3
Moped or motor cycle theft	208	8·4
Breaking-in	180	4·2
Damage	96	3·3
Cycle theft	38	2·2
'Ordinary' theft	183	1·9
Fraud	4	1·5
Receiving	11	1·1

was apprehended was thus only 2·9 per cent. Assuming that her sample was representative. Elmhorn calculated from her results the number of *all* boys in Stockholm who could be expected to have committed various offences in the year 1961 and compared the results with the number of persons known to the police. Table 1:2 shows that with the exception of car theft none of the offences was cleared up in as many as ten per cent of cases. It should be remembered however that these are figures for the number of *persons* known to the police. If we make the general assumption that between a third and a half the crimes *known* are cleared up by convicting persons, we should multiply the figures in column 2 by two or three to get the proportion of these crimes which was known to the police.

Elmhorn's findings are backed up generally by other studies. The most complete figures come from an American study carried out in Utah by Erickson and Empey,[16] although it should be noted that this Mormon area is untypical. Four small samples of boys aged 15 to 17 were selected: 50 high school boys who had never been to court, 30 once-only offenders, 50 repeaters and 50 in an institution. It is particularly important that the latter group should be included, as these offenders may make a disproportionately large contribution to the total amount of recorded crime. Each boy was interviewed and asked if he had committed any of 22 acts ranging from armed robbery to defying parents. If he admitted to any act he was asked how many times he had committed it and how many times he had been caught, arrested or taken to court.

Table 1:3 shows the frequencies with which these 180 young persons claimed to have committed each of the 22 acts, and the proportions which were detected and acted upon by the police. Similarly, in the United States, Witmer, Shirley and Murphy[17] found that only 11 per cent of a group of boys who admitted committing a serious offence had been prosecuted. In Flint, Michigan, Gold[18] found that of a sample of high school children only 16 per cent were caught and 10 per cent booked by the police for their admitted offences. Similarly, in Norway about 14 per cent of admitted delinquents (aged about 18) living in Oslo had been in contact with the police or the courts.[19]

Studies of victims

The use of the survey method to study the incidence of victimisation among the general population is an entirely new approach to estimating the dark figure. The only work so far published is contained in three reports prepared in the United States for the President's Commission in 1967. One report deals with the amount of crime committed against members of a representative sample of 10,000 United States households, another with pilot studies in four precincts of the District of Columbia (Washington), and the third with high and low crime-rate areas in Boston and Chicago.[20]

Major findings of victim studies The Commission's representative national survey found that one in five households in the United States had been a victim of a serious crime in 1966. About twice as many major crimes were committed as were known to the police, as reported in the Uniform Crime Reports by the Federal Bureau of Investigation (FBI). Uniform Crime Reports are made in the United States for all major crimes. The offences are divided into two parts. Part I offences are the most serious, some of these are called Index offences as they are used for Crime Index purposes. Part II offences are generally less serious or are less likely to be reported to the police and so are less reliable for Index purposes. For example, larceny of $50 and over is a part I offence. Under $50 it is a part II offence. These dis-

Table 1:3 Offences admitted by a sample of young persons in Utah, USA, and per cent undetected and unacted upon.

Offence	Per cent admitting	Offences admitted	Unde-tected	Unacted upon
Traffice offences				
Driving without licence	84	11,796	98·9	99·7
Traffic violation	77	12,150	98·2	99·3
Total	—	23,946	98·6	99·5
Theft				
Articles less than $2	93	15,175	97·1	99·8
Articles worth $2 to $50	59	7,396	97·1	99·1
Articles more than $50	26	294	71·0	92·8
Car theft	29	822	88·9	95·5
Forgery	13	512	93·4	97·5
Total		24,199	96·3	99·3
Alcohol and narcotics				
Buying beer or liquor	29	8,890	99·6	99·9
Drinking beer or liquor	74	12,808	98·8	99·8
Selling narcotics	0·5	1	100·0	100·0
Using narcotics	4	74	100·0	100·0
Total		21,773	99·1	99·9
Defiance of authority				
Defying parents	53	8,142	99·7	99·9
Defying others	64	6,497	99·4	99·7
Total	—	14,639	99·5	99·9
Property violations				
Breaking and entering	59	1,622	85·6	94·4
Destroying property	80	10,645	98·5	99·7
Starting fires (arson)	6	11	40·0	90·0
Total	—	12,278	96·8	99·0
Retreatist activities				
Running away from home	38	578	86·8	94·7
Skipping school	83	9,375	93·9	99·8
Total	—	9,953	93·5	99·5
Offences against person				
Armed robbery	5	46	80·4	91·3
Fighting, assault	70	8,980	99·7	99·9
Total	—	9,026	99·6	99·9
Others				
Gambling	85	6,571	99·9	99·8
Smoking (habitually)	42	86	87·1	91·8

tinctions will be seen clearly in some of the following tables and charts.

Figure 1:3 shows that of the more serious offences, the most frequently unknown were burglaries, rapes, aggravated assaults, and larceny of over $50. Only a third of burglaries were known, and 75 per cent of rapes were not reported. While there was twice as much minor crime as serious offences, the dark figure was apparently much smaller (see table 1:4). It seems from the Washington study, however, that interviewees find the greatest difficulty -in remembering any but the most recent serious offences committed against them. The figures for minor offences are therefore probably considerable underestimates.

The Washington enquiry was much smaller and covered only 511 households (plus a further validation study); it was mainly concerned, in fact, with methodological problems. Thirty-eight per cent of the surveyed population were victims of a serious crime within a year, compared with an estimate of ten per cent based on police statistics. For every type of serious crime the dark figure was substantially larger in Washington than in the USA as a whole. This reflected the finding in the national survey that the rate of victimisation was very much higher in the metropolitan centres than in small cities and rural areas. In addition, there are good reasons for believing the methodology of the Washington study was better adapted for gaining reports of victimisation. Figure 1:4 shows overall 5·3 times more serious crime than was known to the police. For serious larceny ($50 and over) the proportion is fifteen times: only about seven per cent is known!

The Boston-Chicago respondents were asked about crimes committed against them in a period of a year from July 1965–6. Table 1:5 compares the number of Index offences found by the survey with those known to the police. In the two Boston precincts there were five and three times as much crime. The figures for Fillmore in Chicago are probably only so different because the survey ran simultaneously with a riot!

Methodological problems of victim studies Because these studies are new there are a number of major methodological problems which must be taken into account in interpreting the results of all three surveys. We shall spell these out in some detail since this kind of research is of great potential value and likely to be used by other investigators in the future.

It should be first borne in mind that only one of the studies pur-

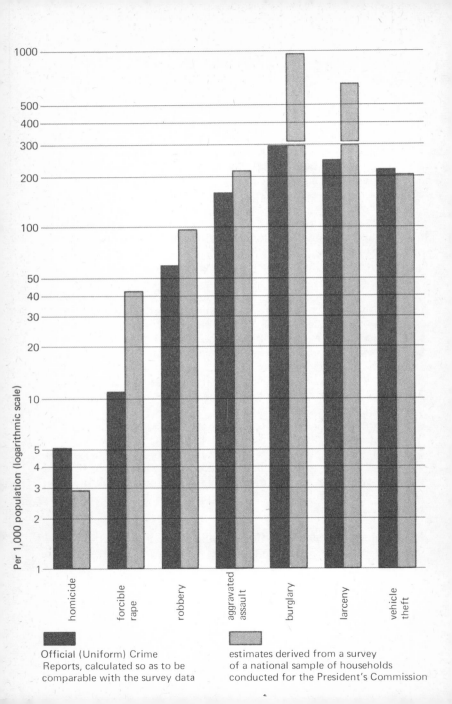

1000
500
400
300
200
100
50
40
30
20
10
5
4
3
2
1

Per 1,000 population (logarithmic scale)

homicide · forcible rape · robbery · aggravated assault · burglary · larceny · vehicle theft

Official (Uniform) Crime Reports, calculated so as to be comparable with the survey data

estimates derived from a survey of a national sample of households conducted for the President's Commission

Figure 1 :3 (left) Rates of serious crime in the United States, 1965 : Comparison of official statistics and survey estimates. The figures for homicides and vehicle theft in the survey are *fewer* than reported to the police. Of course one cannot interview the victim of a homicide, and this crime may break up households. The figures for vehicle theft are not easy to explain, except on the assumption that all thefts are reported to the police for insurance reasons, but some householders fail to report the offence to the survey interviewer.

Figure 1 :4 (below) Estimated rates of offences, per 1,000 residents aged 18 or over : Comparison of police and survey data for three Washington D C Precincts.

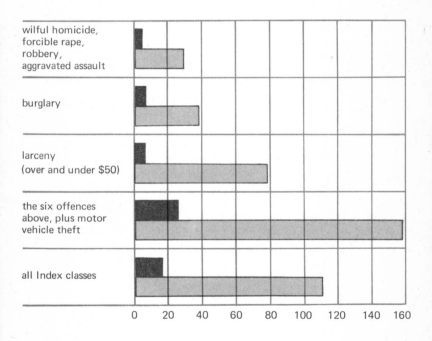

police rate   survey rate

ports to collect a sample representative of the United States as a whole: both the Washington and Boston-Chicago enquiries were limited to specific precincts of these cities, chosen for other than representative reasons, and therefore it is dangerous to generalise from their results. Furthermore, over a quarter of those approached refused to be interviewed and this may be an additional biasing factor.

A survey of households can only ask about a limited range of offences: those specifically against individuals or the household in general. No information can be gleaned about offences where there is no specific victim, such as vagrancy or being drunk and disorderly. It may also be difficult to get information, by this method, about crimes of a consensual or conspiratorial nature – for example those connected with drug use, gambling, prostitution and abortion. In these, the 'victim' (if we can speak of one) is involved in the offence, and would have to be asked to admit to offences for which he could himself be prosecuted. The national survey concluded that it would be quite wrong 'for the survey method to be used as an instrument of confession'. Nevertheless, such an approach has been successfully used in self-report studies, although admittedly not in a doorstep-to-doorstep setting.

Although these are household surveys it is doubtful whether they reveal all the crimes committed against *all* household members. The national survey questioned any adult (over 18) in the household and asked about offences committed against him or her personally and then about those committed against others in the household. This method produced an over-representation of older persons and women in the sample (as they are more likely to be at home). The two other surveys therefore chose at random the adult to be interviewed so as to get a more representative sample of the household. But whichever method is used there is still the problem of estimating the accuracy of the information given by the respondent about other members of his household. In all three studies there was a suspiciously large difference between the number of incidents reported by the respondent about himself and those concerning others. In the national sample it was estimated that the amount of crime committed against Negro families uncovered by the survey was only half of the actual amount of victimisation. It was especially felt that reports about offences committed against young members of the family would be less well known by respondents and therefore in the two city surveys all acts which had been committed against

Table 1:4 Official rates of minor crimes in a metropolitan area compared with survey estimates from metropolitan areas in the United States (1965), (per 100,000 population).

Minor Crimes	Survey Sample	Official Crime Rate
Simple assault	569	528
Petty larceny	1,532	1,462

Table 1:5 A comparison between the numbers of Index offences (and rate per person) reported by victims in a survey of four precincts of Boston and Chicago, and official statistics of crimes known to the police, 1965.

	Boston		Chicago	
	Dorchester	Roxbury	Fillmore	Town Hall
1 Gross estimate of number of Index offences from survey data	9,605	12,612	9,328	17,356
2 Gross estimate of *rate* of Index offences (i.e. proportion per person), from survey data	·16	·24	·11	·13
3 Index offences known to the police, for the same age group	1,881	3,651	6,732	4,372
4 *Rate* of Index offences known to the police	·03	·07	·08	·03
5 Proportion of offences in the survey known to the police (per cent)	18·7	29·2	72·7	23·1

those under 18 years were not taken into consideration.

In comparing the survey-derived data with police records of crime reported over the same period it was necessary to take into account the limited range of offences covered, the age range of the respondents, and other factors such as excluding from police data crimes committed against respondents outside the police jurisdiction. These problems could not be solved precisely and therefore the comparisons between the survey findings and police statistics are estimates, with an uncertain margin of error.

For the future, however, the most important questions centre around the validity and reliability of the information given by respondents: the extent to which they were willing or able to tell the truth. The validity of answers is most difficult to check, but in general there was little evidence of fabrication of events. Two kinds of problems emerged: first whether there was concealment or exaggeration of serious offences; secondly whether respondents reported incidents which were not crimes. All three surveys found that the relative frequency of serious crimes reported by respondents mirrored their frequency in the official Uniform Crime Reports, thus supporting the view that respondents did not exaggerate the incidence of lurid crimes. On the other hand, a much higher proportion of all crimes than would have been expected was in the 'serious' category. As the Boston-Chicago report comments 'if anything, the survey procedure is biased against securing the trivial incident and recall tends to take only the more "salient" serious experiences'. There is, apparently, no over-reporting of serious crime, but a considerable under-representation of petty offences in the findings of these enquiries.

In the national and Boston-Chicago surveys special procedures were built in to check the testimony of respondents to ensure that only 'real crimes' were recorded for comparison with police data. The major criteria used were: Was the respondent credible? Was the event a crime? Was it serious enough to warrant action, or was it committed by a minor? Was there sufficient evidence? Was it committed within the area and time period included in the survey? The national study used two research assistants to evaluate whether a crime had been committed. They agreed that about one quarter of all reports were not crimes, and excluded these and doubtful cases (nine per cent) from the total number of crimes to be compared with police data. But the assistants themselves may not have been entirely accurate in their assessments: a sample of their work was checked by lawyers and policemen who reached the conclusion that only about two-thirds of the events recorded as crime by the assistants were in fact crimes. Similarly, 21 per cent of the reports in Boston-Chicago were excluded – but only 12 of 502 reported incidents were excluded as non-credible. In the Washington enquiry no special procedures were used and a low 'unfounding rate' of 4·4 per cent – the rate of reports the police normally assume not to be real crimes – was deducted from the total number of offences reported. The Washington estimates are therefore probably too high.

The truthfulness of the accounts given by respondents does not seem to be a major problem, but the reliability of their answers is. Respondents were asked to account for all criminal incidents of which they had been a victim within the past year. One problem affecting the reliability of answers has already been discussed – the respondents' ability to report for other household members – but there are three others: the time the respondents were prepared to give the interviewer; the 'telescoping forward' into the survey year of events which occurred in a previous year; and the forgetting of incidents that had happened within the survey year. The first and last of these errors would tend to lead to underestimates of the amount of victimisation, whereas telescoping-forward would lead to an exaggeration.

Part of the Washington study used an interview method in which the respondent was asked for details about each event as he mentioned it. It seems that this led to a considerable under-reporting of incidents. In a survey of an additional precinct in Washington a new method was used: the respondent was asked to say whether he had been the victim of any crime on a list, and only after the whole list had been checked was he asked for details of each offence. In this precinct the number of victimisation incidents per respondent was 2·0 compared with 0·8 for the other Washington precincts with a similar official crime rate. Commenting on the method, the Boston-Chicago report states, 'it soon became clear that a respondent controls the number of experiences he or she had on the basis of what they consider a sufficient amount of time they had given the interviewer'. There was certainly a suspiciously high number of people who were only victims of one crime, as against two, three or four! Thus, again, the surveys probably *underestimate* the amount of victimisation.

By far the most important problem, however, is forgetfulness. Figure 1:5 compares the seasonal incidence of offences that would be expected if there were no telescoping and forgetfulness. They show clearly that although there is apparently some telescoping (about 10 per cent telescoped), the preponderance of reported events is in the recent past: 'most respondents seemed to find it difficult to remember incidents of victimisation other than recent cases'. To check the amount of under-reporting, a separate survey was designed in Boston and Chicago. A note was taken over a period of all incidents in which citizens called the police, and several months later a sample of these citizens was interviewed. Over a fifth of the respondents failed to mention the experience which had been recorded by the investigators!

In summary, it seems that the most satisfactory victimisation study would be one in which a very large sample of the population was asked about incidents which occurred in a period of not more than three months before the interview date. Obviously this would be an extremely expensive method.

All the methodological limitations mentioned above indicate that the estimates derived from these victim surveys *under*-represent the real amount of crime committed within a specified time and area. If respondents had perfect recall, were willing to give an unlimited amount of their time to an interview, and had perfect knowledge of the victim-experiences of their fellow household members, the disparities between survey estimates of crime and police figures shown above would certainly have been considerably larger.

Why is crime unreported or unrecorded?

Although there are substantial differences in the estimates obtained from the self-report and victimisation studies, they nevertheless all show that even crimes generally considered to be the most serious (robbery, aggravated violence and burglary) are under-represented in criminal statistics to a substantial degree. Why is this? Criminological literature abounds with commonsense assumptions about the factors inhibiting the reporting of crime. To begin with, behaviour may not be perceived as 'crime' by the victim or other witnesses. Where lies the difference between unsolicited sexual familiarity and indecent assault? When is a 'lost' wallet assumed to be stolen? Is a stock shrinkage of fifty hair combs due to theft, and if so to fifty thefts or one? Secondly, the victim may know that a crime has been committed, but still not report it. He may have sympathy with the offender – a relative for example; he may dislike or distrust the police

Figure 1:5 Effects of telescoping and forgetfulness on victim's report of crime: the proportions of offences reported in each quarter of a preceding year.

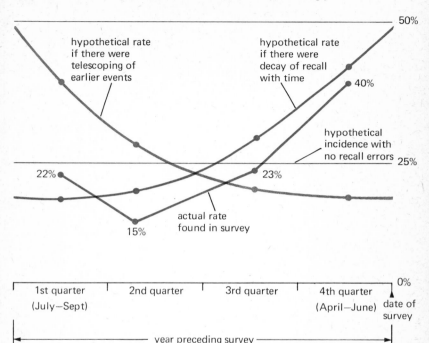

and the courts; he may live in a community where it would be deviant to report a crime – where, for example, if one is hurt in a fight the consequence must be suffered in silence; he may fear reprisals or regard the harm done as too trivial in relation to the consequences for the offender of a conviction; he may fear that his own deviant activity will be exposed (this, for example, is assumed to apply to the victims of theft by prostitutes and their pimps); and there are numerous other possible reasons. Behaviour regarded as criminal by the police may not be so regarded by those involved. This is especially thought to be true of offences such as violence committed in working-class areas and taking small amounts of material from work: this activity may be defined as 'perks' rather than theft. As an example of the latter J. P. Martin found, in a study of businesses in Reading, England, that they drew a line between 'reasonable pilfering' and theft. Half the firms stated that theft only began when the goods were worth £5 or more.[21]

The social toleration of crime is not only high in areas where it is prevalent. It may also be rife in middle-class areas where mis-behaviour by the young can be defined as 'part of growing up' or 'youthful pranks'. Such behaviour may not be reported if it is to lead to the stigma of a conviction. The action of the victim is, of course, not the only variable. The extent of police activity is especially important where there is no specific victim – as in the cases of drunkenness – or where one cannot properly speak of a victim – as in drug and abortion cases. From year to year, therefore, there may be dramatic changes in the proportion of these offences included in the statistics: the figures for abortions known to the police in England and Wales for the three years 1961–3 were 245, 406 and 239 respectively.[22]

Victimisation studies shed a good deal of light on the reasons for not reporting crime and on the disparities between reported acts and those recorded by the police. In each of the three studies referred to above, those interviewed were asked whether the offence committed against them had been reported to the police, and if not, why? In the national sample an attempt was made to trace what happened after the victim had called the police: whether they came, considered the incident a crime, traced the offender, charged him, etc.

In general the results are remarkably similar. As expected, the more serious the offence the more likely the victim was to report it. In Washington, of 121 index crimes committed 32 were not reported to the police, whereas for non-index crimes 83 of 132 were not reported. Even so, as table 1:6 shows, about a third of the most serious crimes which victims claimed to have reported were un-recorded by the police. There is, however, considerable variation from offence to offence. Leaving aside homicide, car theft is the only offence both studies show to be invariably recorded: presumably because of the possibilities of claiming from an insurance company. But here the figures are difficult to interpret as more crime seemed to be recorded than was reported! In comparison, in the Washington study 64 per cent of the minor crimes were not reported to the police.

Why did the victims not report crimes to the police? The reasons varied between persons in different income brackets and more especially between whites and Negroes, as well as for different types

Table 1:6 A comparison of crimes survey respondents claimed were reported to the police and official police statistics of known crimes.

Crime	Survey sample	Police statistics 1965	Percentage difference
Homicide	3·0	5·1	− 42
Forcible rape	30·3	11·6	+ 187
Robbery	60·6	61·4	− 1
Aggravated assault	136·4	106·8	+ 28
Burglary	545·8	296·6	+ 83
Larceny (> $50)	360·8	267·4	+ 35
Vehicle theft	175·8	226·0	− 22
Total	1,312·7	974·7	+ 35

These figures refer to the United States National Sample.

of offence, but over half the respondents felt that nothing would be achieved by involving the police, and over a third felt that it was nothing to do with the police or expressed other negative attitudes. Only two per cent gave fear of reprisals from the offender as their reason. But of course, these findings may not be relevant to societies where there is a tradition of personal retaliation.

After those crimes which were not reported by victims were taken into account there still remained, in all three surveys, substantial discrepancies between the crimes supposedly reported and the police statistics of crimes known. Figure 1:6 shows that in the national study a large 'shrinkage' occurred because the police either did not come when called or they failed to regard the incident as a crime and consequently did not record it. In Washington the police figures accounted for less than half of those respondents claimed to have reported: even when police records were searched for indications of all events recorded by the police that *might* have been crimes, only 74 per cent of citizen reports were accounted for. Similarly, in Boston and Chicago there were between two and three times as many crimes alleged to be reported by survey respondents as could be found in police statistics.

Figure 1:6 The 'shrinkage' of crimes from victim's action to conviction according to survey respondents. It should be noted that, from the fourth circle on, the victim may simply have been ill-informed.

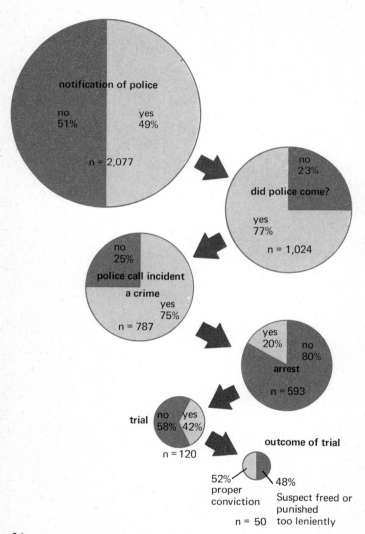

From this evidence, it is clear that either a change in the attitude of citizens towards reporting offences, or a change in police practice, could have a substantial effect on the statistics of recorded crime.

Implications and further evidence

It seems clear that empirical research can be developed to estimate the proportions of different types of crime recorded in official statistics. For many offences the dark figure is so large that even if the errors produced by methodological flaws were up to 20 per cent the general picture would not alter much. On the other hand, the evidence reviewed so far throws some doubt on the assumption that the proportion and 'quality' of serious crimes which are known to the police will remain relatively constant over time and between different areas of the same country. This conclusion is extremely important. As Sellin and Wolfgang point out, it is necessary to make the assumption of stability in the proportion of crimes known if an index is to be constructed from official statistics to compare crime rates at different periods of time and between different parts of a country.

In the Washington survey there were considerable variations in the proportion of offences reported even between 'the fairly similar police districts in this one city': a range of 60-75 per cent was found. The authors suggest that such variations between districts and types of offence also indicate that the size of the dark figure will vary over time: presumably because some of these differences occur because of chance factors. In particular, they note that only a small change in police practice would be necessary to change the crime rate: if two per cent more of the citizen complaints were recorded by the police, the official crime rate would jump eight per cent! There is plenty of evidence that changes in police recording methods can have much greater consequences than this. In both Chicago and New York, a tightening up on police procedures led to a phenomenal change in the crime picture. Wolfgang[23] points out that the re-organisation of the New York city police department in 1950 resulted in a *recorded increase* of 400 per cent in robberies, 200 per cent in assaults with weapons and 700 per cent in larceny over the rates for 1948 and 1949. The picture was capable of even more improvement, for in 1966 New York Police Commissioner Leary found that only 22 per cent of auto theft and rape, 45 per cent of aggravated assault, and 54 per cent of larceny were properly recorded – as against 92 per cent of robbery and 96 per cent of burglary. With these corrections the rate for serious crimes would rise immediately from 1,608 per 100,000 of the population to 2,203: equivalent to an increase of 37 per cent. Similarly, in Chicago, a change of police chief in 1961 led to a 'paper' increase of 83 per cent in the crime rate.

Figure 1:7, which compares crime trends for Chicago and New York for two major crimes, illustrates the marked changes associated with these reforms in police recording practice. Lack of standardisation between local police forces is especially a problem in countries which like the USA, lack a strongly centralised system.

Another study, by Lyle Shannon, of juvenile delinquency in Madison, Wisconsin, showed that the referral rate by the police to the courts changed dramatically between 1951 and 1952, accounting for a large 'paper increase' in offenders. The proportion of juveniles 'contacted' by the police who were referred to court increased from 15 to 47 per cent.[24]

Very much less spectacular changes have taken place in England. A change in the method of recording crimes of violence in 1949 combined with a tightening-up of recording procedures led to a purely statistical (i.e. paper) increase of 13 per cent in recorded crimes between 1949 and 1960.[25] But this was only a small proportion of the total increase of 152 per cent between those years.

There is considerable evidence that the police make wide use of their discretion in deciding whether to book an offence and arrest an offender. There have been few empirical studies of this process, although a considerable amount has been written on the constitutional and legal issues.[26] La Fave[27] points out that the major characteristics of police discretion is its 'low' visibility'. Nothing is recorded and its existence is consequently difficult to prove, let alone measure precisely. There are few examples in the literature of police using their discretion not to book serious cases. The exceptions relate either to officers offering to spare drug offenders in return for information on 'bigger fish' or to the non-booking of violent offences, especially those committed between members of minority groups or between persons of low social status. In the latter cases the police appear to regard violence as a normal part of the daily life of these people, and not properly classifiable as 'crime'. They will especially ignore the offence if the victim is unwilling to press the charge. Newman reports two examples of judicial attitudes towards offences common among certain social groups.[28]

One judge, in dismissing an assault charge against the male

partner in a white, 'hillbilly' common law relationship, explained:

These people couldn't care less about marriage, divorce or other relationships. They are ignorant and their moral standards are not like ours. They come from the backwoods in the South where even incest is the accepted thing. There is no point in this court acting as a referee in these relationships.

Another judge, in commenting on differential treatment of certain sex cases, remarked:

In certain types of cases you must take into consideration the social standards of the offenders. For example, in statutory rape or carnal knowledge cases the man might be just above the legal age and the girl just below. Usually in such cases, particularly among the Negroes, there is mutual consent and in the Negro group this type of behaviour is not particularly frowned upon and is felt to be normal. You have to take this factor into consideration.

More rigid law enforcement would undoubtedly, in the short run, bring more crimes of violence to light. In the long run, however, it may be likely to lead to a reduced willingness to notify the police. When police in California decided to prosecture all crimes of violence, whether or not the victim wished to proceed with the case, the number of reported cases dropped 11 per cent in a year.

Of course, besides not reporting offences the police may downgrade them to something less serious. In a study of robberies in London, McClintock and Gibson[29] showed that police classified a considerable proportion of aggravated robberies as less serious types of robbery (see table 1:7).

Some observers suggest that the amount of crime recorded will simply reflect the deployment of police resources and some even suggest that the police hold a vested interest in maintaining increasing crime rate. Biderman and Reiss state that

operational organisations such as the police ... choose not to observe more than they can process with given resources, and they selectively screen observations to fit organisational goals, strategy and tactics.[30]

This is not just a question of the best use of scarce personnel, or of decisions about the priorities of law enforcement. There may be other pressures, such as the necessity to present a good image of a crime-free city or to show efficiency through a substantial clear-up rate. These factors will operate particularly strongly where the police are under strong local political control. Skolnick made a detailed study, through observation, of the 'Westville' police department in California.[31] He found that between a fifth and a quarter of the burglary complaints processed by patrolmen were recorded only as

Figure 1:7 Robbery and burglary trends for Chicago and New York, 1935-66.

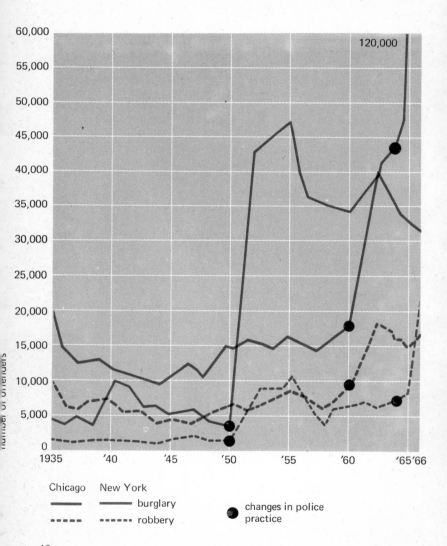

Chicago New York
—— —— burglary
----- ----- robbery
● changes in police practice

Table 1:7 A comparison between police and legal classifications of robbery in London, 1957.

	Police classification		Legal classification	
	No.	%	No.	%
Aggravated robbery	280	70·4	400	95·5
Other robbery	118	29·6	19	4·5
Total	**398**	**100·0**	**419**	**100·0**

suspected offences with 'suspicious circumstances'. These offences would not appear as burglaries in police statistics but would be counted as crimes cleared up. As Skolnick points out: 'in effect, therefore, every time a complaint is filed as a suspicious circumstance instead of as a reported offence, the clearance rate rises (since it is based on the ratio of cleared to actual offences)'. Officers in this city were under strong pressure to produce a high clearance rate. In contrast, the police in an East coast city virtually recorded every complaint received as an actual offence. Clearly, any comparisons between the crime rates of these two American police districts would be extremely misleading.

Presumably, the two most important factors likely to lead to reporting are first a belief that the offence is sufficiently serious for some official action to be taken to recover property or deal with the offender and secondly a feeling that reporting will be a useful thing to do – either in leading to the apprehension of the culprit or to the development of better preventive measures. In other words, changes in public perception and evaluation of deviant activity, changes in the extent to which they feel the need for 'outside assistance' in dealing with the deviant, and changes in the level of confidence in the police can all have a marked effect on the proportion of crimes reported.

Sellin and Wolfgang argue that the offences most likely to be reported in a constant ratio to the total committed were those which 'cause harm to persons directly'. These are offences which 'inflict some bodily harm on a victim and/or cause property loss by theft, damage or destruction'. The examples they give in their book cover a wide range of offences including assaults occasioning minor injuries and fairly petty larcenies of goods worth five dollars. There is need, however, for empirical evidence to determine whether the assumption of a constant reporting rate over such a wide variety of offences is valid.

In a study of all violent offences committed in London in 1950 and 1957, McClintock[32] concludes, on the basis of a subjective assessment:

> It would be erroneous to assume that most, or even a large part, of the *recorded* increase is due to an *actual* increase in violent behaviour. ... Most crimes of violence *recorded* by the police are not committed for the purposes of pecuniary gain but are the outcome of patterns of social behaviour among certain strata of society. The fact that more of the 'dark figures' are now coming to the notice of the police indicates a new situation. ...

In particular, he argues that violence arising from domestic strife, neighbourhood quarrels and fights in bars and cafés are now being reported much more frequently than even twenty years ago. He suggests that the main reasons for this change are an increasing awareness of individual rights, especially among women, and to some extent a break-down of close community ties which led to solidarity against the police and fear of retaliation from the offender. When it is recognised that these offences account for over 50 per cent of all crimes of violence, it is clear that a change in reporting behaviour can increase the crime rate substantially. There is indeed evidence from this study that in the seven years 1950 to 1957 the increase in violent crimes was higher for offences involving minor injuries – bruises, abrasions and small cuts – than for serious injuries. This was especially true for assaults arising from domestic and neighbourhood quarrels. The proportion of reported offences in which there were only minor injuries increased from 21 to 31 per cent of the total crimes of violence. At a more impressionistic level other observers have noted that an increase in reported violence may even be associated with a decrease in actual violence. Downes[33] reports a London East End youth club worker as saying:

> You can read the statistics any way you like. A twenty per cent rise in juvenile crime would mean just that the kids don't get away with it ... Thirty years ago, you honestly couldn't walk through Stepney without fear of being molested ... Well I've been here ten to fifteen years and I've never been beaten up yet, even in the worst districts. There's a lot of exaggeration. There's less *real* delinquency than ever before.

In fact a decrease in the tolerance of violence by the population will probably lead people to *expect* not to be molested. If they are nevertheless assaulted, they are likely to perceive the offence more seriously than if they had learned to accept it as 'part of life'. A good example of this is cited by McClintock:[34]

An officer of senior rank said that there 'is a smaller toleration of violence all round and that quite a lot of the increase in crime recording reflects this'. He illustrated his point by telling a story of what happened soon after he joined the police force. 'I was on beat duty and saw a burglar leaving a house; I gave chase and came to grips with him. We both rolled over in the dust; after a struggle in which I received a cut lip and several bruises I was able to get him back to the station, where he was put in a cell. I made my report to the station sergeant and dwelt upon the fight and the injury received. When I was finished there was silence for a few minutes and then the sergeant said, 'You've done well my lad, but don't expect burglars to be gentlemen. You'd better brush your uniform, wash your face, have a cup of tea and get back on your beat'. There was no question of recording a crime of violence or even an assault. Today this would be recorded as an indictable offence of assault, either causing actual bodily harm or with intent to resist apprehension.

Increases in education, affluence and civil rights for minority groups, the break-up of traditional slum life and increasing opportunities for social mobility as well as the influence of mass communications are all factors which might affect the reporting of crime. This is part of what Biderman[35] means when he claims that 'year-to-year increases in crime rates may be more indicative of social progress than social decay'.

Conclusions

In summary then, hidden delinquency and victim surveys have cast doubt on the assumption of a constant ratio of reporting crimes in general. For the very serious offences such as bank robberies or thefts of large amounts of money we do not doubt the criminal statistics accurately reflect the true state of crime. But most offences are not like this. The vast majority of thefts and breakings and enterings (the largest single category of crime) involve relatively small sums of money and the American victim surveys have shown that only a third to a half of the most serious (Part I offences) of these crimes are reported. There is obviously much room for changes in reporting behaviour. The reportability rate of minor crime, which figures so largely in the total criminal statistics would only have to

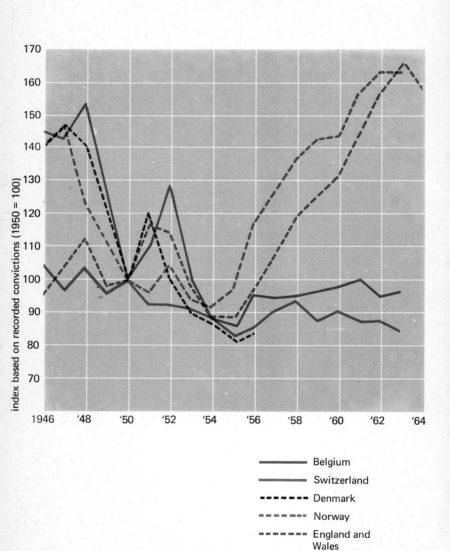

Figure 1:8 Variations in offences against property: certain European countries, 1946-64. (For years prior to 1955 comparable information is not available for other European countries.) Christiansen's data.

index based on recorded convictions (1950 = 100)

Belgium
Switzerland
Denmark
Norway
England and Wales

increase at a relatively slow rate to produce an annual increase in the total criminal statistics of about eight per cent per year – which has been the annual rate, for example, in England and Wales for the decade 1955-65.

It should be remembered, however, that not all changes in the official crime rate are upwards. Nearly all western countries had a slight fall in their rates during the early 1950s (see figure 1: 8). It is doubtful whether this was caused by a decline in reportability. Certainly, rising crime rates must reflect *some* real change in the pattern of crime. The problem for criminology is to find exactly what this change is.

We do not in fact have any hard data on the crucial question of the extent to which reporting of offences by victims and other witnesses of crime is constant over time. What is needed is a series of victimisation studies of the same population over intervals of (say) five years. At the moment we must rely on a series of impressions, gained from a number of studies, which suggest that changes in reporting behaviour have occurred in some major crimes over relatively short periods.

But the fact that these studies show much crime to be hidden should not lead the zealous automatically to campaign for more rigid law enforcement. Rather it should be used as one kind of 'social indicator': namely a measure of the extent to which perceived deviant activity is handled differently according to its seriousness and the social context within which it takes place. In other words perhaps the real value of hidden delinquency and victimisation studies is not to warn us of the evils lurking beneath the surface, or even to help us get into perspective our concern over published statistics of crime, but rather to provide data to aid our understanding of the way in which deviance is perceived and dealt with in varying social contexts. This is surely vital information for the investigation of what Kitsuse and Cicourel[36] have called 'the difference between social conduct which produces a unit of behaviour and the organisational activity which labels this behaviour distinctively deviant'.

2 Official and hidden delinquents

From the point of view of criminological and penal theory, self-report studies of delinquency serve three important purposes. First, they make possible an assessment of the *number of people* in the population as a whole who commit (or have committed) various deviant acts and the frequency with which they have done so. Secondly, by abolishing the artificial dichotomy between delinquents and non-delinquents under which all the latter are presumed 'innocent', they lead to the conception of delinquency as a *variable* and thus to the development of a scale on which to measure individuals' involvement in delinquency – ranging from the completely innocent to the completely committed. Thirdly, and most important of all, they enable a comparison of those who have been officially labelled as delinquent – who have a 'record' – with those who have not. Cohen has stressed the importance of this for delinquency theory:[1]

First and foremost, we must overcome the limitations inherent in all official or quasi-official data on juvenile delinquency. The defect of these data, of course, is not that they represent too small a sample but that we cannot tell what sorts of delinquents and delinquencies may be over-represented or under-represented. We can never lay to rest the ghost of unrepresentativeness as long as our statistical base of operations is delinquencies known to the courts, the police, or even the schools and the social agencies. Until this defect is remedied, comparisons between delinquents and non-delinquents with respect to their developmental histories, personalities and social position must be received with some scepticism and reserve. In order to remedy this defect, we must start, not with known delinquents, but with *representative samples of the juvenile population* drawn without regard to their known or probable delinquent histories. *Then*, on the basis of interviews, questionnaires and tests we must differentiate these samples into delinquents and non-delinquents of various degrees and kinds. In this manner alone can we achieve a valid conception of the distribution, by degree and kind, of delinquency within sectors and strata of the population.

Instead of adding innumerable methodological caveats to the findings of each study, we shall review the major conclusions first before considering methodological issues. However, these methodological problems are of great importance and the findings of the various surveys should not be interpreted without a thorough study of the methods through which they were obtained. Finally it should be borne in mind that nearly all the studies mentioned in this chapter refer to juvenile delinquency. Although we have referred to the few studies of adults, the general conclusions apply to juveniles only.

The incidence of delinquency

Numerous investigations have shown delinquent conduct to be far more widespread than official records indicate. Large proportions of all population studies admit to at least some acts for which they could have appeared before a court. While many of these acts are of a trivial nature there nevertheless appears to be a substantial number of persons who are officially non-delinquent and who admit to relatively serious acts, sometimes committed more than once.

As we noted earlier, the majority of studies have concentrated on young schoolchildren, although in Scandinavia young adults have also been extensively surveyed (see page 19 above). In the 1940s Wallerstein and Wyle[2] sent a mail questionnaire to 1,800 men and women in New York State asking them to tick any of 49 offences against the penal law which they had committed. Table 2:1 shows the replies for men and women, separately, for the most serious offences. Altogether 64 per cent of the men admitted committing a felony. The average number admitted since the age of sixteen was eighteen. Even ministers of religion admitted an average of 8·2! It should be noted that like most studies, these figures are an underestimate of the number of delinquents in the population as a whole as it excludes those in penal institutions at the time of the survey.

Both in the United States and England it has been suggested that by the age of eighteen somewhere between 10 and 20 per cent of the male population will have been convicted by a court of a criminal offence (although the proportion varies a good deal between different races and areas in the United States).[3] Self-report studies indicate that they represent on average only a quarter of those who have actually committed these offences. Dentler and Monroe found that between 38 and 46 per cent (depending on where they were living – suburb, urban, farm or small town communities) of 644 Kansas junior high school pupils admitted having committed a criminal offence.[4] Similarly in the Utah study (see page 22) Empey and Erickson found their respondents 'reported a tremendous number of violations running into the thousands on all but a few serious

Table 2:1 Percentages of men and women from New York State who admitted committing various crimes.

Offence	Per cent Men	Per cent Women
Malicious mischief	84	81
Disorderly conduct	85	76
Assault	49	5
Motoring offences	61	39
Indecency	77	74
Gambling	74	54
Larceny	89	83
Grand larceny (except car)	13	11
Car theft	26	8
Burglary	17	4
Robbery	11	1
Concealed weapons	35	3
Perjury	23	17
Falsification and fraud	46	34
Election frauds	7	4
Tax evasion	57	40
Coercion	16	6
Conspiracy	23	7
Criminal libel	36	29

offences such as arson, selling and using narcotics, forgery and armed robbery'.[5] Over 90 per cent were undetected. The Scandinavian studies of entrants to the armed forces yield similar results. Residents of Oslo and Helsinki admitted the offences shown in table 2:2. In Helsinki only between 3 and 7 per cent of the thieves were known to the police![6] In Stockholm, 92 per cent of school children admitted an offence and 53 per cent a 'serious' crime such as larceny. Although on average they had been involved in three such offences 93 per cent were without an official record.[7]

A recent English study of adolescents[8] also found that less than

Table 2:2 Percentages of entrants to the armed forces from Helsinki and Oslo who admitted committing various crimes.

Crime category	Helsinki 1,973 Entrants	Oslo 1,820 Entrants
Shoplifting	39·6	56·2
Smuggling of alcohol or tobacco	33·8	36·7
Taking items from a restaurant	21·4	38·0
Sex offence against a minor*	18·3	14·9
Receiving stolen property	17·9	22·2
Drunkenness resulting in a disturbance	17·1	6·6
Breaking and entering	16·0	11·9
Taking parts from a motor vehicle	15·5	8·2
Drunken driving	15·3	13·4
Theft of bicycle	6·7	13·1
Theft of other motor vehicle (except car)	5·1	8·7
Illegal distillation of alcohol	4·5	15·2
Leaving a restaurant or a hotel without paying	3·5	6·8
Car theft	2·9	7·9
Robbery	2·4	1·8

* under 17 in Helsinki, and under 16 in Oslo.

three per cent admitted to none of 40 types of offence. Between 70 and 84 per cent admitted traffic violations; 16 to 20 per cent, vandalism, gang fighting and larceny; but only 1·7 to 3·3 per cent admitted serious offences – breaking and entering, fighting the police and attacking unknown persons. It should be borne in mind that in this study 29 per cent of those approached refused to participate. There was evidence to suggest that these were more likely to have committed a greater number and variety of offences: in other words the figures both distort the population being studied and *underestimate* the amount of delinquency in the population as a whole. A more

Table 2:3 Percentage of 1,400 London boys committing certain types of theft at least once.

Nature of theft	Percentage*
I have kept something I have found	89
I have stolen something belonging to a school	63
I have had something that I knew was stolen	60
I have stolen something from a shop	53
I have stolen money	51
I have cheated someone out of money	46
I have stolen fruit or some other kind of food	41
I have stolen a book or newspaper or a magazine or comic	39
I have stolen something from someone at school	35
I have pinched something from my family or relatives	35
I have stolen something out of a garden or yard of a home	31
I have stolen something from a bike or motor-bike	29
I have stolen from a building site	28
I have got things out of a slot machine without paying	28
I have stolen from work	25
I have stolen something from a car or lorry or van	23
I have stolen cigarettes	22
I have stolen from a cafe	21
I have stolen something from a stall or barrow	20
I have got into a place and stolen	17
I have stolen from a club	17
I have got something by threatening others	15
I have stolen from a changing room or cloakroom	15
I have taken a bike or motor-bike	14
I have stolen something from a telephone box	11
I have stolen from someone at work	7
I have taken a car or a lorry or van	5

* excluding minor items which were regarded as items worth less than 1s. 6d.

recent study by Belson and his associates of 1,400 London boys, aged 13 to 16, shows that between half and a third had stolen in a variety of different situations (see table 2:3).[9]

It seems that the majority of children do something at some time against the law: a large proportion even admit to stealing. On the other hand, a low proportion admit to *persistent* misbehaviour of this kind. In a study of over three thousand teenagers from the public high schools in the State of Washington, Slocum and Stone found that although 63 per cent of the boys admitted 'taking things belonging to others', only 11 per cent admitted to doing it 'several times' and two per cent to 'doing it often'.[10] Similar results were obtained by Short and Nye (see figure 2:1)[11] for mid-west high school students, by Akers for students in a large mid-western city[12], by Anttila in Helsinki, Christie in Oslo for entrants to military service[13] and Elmhorn for Stockholm schoolboys (see figure 2:2). While it may be correct to say that to commit one or two delinquent acts is 'normal behaviour' for boys, to be involved in frequent criminal acts is apparently relatively rare.

Official and unofficial delinquents compared

In general, the extent to which information about known offenders is representative of all offenders will depend first on the amount of crime actually reported and secondly on the amount cleared up by prosecution. This is not, however, true for all offences. Some crimes are cleared up in all cases simply because they only come to the notice of the police when an offender is found. These include those crimes of a consensual or conspiratorial nature, hidden personal offences or offences against public order. There are many examples – receiving stolen goods, abortion, most homosexuality, being drunk and disorderly, carrying an offensive weapon. No one reports such offences without identifying an offender. In general, the greater the dark figure of unknown offences, and the lower the clear-up rate, the greater the chance that known offenders will be an unrepresentative sample of all those who commit crimes.

How typical is the convicted offender in terms of sex, social class, race, family background, educational performance and criminal involvement? Some of these questions, but not all, can be answered from the evidence of self-report studies. In addition there is an increasing body of evidence, based on observations of, and interviews with, the police about the way in which they use their discre-

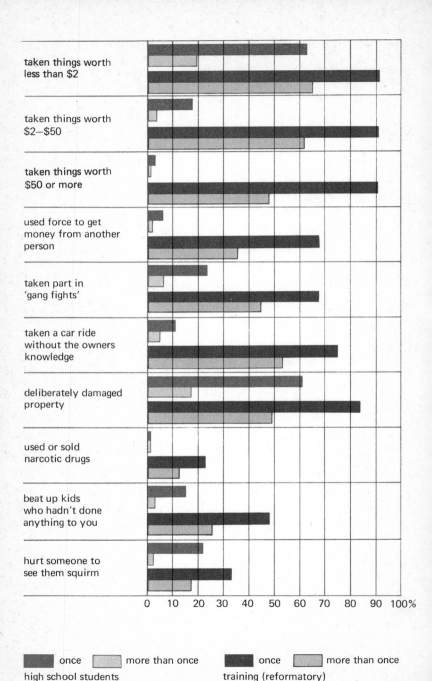

	0	10	20	30	40	50	60	70	80	90	100%

taken things worth
less than $2

taken things worth
$2–$50

taken things worth
$50 or more

used force to get
money from another
person

taken part in
'gang fights'

taken a car ride
without the owners
knowledge

deliberately damaged
property

used or sold
narcotic drugs

beat up kids
who hadn't done
anything to you

hurt someone to
see them squirm

■ once   ▢ more than once   ■ once   ▢ more than once
high school students   training (reformatory)
                              school delinquents

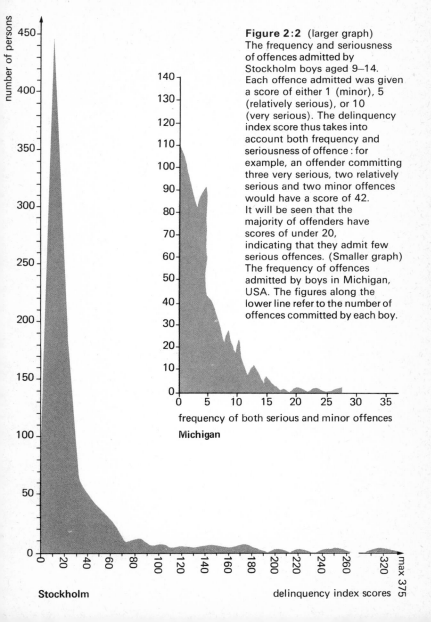

Figure 2:1 (left) Reported delinquent behaviour among boys in two mid-west USA samples comparing those who admitted the offence once with those admitting it more than once.

number of persons

Figure 2:2 (larger graph) The frequency and seriousness of offences admitted by Stockholm boys aged 9–14. Each offence admitted was given a score of either 1 (minor), 5 (relatively serious), or 10 (very serious). The delinquency index score thus takes into account both frequency and seriousness of offence : for example, an offender committing three very serious, two relatively serious and two minor offences would have a score of 42. It will be seen that the majority of offenders have scores of under 20, indicating that they admit few serious offences. (Smaller graph) The frequency of offences admitted by boys in Michigan, USA. The figures along the lower line refer to the number of offences committed by each boy.

frequency of both serious and minor offences

Michigan

Stockholm

delinquency index scores

max 375

tionary power to initiate or drop proceedings against known offenders. We shall deal first with the self-report evidence.

Most commentators, working either from official statistics or research material based on court records, describe delinquency as characteristically a phenomenon mainly restricted to male working (or lower)-class adolescents living in large urban areas. To what extent is this picture challenged by the confessions of the respectable?

The sex ratio Taking the total number of offenders convicted in one year men outnumber women in the ratio between five and seven to one. This ratio is fairly constant over time and between countries. Although the proportion of female offenders obviously varies for different types of offence – being very low for robbery and burglary and being above that of men for shoplifting – there are at any time at least four times more men in the population with a criminal record than women.

Some explanations of this difference have attempted to show that women commit offences that are more likely to be hidden – of the conspiratorial and consensual kind – and that they also express their deviancy through alternative non-criminal acts such as promiscuity and prostitution. There is also the possibility that they are less often proceeded against by the police. It is difficult to test the first suggestion through the self-report studies done so far, as the lists of offences used tend to be biased towards those characteristically committed by boys. As far as these are concerned, the self-reports mirror the official records. Both the American high school and the Scandinavian student studies have found boys much more likely to admit offences.[14] Martin Gold's evidence shows that at all status levels, for whites and for Negroes, the frequency rate of female delinquency is two to four times lower than that for boys[15] (see figure 2:3). This may, of course, be due to a greater reluctance on the part of girls to admit delinquency involvement (as Gold himself suggests), and certainly the admitting of sexual relations may do harm to a girl's self-image while it bolsters the boy's.

Social class There is no doubt that the incidence of official delinquency is higher in the lower than in the middle and upper classes. Figures from a cross section of British children born in March 1946 are shown in figure 2:4.[16] The social-class distribution of adult offenders is probably much the same.

Attempts to study the incidence of hidden delinquency among different social classes have been castigated by Albert Cohen as being motivated by 'egalitarian proclivities and sentimental humanitarianism'. Yet their findings have had a definite impact on criminological theory.

In 1946 Austin Porterfield compared the offences reported by 337 students at Texan Christian University with those reported by over 2,000 children charged at Fort Worth juvenile court. He was surprised to find that the delinquencies of the students were as serious as those of the court cases.[17] Two hypotheses were put forward: first, that social background is used by the police in deciding whether to prosecute – the police using their discretion to favour middle-class children – second that the court cases may have been more frequently involved in delinquency than the students, thus increasing both their chances of detection and, once detected, the likelihood of prosecution as serious delinquents. Most of the other evidence supports Porterfield's findings and his two hypotheses.

Many studies have shown as absence of, or a negligible correlation between social class and the proportion of respondents admitting delinquency, but others have found significant positive correlations. For example, Short and Nye's and Dentler and Monroe's high school studies found no differences between boys from low, medium or high status family backgrounds. The Utah enquiry concluded: 'most respondents on one status level were no more or no less delinquent than most respondents on another'. The same conclusions were found by Edmund Vaz[18] in a Canadian small town, by Akers in a large Ohio city and by Voss in Honolulu.[19] The Scandinavian studies produce similar evidence. In Norway, Christie concluded: 'Instead of any concentration of high degrees of self-reporting at the lower ends of the class scale we found a slight but persistent tendency in the opposite direction'. These results were mirrored in Finland. Voss in Honolulu and Arnold in Texas[20] reported that crimes of property destruction were higher in the upper socio-economic groups and in Utah the middle status delinquents who were incarcerated were especially frequent offenders. 'This group, rather than middle status respondents across the board, seems to have contributed to the disproportionate number of serious and destructive offences reported by the middle status group. The lower status group, on the other hand, was over-represented in using alcohol and narcotics and fighting and assault.[21]

Christie suggested that his inability to find social class differences

Figure 2:3 Percentage of youngsters at four levels of frequency of admitted delinquent acts: by social status and by race and sex (in a Michigan study).

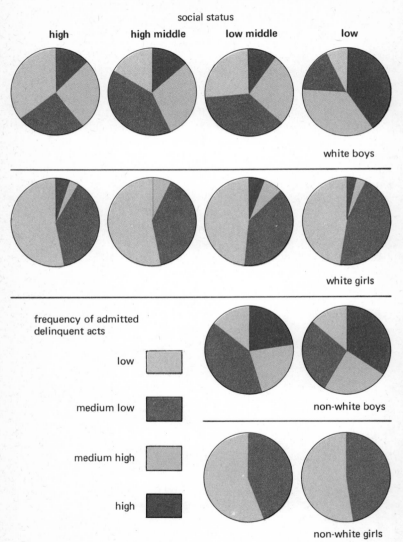

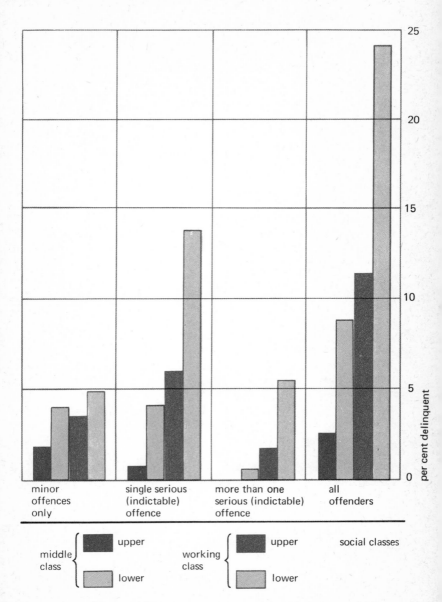

Figure 2:4 Incidence of delinquency up to the age of seventeen among different social classes in a national sample of children in Great Britain. (Based on official statistics).

minor offences only

single serious (indictable) offence

more than one serious (indictable) offence

all offenders

per cent delinquent

middle class { upper / lower

working class { upper / lower

social classes

in delinquency may have been due to the 'seriousness of the acts themselves' being different, or that middle-class youths reported all acts they had committed while the working-class youths had forgotten most of theirs. He found, on the contrary, that middle-class offenders reported recent acts. Supporting data for Christie's first hypothesis was found by Martin Gold in his study of over 500 schoolchildren from the town of Flint in Michigan. Using an interview designed to probe into the details of admitted offences, Gold found that one quarter 'could not conceivably be called chargeable offences – the proportion of confessions of accidental and trivial acts of property destruction was significantly higher among wealthier than among poor white boys'. Nevertheless official records did exaggerate the difference in delinquency among boys of different social status. The ratio of low to high status boys with official records was five to one: on the basis of self-reports it should have been 1·5 to 1. On the other hand, the low status boys were more frequently delinquent and committed more serious offences. Looking only at those boys who commit offences most frequently (and who are at the top of a seriousness scale) Gold found three or four times more low than medium or high status boys. Rather similar results were reported by Reiss and Rhodes from Tennessee;[22] lower status boys were more frequently and seriously delinquent and career-orientated delinquents were only found in this social class – although only 1·3 per cent of boys were so designated. Gold's study is one of the few to compare differences between races. In the lowest social class there is a slightly higher rate of self-reported crime from whites, but the difference is small (see figure 2:3). *In other words, if the purpose of law enforcement is only to deal with the more serious delinquents, then self-report studies fairly accurately reflect social status differences in the incidence of serious delinquency*. Similar results were found by Empey and Erickson: there were more serious offences admitted by the middle and low status boys than the high status ones. However, as already shown, the few middle status boys who were frequently delinquents were the most highly involved group in serious delinquency.

There are two possible explanations for this rather contradictory evidence. First, these studies cover a wide range of populations in very different kinds of community. Within these communities social class differences may be more or less important in the way they affect the life-chances of the population: this is especially true in relation to education, work, housing and leisure opportunities.

Table 2:4 Percentage of boys in four different school 'streams', ranked by educational performance, who admitted delinquent acts in an English secondary school.

Form	At least one appearance in court	Current petty thieving	No.
4A (best performance)	3	7	30
4B	14	43	28
4C	37	73	22
4D (worst performance)	55	64	22
All	24	43	102

There is a great deal of difference between the social situation of the 'lower class' in a small mid-west town or in Scandinavia and in the slums of metropolitan centres. Being working-class in a tight-knit, religiously-orientated, one-community-school, full employment area obviously is an entirely different experience from growing up in an urban slum. In fact, social class may be a poor indicator in some areas of the factors most likely to be associated with delinquency: better ones may be educational performance, work skills or opportunities and family relationships. Some of these will be discussed more fully below.

The second explanation is that interview methods have found social class differences whereas the self-completion technique has not. This may be due to the greater ability of the interview to elicit responses, or to exaggeration of delinquency by lower-class boys in the situation of interview. On the other hand, the difference could be the result of genuine variations in the populations studied.

A number of enquiries have found self-reported delinquency related to educational level. In a small study of London schoolboys Gibson[23] found that while grammar school boys admitted committing, on average, 18 of a list of 42 delinquent acts, the corresponding figure for secondary-modern boys was 32. While on average the former group had committed 0·5 serious acts each, the latter admitted to 3·5. In a study of one secondary school in an industrialised city

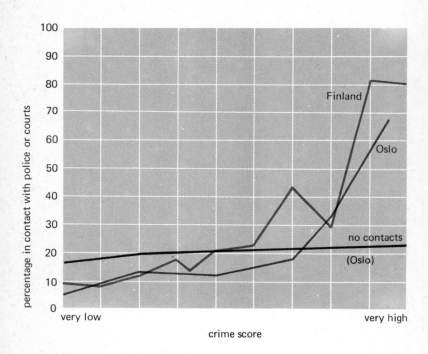

Figure 2:5 The relationship between frequency and seriousness of admitted crimes and admitted contacts with the police or courts. Each offence was rated according to its seriousness. The crime score thus reflects both the frequency and the seriousness of the offence.

of north-east England, David Hargreaves asked 14 year-old boys in different ability-streams whether they were currently involved in petty thieving. Table 2:4 compares the proportion who had been in court with the proportion admitting theft.[24] There is a very strong correlation between educational performance and delinquency. Comparable data are unavailable from most of the studies. There was some evidence in Norway that those in the higher social classes with high crime scores were those with relatively low educational attainment. But this correlation between educational level and self-reported crime was not found elsewhere in Scandinavia.

Although both Short and Nye's and Dentler and Monroe's studies failed to find social class differences they did show an association with family relationships. In particular those who had less good relations with their parents, where there was lack of supervision and discipline, reported more misbehaviour. Dentler's figures show that strained relations with parents is a more important factor than social class. It is interesting to note that in the British Social Survey enquiry it was suggested that the high number of delinquents who refused to take part were much more likely to be out of the home and unavailable for interview.

Frequency and seriousness Nearly all enquiries have shown that convicted offenders admit a much greater frequency of offending than non-official delinquents. Besides Gold's study noted above, the Scandinavian studies provide the best evidence of this. In Norway, Sweden and Finland the subjects' responses were rated on an index of 'crime-points'. Those with the highest points admitted the most serious offences most frequently. In Norway there were ten times more people reporting conflict with the law in the highest crime-point groups than in the lowest. Almost exactly the same results were reported in Finland (see figure 2:5), and in Stockholm Elmhorn reported that the culpability (again in terms of position on a crime score) of official offenders was over four times that of the others. Their average crime score was 88 points as against 20 for the whole sample.

Rather similar results were found in Utah. Although there was a large amount of admitted delinquency by the sample of ordinary schoolboys they did not compare with the boys in training school in terms of the frequency with which serious offences were committed. A far smaller proportion of non-offenders and one-time offenders committed offences of a 'serious' nature than did persistent offenders who were either in the community or incarcerated: for example, two per cent of the former group committed thefts of more than 50 dollars compared with 46 and 54 per cent of the latter groups (see table 2:5). In London, Gibson reports that while secondary modern schoolboys admitted an average of 3·5 serious acts each, the figure for approved schoolboys was 8·25.

Most writers regard these findings as showing that the system of law enforcement only processes the more serious and frequent delinquents. Christie concludes 'The official system does not select its cases at random. By and large it is the case that the small group of officially registered criminals have also been involved in the largest amount of crime'. Elmhorn thinks:

Table 2:5 A comparison between the number of delinquent acts admitted by non-offenders and various groups of officially known offenders.

Offence	Subsamples in groups of 50			
	Non-delinquents	One time offenders	Delinquents in community	Delinquents incarcerated
Theft				
Articles less than $2	966	1,738	7,886	4,585
Articles worth $2 to $50	60	80	4,671	2,585
Articles more than $50	1	2	90	201
Car theft	4	0	169	649
Forgery	0	0	60	452
Total	**1,031**	**1,820**	**12,876**	**8,472**
Property violations				
Breaking and entering	67	102	527	926
Destroying property	477	800	4,927	4,441
Starting fires (arson)	2	2	0	7
Total	**546**	**904**	**5,454**	**5,374**
Offences against person				
Armed robbery	0	0	22	24
Fighting, assault	354	103	2,207	6,316
Total	**354**	**103**	**2,229**	**6,340**

It is possible that the advantages outweigh the drawbacks. It may be hoped that the high incriminated category of offenders who are caught serve to provide the general preventive effect which is desirable, and which is assumed to be bound up with discovery. From the point of view of individual prevention, and taking a long view, it is perhaps for the best that most of the ordinary incriminated escape discovery, with the social stigmatization it brings in its train, and the risk of identifying themselves with the anti-social elements in the community.

Obviously, two factors are at work here: chance, which favours the once-only offender, and public policy as put into practice by the decisions of the victim and officials – schoolteachers, social workers, police and judges.

On the basis of this evidence it seems that official records include a higher proportion of the more serious and committed offenders than are found in the population as a whole. Erickson and Empey point out that there was little difference in their Utah study between unofficial and one-time only offenders, but very large differences between the one-timer and the persistent offender. On the other hand, as Gold points out, 'the one third of the most delinquent boys who *are* caught may be a highly selected group of youngsters – two thirds, after all are not caught'.

One should not assume that the most involved in crime are easily caught. In fact there is good reason to believe that those professionally involved in crime as a way of life are much less easy to catch. There are no examples from studies of young offenders, but in their study of robbery in London, McClintock and Gibson discovered that those who had been involved in big wage snatches had the lowest incidence of reconviction after leaving prison.[25] This they attributed not to these men's reform, but to their elusiveness. When, and if, such persons are caught one must not therefore regard their official record as giving a true indication of their real involvement in crime. Erickson and Empey found that the more delinquent a boy was the less the official record reflected his most commonly admitted offences. In the Social Survey Study, offenders who were caught for breaking and entering or joyriding admitted between two and six offences per conviction. This finding must account for the seeming innocence of many juvenile offenders. Officially about 80 per cent of all who appear before a court never appear again. It would be ridiculously naive to assume all were *real* first offenders or that all the 80 per cent were true 'successes'. Attempts to explain this apparent innocence should obviously take the findings of self-report studies into account.

In addition we should bear in mind that the crime for which the person is convicted may not be the same thing as the one he committed. It may be difficult to prove a serious offence rather than a minor one, or a serious offence may be dropped in consideration for information of use to the police, as Skolnick points out.[26] Furthermore, in some countries there is a more or less open system of plea-bargaining whereby an offender pleads guilty to a lesser charge in return for less punishment. This process speeds the administration of justice but hides the true nature of offenders' crimes.

Methodological problems of self-report studies

Two fundamental methodological issues are raised by the self-report method. First, when respondents admit to having committed an offence, is their answer true? Was what they did really a crime? Did it have the important component of intent to do harm (where the law requires this)? Was it something that the victim or anyone else who knew about it would have defined as a crime? Secondly, to what extent is the method reliable? Are large numbers of offences concealed? Do respondents take the opportunity to exaggerate their criminal behaviour for fun or fantasy? How reliable are estimates of the frequency with which respondents have committed acts, especially when they are asked to recall their behaviour over considerable periods – sometimes a lifetime? To overcome these problems two different techniques have been developed for self-report studies. The method used most frequently is to present groups of individuals with a list of items and ask them to tick, in complete anonymity, those which they have committed – sometimes they are asked to say how often. The second method involves interviewing each person. Here a technique has been used in which the respondent is given a pack of cards on each of which is written an offence category: he then sorts them into those he has committed and those he has not. The interviewer then asks probing questions about the details of each act – exactly what happened, when it happened and how often. There is a good deal of controversy over which is the most useful technique. The arguments are reviewed below.

Was it a crime? At a fundamental level, it is difficult to know whether to describe these studies as hidden *delinquency* enquiries. Lists of offences only contain a brief title, often little more than a legal label, such as 'stole from a shop', 'attacked another person causing him harm'. But whether or not an act can be regarded as *delinquent* rather than naughty or stupid or 'deviant', depends upon the social situation in which it is committed, and the person who is making the judgment. An act of violence against an unknown stranger would usually be classed as delinquent, a fight between two boys at school as 'troublesome'. In the same way, taking things from home without permission will rarely be classed as theft (although legally, of course, it is); taking things from a store is something different – although even in this case we have already examined evidence which shows that shopkeepers are often unwilling to call the police or prosecute, since *they* do not consider it a crime. Similarly, most office workers would certainly not perceive their private use of office note-paper as larceny by a servant – yet legally it may be.

In the lists of offences which respondents are asked to check there often occur items which are probably rarely regarded as 'delinquent'. In research recently carried out by the British Government Social Survey, and in H. B. Gibson's study, 'taking money from home with no intention of returning it' occurs among the list of 'serious offences' whereas in Elmhorn's enquiry it was merely listed as a 'petty offence'. The problem is even more pronounced with sexual offences. Glaser uses material from a study of a mid-west United States University by Kirkpatrick and Kanin to show a high incidence of hidden sexual crime. He states: 'A tactfully administered enquiry, guaranteeing anonymity, revealed that of 291 female students ... 10·9 per cent in the previous academic year suffered "forceful attempts at intercourse" and 6·2 per cent "aggressively forceful attempts at sex intercourse in the course of which menacing threats or coercive infliction of physical pain were employed", yet none was reported'.[27] Surely all these results indicate is that college sex relations are rather aggressive, not that those participating define their experience as attempted rape. In most studies of school-children in the United States (where the definition of 'delinquency' is extremely wide and not, as in Europe, a synonym for crime committed by the young), the lists of offences include such items as 'had fist fight with one person', 'defied parent's authority', 'taken things you didn't want', 'hurt someone to see them squirm' (Short and Nye), 'took things that belonged to others' (Slocum and Stone), 'took articles less than $2', 'defying people other than parents' (Empey and Erickson). Without a detailed investigation of the situations in which such acts took place – who was the 'victim' and what was the relationship between the respondent and victim – it is difficult to know whether these actions can properly be classified as delinquent.

Respondents in different social classes are likely to perceive the items differently. For example, 'assault' for the middle classes may include behaviour that would be regarded as an everyday occurrence by the working class. Wallerstein and Wyle admit that their postal survey suffered from this defect. Middle-class respondents included such incidents as opening their son's mail as a crime of malicious mischief: many of their offences appear to have been committed against friends or relatives who would not have perceived them as crimes. As Christie and his colleagues point out, 'as long as we do not know if we have sampled delinquent acts that are equally relevant for different strata of the population'[28] we cannot use self-report studies for comparison between different social groups. In reporting theft, those who are 'honest citizens' will include trivia which are neither recognised as theft nor remembered by those who engaged in stealing larger items for personal gain. Thus, the different classes, and the lack of precision with which most items on self-report studies are defined may lead to the inclusion of a great deal of trivial behaviour. If the object of these studies is to compare crimes known and defined as such with similar behaviour *that would be so defined if known,* the inclusion of trivial items simply exaggerates the 'dark figure'.

The most obvious way to overcome this difficulty is for each person to be interviewed about his deviant acts. In his Michigan study, Gold asked each respondent detailed questions about the event and concluded that there was a differential response between socio-economic groups:

Half of the acts of property destruction, one fourth of the confidence games, and one fifth of the personal assaults to which our sample initially admitted could not conceivably be called chargeable offences ... The proportion of confessions of accidental or trivial acts of property destruction was significantly higher among wealthier than among poorer white boys.[29]

Reliability, concealment and exaggeration The arguments for and against a self-completed check-list or an interview are at the moment inconclusive. Those who favour interviews claim that respondents are less likely to exaggerate and that errors due to poor motivation, reading ability and general comprehension can be corrected. On the other hand, there is little evidence that these are major problems with the self-completion method. Dentler claims that only three to four per cent of papers were lost for these reasons.[30] Elmhorn, in Stockholm had a misconception rate of only 0·5 per cent. On the other hand, Erickson and Empey had to interview institutionalised offenders because of their poor comprehension, and even high school students found the listed items difficult to understand.

Another argument is that respondents are more likely to exaggerate their delinquency in the anonymous situation than when confronted with an interviewer. There is little evidence for this either.

Elmhorn found that the relative frequency with which different types of offence were admitted varied very little between the various schools from which the respondents came. It is perhaps unlikely that they all exaggerated in exactly the same way. Furthermore, all those researchers who have relied on the self-completion method have reported that their subjects appeared to take the exercise seriously. Exaggeration may occur among a few isolated individuals but there is no evidence of consistent exaggeration. In the few studies where the subjects have been re-tested after a reasonable period of time, very similar results have again been found – Dentler produced test-retest correlations of between 80 and 92 per cent for theft scales (but the much lower rate of 64 per cent for aggression scales) and in a Norwegian study 94 per cent of subjects who were interviewed six to nine months after a self-completion test insisted that they had answered honestly.[31] Admittedly this kind of evidence is not very conclusive, but the fact that all researchers have reported similar experience does suggest that these studies are not especially unreliable.

If there is a problem it is much more likely to be one of concealment, either deliberate or due to faulty memory. Nye reported definite evidence of defensiveness among his subjects, and in one of his enquiries Dentler excluded a third of the respondents for over-endorsing items which were socially desirable.[32] The Utah high school students also concealed offences until probed by sceptical questioning. Nevertheless, when investigators have compared the self-reports of those known to the police with their official records they have found no evidence of respondents failing to describe the offences for which they have been charged (Erickson and Empey). Martin Gold used an ingenious method for checking the validity of his respondents' answers. He obtained the co-operation of a small group of 'informants' in the community who provided detailed information of acts committed by 125 of his 522 respondents. When questioned, 72 per cent of these 125 admitted the acts specified by the 'spies'; 11 per cent gave doubtful answers, which in some respects contradicted the spies' reports, and 17 per cent definitely concealed offences reported by the spies. These offences tended to be among the more serious – breaking and entering, property destruction and carrying concealed weapons. An even more ingenious check was made by Clark and Tifft,[33] who used both a follow-up interview and a polygraph (lie-test) to check the self-completed responses of 40 mid-western American university students. Comparing the initial responses with the lie detector it appeared that all changed at least something. Three-quarters of the changes increased the amount of deviant behaviour admitted. The average accuracy of initial response was 81·5 per cent over 35 items, but there was a range from 47–97 per cent. Clark and Tifft point out that those items most frequently used – those comprising the Short-Nye and Dentler-Monroe scales – are rather inaccurate. Under-reporting was especially noted in respect of truanting and stealing small amounts, and over-reporting for offences involving violence and sexual exploits in which the respondents might tend to 'role-play' the masculine ideal.

The obvious advantages of interviewing are the opportunities to check details of the offence in order to establish whether criminal intent was involved, to question possible exaggerations and fantasies, and to interpret items which may be misunderstood by the less well-educated. Its disadvantage is that it clearly makes it more difficult to convince the respondent that he is protected by anonymity. As one of Gold's respondents said: 'You have enough on me to send me up for thirty years'. The interviewer who attempts to gain *rapport* by a sympathetic approach may produce concealment on embarrassing items, while a more cold and authoritarian approach may engender lack of trust. The interviewee has certainly both more to gain and lose than the 'self-completer'. He is likely to have something to gain from exaggerating his behaviour by projecting an image of toughness or manliness. He will 'lose' it if he feels guilty. James Coleman noted that when high school girls in Illinois were asked by an adult about drinking and smoking 15 per cent said they drank and 23 per cent that they smoked. In a similar study in Baltimore, high school girls were asked the same question by other high school juniors and there 30 per cent admitted drinking and 58 per cent smoking. Despite the differences in area, Coleman suggests that there may have been considerable concealment in his study through using adult inter-viewers.[34]

So far, there is no firm evidence to indicate that in general one method is better than another. What is clear, however, is that the interview is probably preferable for certain purposes, especially when the enquiry is concerned to classify hidden crime in terms of its seriousness and frequency. A seriousness scale must be based on an assessment of the actual circumstances of the offence, and frequency counts, relying on memory as they do, can be checked more thoroughly through the searching promptings of an interview.

Some of the self-completion studies have devised an index of seriousness for the offences in their lists. In Norway this was done by two criminal law professors, and in Stockholm on an arbitrary basis by the research staff. In each case a score had to be given to a very crude description of the offence – such as taking things from cafés and restaurants, breaking and entering, taking by force or threat of using force. Obviously there could be a very wide range of circumstances involved under any one of these general headings – the object taken from the restaurant could be a menu or a complete set of cutlery! In contrast to this crude method of scoring, Gold was able to use the method developed by Sellin and Wolfgang[35] to give specific weights to the offence depending on the amount of property stolen, the degree and the extent of violence used. In such a system it is possible to distinguish clearly the petty from the major theft, the minor from the major damage and the slight assault from the serious attack.

It is also likely that interviewing will increase the reliability of information on the frequency with which acts have been performed. If questions are asked about a restricted number of items the interviewer can aid the respondent considerably in problems of recall. In the self-completion situation either he will simply guess at an approximate number (and the frequent offender may give a wildly inaccurate estimate) or plump for a simple category such as 'occasionally' or 'frequently'. Whichever method is used, it is clear that attempts to get respondents to remember all acts committed over a period of years are unlikely to be very accurate. In general, we must agree with Dentler's view that these studies are a better guide to who admits 'an' offence. Certainly, attempts to get a total recall of criminality should be restricted to a very specific period, probably one year at the most.

One of the main contributors to self-report research, Robert Dentler, has recently announced his decision to discontinue this type of study. There appear to be two main reasons. First, Dentler and his associates have found little relationship between scales isolating different aspects of deviant behaviour – for example, an individual's score on a theft scale is not a good predictor of his score on a vandalism or an aggressive behaviour scale. This seems to show that there is some evidence of specialisation in specific types of delinquency, and they therefore doubt the value of lists which lump together all these offences. Secondly, they have failed to find an expected relationship between such factors as 'sexual experience, deprivation, alienation, mother punishment and father punishment' and self-reported misconduct. Thus they are placed in the dilemma of not knowing whether this result should be interpreted as evidence to reject these hypothesised relationships, or as *prima facie* evidence of the invalidity of the self-report method. They conclude that 'some of the findings are reliable and valid, and that a few ... challenge current social theories of delinquency causation. But the method seems too shaky and equivocal to deserve further effort'.[36] In our opinion, this conclusion is too pessimistic. Undoubtedly, researchers will improve their methodology and when self-report studies are used in conjunction with studies of the law enforcement process they will enrich our understanding of the relationship between the incidence and distribution of deviant behaviour in the population and its definition and enforcement as 'delinquent' or 'criminal' through the legal system.

Self-report studies, however, can only look at the results of a process which discriminates between those who become known and those who remain hidden delinquents. In recent years there has been a large increase in research which has attempted to look in detail at the process through which young offenders become officially labelled 'delinquent'. These studies are reviewed in the next section.

Studies of the law enforcement process

Empirical studies of the way in which the police use their powers in deciding whether to arrest or initiate prosecutions against offenders are rare and restricted entirely to the United States. In some police forces in England and other countries there exist sets of agreed instructions to guide the police in the use of their discretion, but no enquiries have been carried out into the way they operate in practice.

In many police jurisdictions a large proportion of offenders is released without proceedings being taken against them. The police may either release them with an informal caution or they may be formally cautioned. If the first procedure is used it is unlikely that the event will be recorded. Available statistics only deal, therefore, with those offenders who have been released after a formal police enquiry.

La Fave[37] reports that in Detroit in 1940 only one in seven juveniles arrested is eventually brought before the court. Robert Terry, in a mid-west industrial city of about 100,000 population, reported that over four-fifths of offenders were released by the police and of the remainder over a quarter was released after being referred to a probation department (see figure 2:6).[38] Similarly, in a study of three different jurisdictions in the eastern United States, Nathan Goldman[39] found that 64 per cent of a sample of over a thousand young people were released without court appearance.

There are, of course, substantial variations between police forces. James Wilson[40] shows that a highly professionalised force in Westville (western USA) used discretionary powers much less frequently than a non-professional 'fraternal' force in an eastern city. He attributed the large use of discretion in Eastville to the lack of bureaucratic pressure for records, police sympathy with lower-class youth, from whose ranks they had been recruited, and a belief that most offences were not serious enough to warrant official action:

Most of the kids around here get two or three chances. Let me give you an example. There was this fellow around here who is not vicious, not, I think, what you'd call bad; he's really sort of a good kid. He just can't move without getting into trouble. I don't know what there is about him … I'll read you his record. 1958 – he's picked up for shoplifting, given a warning. 1958 – again a few months later was picked up for illegal possession [of dangerous weapons]. He had some dynamite caps and railroad flares. Gave him another warning. 1959 – the next year he stole a bike. Got a warning. 1960 – he broke into some freight cars. [Taken to court and] continued without a finding [that is, no court action] on the understanding that he would pay restitution. Later the same year he was a runaway from home. No complaint was brought against him. Then in 1960 he started getting into some serious stuff. There was larceny and committing an unnatural act with a retarded boy. So, he went up on that one and was committed to [the reformatory] for nine months. Got out. In 1962 he was shot while attempting a larceny in a junk yard at night … Went to court, continued without a finding [that is, no punishment]. Now that's typical of a kid who just sort of can't stay out of trouble. He only went up once out of, let me see … eight offenses … I wouldn't call him a bad kid despite the record … The bad kids: we don't have a lot of those.

In 1965 over 10 per cent of all known male offenders in England and Wales were formally cautioned, and the proportion was as high as 31 per cent for those aged 10 to 14, and 15 per cent for 14 to 17 year olds (see figure 2:7).[41] It is not known what proportion are dealt with informally, but it is probably substantial.

Obviously, with police discretion such an important factor in determining who enters the criminal statistics as a recorded offender, it is important to examine the criteria being used.

For example, in a police juvenile liaison scheme in London, under which children are dealt with informally, the kinds of cases thought

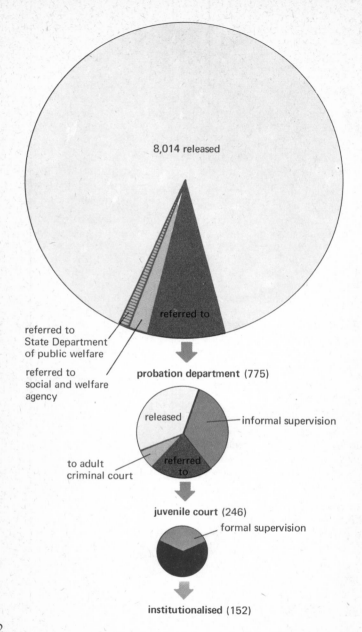

8,014 released

referred to

referred to
State Department
of public welfare

referred to
social and welfare
agency

probation department (775)

released

informal supervision

to adult
criminal court

referred
to

juvenile court (246)

formal supervision

institutionalised (152)

Figure 2:6 (left) How delinquents were dealt with in a mid-west industrial city in the United States.

Figure 2:7 (below) The proportion of known male offenders in different age groups, cautioned in England and Wales, 1965.

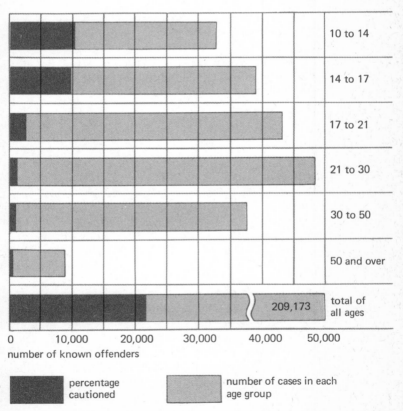

number of known offenders

percentage cautioned   number of cases in each age group

suitable are those involved in hooliganism or minor damage where the owner is unwilling to take action, those known to frequent undesirable cafés or associate with undesirable persons, those committing petty larcenies who admit the offence. The factors that are supposed to be taken into account are age, seriousness of offence, admission, previous record (those who have already been before the court are usually excluded), home background, likelihood of recurrence, wishes of the aggrieved party, welfare and safety of the offender and the offender's 'general suitability for treatment by caution'. In Canada, a court official decides whether a child should be charged. It is laid down that those who create a risk of serious bodily harm to another person should always be charged, as should those who have a previous conviction.[42] No wonder that one criminologist, Harwin Voss, goes so far as to state that 'records describe the behavior of officials – policemen, judges and probation officers – rather than the behavior of adolescents'.[43]

The use of informal cautions is likely to vary according to the information the officer has about the offender. La Fave points out that the policy of not charging juveniles for relatively minor offences is affected by the size of the community – in a small town the officer is likely to know all those who have previously appeared in court but in a city it will be necessary to take the offender to the police station, check his record and administer a formal caution.[44] Another major factor is the police perception of the function and effectiveness of the juvenile court. Where the court is thought of as a valuable body, fully competent to make decisions in the best interests of the offenders, cautioning will be rare. This has, for example, been the official view of the Metropolitan police in London until recently: in 1966 over 11,000 juveniles were prosecuted and only 93 formally cautioned. In contrast, Piliavin and Briar[45] in a study of a highly reputed California police force, found officers generally reluctant to stigmatise offenders with a court appearance, and sceptical of the value of the 'rehabilitative techniques' available to the court. They conceived their role, in relation to juvenile offenders, as preventive, avoiding court referral as frequently as possible – rather than leaving the selection process to the court itself. Nathan Goldman found similar attitudes in the eastern United States. At the other end of the scale, police officers may fail to prosecute because they regard the court as generally too lenient with offenders. La Fave found Detroit officers frequently expressing this view:

Table 2:6 Percentage of arrested offenders taken to juvenile court in certain areas of eastern USA.

Offence	Total arrests	To juvenile court	
Larceny	284	37·3	} 38·1
Receiving stolen goods	10	60·0	
Burglary	138	73·2	} 75·0
Robbery	10	100·	
Car theft	46	91·3	} 91·1
Riding in stolen car	10	90·0	
Assault	2	100·	
Sex	42	83·3	} 82·9
Carrying concealed weapons	3	66·7	
Incorrigible delinquent	42	80·9	} 69·5
Runaway	40	52·5	
Disorderly	54	35·2	
Vagrancy	4	25·0	
Prowling	1	100·	
Drunkenness	8	12·5	
Gambling	31	3·2	} 11·6
Trespassing	39	0·	
Violation boro ordinance	153	5·2	
Motor law violation	20	20·0	
Army uniform violation	1	100·	
Mischief	64	4·7	
Malicious mischief	104	13·5	} 10·7
Property damage	128	10·9	
Arson	2	50·0	
Total	**1,236**	**35·4**	

We may go around here for months trying to figure out who the hell is committing a bunch of petty crimes. We finally apprehend the guy and bring him before a judge. But since he is a juvenile, he gets off easy.[46]

Nearly all commentators agree that the major factors taken into account by the police are: seriousness of the offence, previous convictions, quality of parental control, styles of dress and hair and, most important, the attitude of the offender when confronted by the police.

Goldman's enquiry revealed that 91 per cent of young car thieves were prosecuted compared with only 38 per cent of thieves and 11 per cent of those committing damage (see table 2:6). Looking at four different areas the variation in the proportions prosecuted was much greater for minor than for serious offences. Piliavin and Briar suggest that officers regard a serious offence such as robbery, auto theft, arson and rape as evidence of confirmed delinquency although even so, in one year 30 per cent of juveniles involved in burglaries and 12 per cent in auto theft were not charged. On the other hand most offences are relatively minor and here previous record and personal factors are important. Those with a record are usually regarded as confirmed delinquents and charged, but the situation in which the offence occurs may be an important additional variable. Where boys are fighting within a gang structure, or where violence is committed between members of minority groups it is, according to La Fave, often ignored. Where such offences are committed against persons outside the offender's social group, there is far more likely to be official action.

Goldman also found that a lower proportion of middle-class children were prosecuted and a group of 90 policemen when interviewed admitted taking family background into account. Those with 'bad homes' were taken to court either 'for their own protection' or because it was considered that the family could not control recurrences of the behaviour: Martin Gold, in his self-report study also found that 'police station adjustment' rather than referral to court was more frequent for middle than lower status boys. While middle-class children are believed to stop delinquency after a warning and discipline from their parents, working-class children 'need' the discipline of the courts. In other words the police are engaged in predicting the probabilities of the offender becoming a recidivist. The same kind of reasoning can perhaps be seen in the practice of arresting a higher proportion of Negroes in the United States. Cameron[47] noted that whereas Negro shoplifters outnumbered

76

whites by the ratio of 1·8:1, 4·8 times as many were arrested. Jerome Skolnick[48] in his study of a California police department found Negroes arrested far more frequently than whites for failing to pay traffic fines. This he attributed not to racial bias, but to the fact that a higher proportion of Negroes exhibit characteristics that seem to be associated with a high risk of failing to pay – such as being un-employed and on welfare assistance. James Wilson, similarly found the police in 'Eastville' more frequently arresting Negroes, but apparently because the officers considered they lacked decent homes and needed institutional discipline and treatment. It may be true that the police regard Negroes more often as potential recidivists, and there are statistics to show a higher Negro crime rate – but by enforcing the law in this way they are, of course, simply ensuring a self-fulfilling prophecy.

The Negro is, in fact, in an analogous situation to any sub-group with both a high crime rate and distinguishing physical or attitu-dinal characteristics. American studies show how gang boys, hang-ing around street corners, are constantly singled out for interroga-tion: in the same way Negroes feel themselves to be harassed by the police.

The police do not respect Negro juveniles as human beings; he is picked up if he has a beard, picked up if he has the wrong clothing on, picked up if he's a 'beatnik', and picked up if he's out after curfew hours without a chance to explain or give a reason; if he has a motorcycle, he is likely to be stopped.[49]

Werthman and Piliavin point out that the police tend to use their powers under vagrancy, loitering and curfew laws to arrest juveniles who are under suspicion because of their general behaviour. In doing this they will rely on various 'cues'. They are especially suspi-cious of street corner groups, youths on the street during school or working hours, and those who wear distinctive clothes and hair styles:

The police more or less correctly assess the long hair, black leather jacket, blue-jeans complex as fair warning that its owners are making claims to being 'tough' ... a delinquent is therefore not a juvenile who happens to have com-mitted an illegal act. He is a young person whose character has been negatively assessed.[50]

According to Piliavin and Briar the most important cue is the way the boy responds to the police. If he confesses quickly, appears penitent and anxious he will be classed as a 'victim of circumstance' or 'salvageable' and consequently dealt with informally. If, on the other hand, the offender's demeanour is hostile, lacking in respect and unco-operative he is more likely to get himself defined as someone who 'doesn't respect the law'. Most of the officers interviewed by Werthman and Piliavin felt that the attitude of the offender was the major determinant of the decision to prosecute in about half their cases. Similarly Piliavin and Briar's study shows that of the 21 youths in their study who were classed as unco-operative 14 were arrested compared to only two of the 45 who were co-operative.

This evidence does not mean that the police are necessarily prejudiced. The 'cues' they use in deciding to arrest and prosecute may all be highly correlated with previous criminality and a poor prognosis. Robert Terry, in a study of over 9,000 cases in mid-western USA, found that the seriousness of offence committed, number of previous offences and age of offender were all related to the police decision to refer to the probation department or the court. However, socio-economic status, race (whether Anglo-Saxon, Mexican-American or Negro) and sex were not related to the use of police discretion *when previous record was taken into account*. It should be remembered that this is a study of formal use of discretion, and does not indicate what factors led the police to decide to take initial action.[51]

In summary, it appears that both the police and the public have definite stereotypes about the kinds of offence and offender which should be dealt with by the criminal law: seriousness of offence is certainly a major criterion for official action, but so also are persistence in offending, lack of family support, membership of street corner groups, and dress and demeanour that indicate a self-image of toughness and anti-authoritarianism. In the enforcement of the law, three different factors are being taken into account – societal reaction reflected in the criterion of the seriousness of the offence; the need to provide help or guidance – reflected, for example, in the criteria of family conditions and status; and the probability of offending in the future, reflected in the criteria of previous record, companions, work record, dress and demeanour.

These findings illustrate one major flaw in the arguments of those who see self-reported deviant conduct as 'hidden delinquency'. Gibson for example suggests that his study shows that over half the grammar school boys admitted serious offences 'which would have landed them in serious trouble had they been detected, in which case they would have been officially classified as delinquents'. Just as many offenders known to the police are not proceeded against, many 'hidden deviants' would probably not become official offenders even if their misconduct were known.

In the same way that the factors outlined above are important in the decision whether or not to prosecute, they occur again at each stage of the penal process. Similar factors are taken into account in sentencing, so that studies based on (say) men serving long sentences of imprisonment obviously can only represent a tiny proportion of the offending population. Generalisations from such populations about offenders in general must be viewed with the greatest caution.

3 Subcultural and gang delinquency

We began chapter 1 by complaining that criminological theorists often did not pay enough attention to the facts they were supposed to explain. In that chapter and the last one, we outlined some major findings on 'hidden' crime which have shed new light on the problem of delinquency. We showed that a large proportion of crime – even quite serious crime – is hidden; that a large proportion of young people admit to at least one delinquent act during their adolescence, but that a much smaller proportion persist in frequent and serious delinquency; that few young offenders are caught and even fewer proceeded against, but that those who are most persistent are more likely to be caught and officially judged delinquents; that in reality delinquency is much more widely spread through the social classes than one would suppose from official figures, but that the more serious and frequent delinquencies are more likely to be committed by the lower socio-economic groups; and finally, that the process of law enforcement takes into account, to some extent, an assessment of the probability of future delinquency as perceived by the police and others in authority, the criteria used being related especially to social class, styles of dress, manner and demeanour on arrest.

But the whole picture of delinquency is by no means filled by these studies. Sociologists emphasise that delinquency is not just a conglomeration of individual acts, but that much of it is learned in association with others, just as other values, norms and standards of behaviour are learned. Even though hidden-delinquency studies in small towns have shown little difference in the rate of delinquency between children from different social backgrounds, there is overwhelming evidence that those who are persistent delinquents mainly associate with other delinquents, and in doing so, share 'certain ways of looking at the world'.[1] It is these ways of 'looking at the world', which have through time become traditional in delinquent groups, that sociologists have called 'the delinquent subculture'. The subculture contains certain beliefs, values, norms (expectations members have of each other) and forms of behaviour which are generally condoned, approved or even required of members. One facet of delinquency which it is essential to understand is the nature of social relationships within the delinquent subculture, for as Short[2] points out, 'the influence of particular subcultures on an individual's behaviour depends, to a considerable extent, on the nature of his relations with other carriers of these subcultures'. What is often at issue is whether this subculture is a peculiarly lower-class pheno-menon or whether similar social relations and patterns of behaviour exist among middle-class youth.

There has been a great deal of theorising about the factors leading to the establishment and maintenance of the delinquent subculture and about the values and norms governing behaviour within the group. But – except for work carried out in the thirties – there was until recently a dearth of empirical research aimed at describing the social relationships within which delinquency commonly takes place. Research of this kind is of vital importance, because as we shall see there are major theoretical disputes about the nature of the subculture and the forces which maintain it in being which need verifying by research. Before reviewing the main findings of such research, we shall first briefly outline the major theoretical issues. There are four broadly different explanations given for the occurr-ence of delinquent subcultures.

1 The Chicago school of the late thirties and early forties described the subculture as a product of social disorganisation and lack of cohesion in the slum. A general breakdown of social controls, the concentration of persons with few social ties – such as immigrants, the mentally ill and the destitute – and a consequent lack of parental control over the young, were seen to lead to an autonomous 'society' of children in the street. In Frederick Thrasher's classic description of the gang,[3] delinquency is seen as a natural progession from, and consequence of, a childhood search for excitement in a frustrating and limiting environment.

A related view of social disorganisation is put forward in a num-ber of British studies. Morris[4] in Croydon and Jephcott and Carter[5] in 'Radby', an English Midland town, attributed most delinquency to pockets of 'problem families' with little social control over their children, low standards of child care and a lack of emotional stability in the home. In this situation as well, the young adolescent becomes 'free' to join the street corner group.

2 A second theory has been suggested by the anthropologist Walter Miller, who has made intensive investigations of lower-class life and gangs in Boston.[6] Miller sees delinquency as a variant of traditional lower class behaviour. The delinquent gang is, he claims, not a legitimate unit of study *per se*. Miller stresses that the typical structure of social relations in the lower class of large cities is the 'one sex' peer group: males and females may come together for casual associations, but these are rarely stable. The boy is usually reared in a female-dominated household, and so in adolescence the street-corner group 'provides the first real opportunity to learn essential aspects of the male role in the context of peers facing similar problems of sex-role identification'. The peer group is, Miller claims, in many cases 'the most stable and solidary primary group he has ever belonged to'. He further asserts that:

The activity patterns of the group require a high level of intra-group solidarity; individual members must possess a good capacity for subordinating individual desires to general group interests as well as the capacity for intimate and persisting interaction. Thus highly 'disturbed' individuals, or those who cannot tolerate consistently imposed sanctions on 'deviant' behaviour, cannot remain accepted members ... This selective process produces a type of group whose members possess to an unusually high degree both the *capacity* and *motivation* to conform to perceived cultural norms.

The norms and values to which members of the peer group conform are seen by Miller as being 'focal concerns' ('areas or issues which command widespread and persistent attention and a high degree of emotion involvement') common to the lower class. They revolve around concern about getting into trouble, toughness, 'smartness' or quick-wittedness, excitement or thrills, a tendency to consider factors affecting one's life as due to fate, fortune and luck, and lastly an ambivalence towards being individually autonomous or being controlled by social institutions. Delinquents are simply seen as being more involved with these concerns than other lower-class youth.

3 The third view is markedly different. Its main exponents have been Albert Cohen[7] and Richard Cloward and Lloyd Ohlin,[8] and their theories have been the main focus of recent discussion and empirical research. Broadly, their contention is that delinquency is the collective solution of young lower-class males placed in a situation of stress; a situation where opportunities for advancement in wealth or status through legitimate channels are blocked. The subculture is described by Cohen and Cloward and Ohlin as being the culture of the lower-class gang; its values and norms, or prescrip-

tions for behaviour, are oppositional, that is, they are in conflict with those of conventional society. In their view the delinquent subculture is really what Yinger[9] has called a *contraculture*.

Cohen suggests that lower-class boys are not equipped by their upbringing to be able to compete successfully for high status through the educational system. They are not trained, as middle-class children are, to forgo immediate gratification; nor are they taught the value of rationality and the control of aggression. Furthermore they are more independent of their parents and are less likely to conform to parental expectations, for they commonly get much of their gratification through emotional relationships with other children of a similar age. Their consequent low educational performance, when compared with their attempts to achieve status in academic terms, is seen by Cohen to lead to frustration and anxiety which is resolved by a 'reaction-formation' through which middle-class values and norms (by which the school measures status) are replaced by a collective subcultural solution. In the subculture boys gain status through behaviour they *can* achieve, emphasising the antithesis of school values: non-utilitarian, malicious, negative behaviour – all done for purposes of short-run gratification. Thus the delinquent subculture provides a group solution for all those suffering 'status frustration'. Cohen is careful to point out that he is explaining the *genesis* of the subculture: why the values and norms are what they are. But he also suggests that the core of the delinquent group do share these problems of adjustment, even if all who join do not. In Cohen's view, the subculture is found in the institution of the gang which is described as having extremely cohesive relationships:

Relations with gang members tend to be intensely solidary and imperious ... the gang is a separate, distinct and often irresistible focus of attraction, loyalty and solidarity.[10]

Cloward and Ohlin describe the subculture rather differently. They see most delinquency as activity with a definite aim: to gain wealth by illegitimate means. Their explanation of the subculture (following Merton's theory of *anomie*[11]) differs from Cohen's, in that they explain delinquency mainly as a reaction to lack of opportunity to reach the success-goal of high income through employment or other legitimate channels, and the consequent adoption of illegitimate means to achieve this goal. Delinquency is not a reaction to middle-class standards, but a 'withdrawal of legitimacy' from them. But like Cohen, they see the subculture as existing in the form of the gang, and regard membership as making delinquency mandatory: 'certain forms of delinquent activity are *essential requirements* for the performance of the dominant roles supported by the subculture' (our italics).[12]

Cloward and Ohlin suggest that not all lower-class youth will be able to achieve success through illegitimate means, and that whether or not they do will depend upon local opportunities. There are, they claim, three distinct types of subculture: criminal, conflict and retreatist. The 'criminal subculture' is to be found in stable working-class areas where youthful delinquency can be integrated with adult 'rackets' (organised crime). The main aim in this criminal sub-culture is to make 'the big score' and graduate to the successful adult criminal class. Where these opportunities do not exist, such as in 'disorganised' areas of new immigrants, there is a 'conflict sub-culture' with emphasis on the delinquent 'winning by coercion' the attention and opportunity he lacks. This culture emphasises the warrior cult: 'rep' (reputation), 'heart' (courage) and 'turf' (one's local territory) being crucial aspects. The third subculture is said to exist for the 'double failure', the boy who neither has criminal opportunities, nor can gain status in the conflict group – he 'retreats' to the subculture of drugs. A rather similar elaboration has been suggested by Cohen and Short[13] but they suggest that different styles of subculture grow out of a 'parent-male' subculture shared by all youth in their early teens.

While it is clear that the *explanations* for the existence of sub-cultures of Miller and the Social Disorganisation school are sub-stantially different from Cohen's and Cloward and Ohlin's, they are in substantial agreement on one basic issue. All see the delinquent subculture as a specifically lower-class phenomenon. They all emphasise that gangs, poor school and work performance and loose home ties are special attributes of the members of this lower class and that delinquency must be explained in terms of the social conditions in which lower-class youth are placed. Middle-class delinquency, insofar as it is admitted, is seen as an entirely different phenomenon.

4 It is the third view, of the subculture arising from the frustrations of the lower class as an oppositional system of behaviour, which has been attacked by David Matza in *Delinquency and Drift*[14] and other essays. Matza's main concern is to emphasise the similarity

84

between delinquents and other youth. There are three main reasons why he does not accept the view that the delinquent subculture is a peculiarly lower-class conflict-orientated phenomenon. First, he believes that most delinquents recognise that what they do is wrong and feel guilty about it: in order to deal with this the subculture contains all kinds of rationalisations which are designed to make delinquency acceptable to its members. These he calls 'techniques of neutralisation', by which he means such justifications for aggression as the claim that it was necessary for self-defence.[15] Secondly, he believes that the idea of a fully-fledged delinquent subculture in which members are _required_ to commit crimes explains 'too much delinquency'. He suggests that boys are not committed to full-time conflict with conventional society: their delinquencies are episodic, they 'drift' occasionally into them. Thirdly, Matza suggests that delinquency is an activity that is easily given up – and that the sub-cultural thesis makes this difficult to explain.

He therefore argues that delinquency occurs because adolescents are in a state of suspension between childhood and adulthood, spend most of their time with their peers, and are anxious both about their identity as males and their acceptance by the peer group. They conform to the norms of the group because not to do so would threaten their status. Each individual thinks that the others support delinquent activity, and so he himself supports it. In reality, Matza suggests, this is a 'comedy of errors', for each person is under a misapprehension that others around him are committed to delin-quency, whereas in reality they are not. These 'shared misunderstand-ings' are not challenged because of status anxiety. Matza and Sykes[16] suggest that these misunderstandings are about delinquency because the dominant theme of adolescent activity is leisure, and leisure pursuits emphasise the importance of toughness and masculinity:

A number of supposedly deviant values are closely akin to those embodied in the leisure activities of the dominant society. To view adolescents in general and delinquents in particular as members of the last leisure class may help us explain both the large amount of unrecorded delinquency and the occurrence of delinquency throughout the class structure.

The values of the delinquent, they claim, are the same as those of the gentleman of leisure – concern for adventure, excitement, disdain for regular hard work, desire for quick financial success, verbal and physical aggression demonstrating toughness and masculinity. Matza and Sykes' view is that the 'quality of the values is obscured by their context'; they draw attention to Merton's important observation that what are seen as virtues in the 'in group' may be perceived as vices when done by the 'out group'. The values of leisure are seen as co-existing with those of 'security and routinisation', but in middle-class society they are limited to specific socially-approved contexts. The delinquent, in contrast, lives by these values at inappropriate times: what is deviant is his 'bad timing'. Delinquency is considered to be, therefore, only 'a disturbing reflection or a caricature' of society.

We can see that criminologists are now faced with a number of rival theories of the subculture. Each of these rests upon a number of assumptions about what the subculture is really like. Cohen and Cloward and Ohlin see it as a more cohesive set of relationships, demanding conformity, than Matza does. On the other hand, Matza seems to be claiming that lower-class background, poor school and work performance are irrelevant factors in delinquency. Indeed it seems as if theory has outstripped research and that what is needed is more detailed investigations to establish more precisely what behaviour is characteristically committed by delinquent groups, what the nature and structure of peer groups is, what social bonds exist within the group and what values, beliefs and norms members share. Furthermore as Albert Cohen pointed out in 1955:[17]

We need much more full and detailed data on the delinquent action itself ... we need to know more about the collective or individual nature of the delinquent act and how delinquency varies in individual and group situations   it would be desirable to continue and expand research on delinquent groups as social systems, that is research whose object is the structure, the process, the history of the subculture of the group as such rather than the delinquent individual. ... Such research should investigate systematically the origin and dissolution of these groups, their status systems, their spirit and ideologies, their systems for control and maintenance of morale and their attitudes towards and interaction with other agencies and groups in the wider community ... Needless to say, this type of research is fraught with great difficulty. Our techniques for the study of small groups in action are crude and the problems of 'getting close' to live delinquent groups and observing them at first hand are enormous. On the other hand no type of research is of potentially greater value for throwing new light on delinquency ...

In the last ten years there has been an increasing amount of research which has challenged basic assumptions about the subculture and led to new insights. Nearly all of it has, however, been in the United States and almost all has dealt with the delinquent gang rather than the subculture in a more general sense. This research has cast doubt on the concept of the highly organised gang, the existence of a 'criminally-orientated' subculture, the notion of internal solidarity and group loyalty within gangs and the idea that delinquency is simply negative, malicious and consciously in opposition to middle class standards. Researchers have aimed to describe the gang boy in more detail and in particular to examine his values and aspirations and the norms controlling his behaviour. We shall deal in turn with research concerned with the structure of groups, their behaviour, their solidarity, their values, aspirations and norms.

The structure of delinquent groups

There is no doubt that the vast majority of early and mid-adolescent delinquency is carried out in groups. In the United States, Shaw and McKay found that nearly 90 per cent of offenders had accomplices; the Gluecks found 70 per cent. There have been similar results in Germany, Switzerland, France, England and Scandinavia (see Sveri[18]). Nearly all these studies, which have been of convicted delinquents, have found the normal number of persons involved to be two or three. They have also shown that as delinquents grow older they are more likely to commit offences alone, but until their twenties over half of offenders are still likely to have known associates. The following graphs show figures for Norway and London (see figure 3:1). They are remarkably similar. Of course these figures are based on police knowledge and do not necessarily reflect the group structure in which delinquency takes place. Yet they do seem to be supported by observation of delinquent groups or gangs. Miller[19] in a detailed observational study of Boston gangs notes that the average incident of theft had two participants, and that 40 per cent of thefts were committed by persons acting alone. Other experienced observers have also claimed that most offences are committed by groups of two or three.

But, while much theft and hooliganism may be committed by small groups of friends, these may still be members of larger groups from which they get 'moral support' for their actions. The most institutionalised form of the subculture is the organised 'gang'. Gangs are written about as widely in the academic literature of criminology as in the popular press, and yet surprisingly little is known about their organisation, structure and interpersonal relationships. In fact there seems a great deal of disagreement at the purely descriptive level.

87

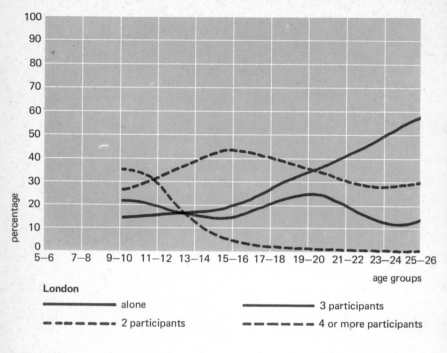

London

——— alone		——— 3 participants
- - - 2 participants		– – – 4 or more participants

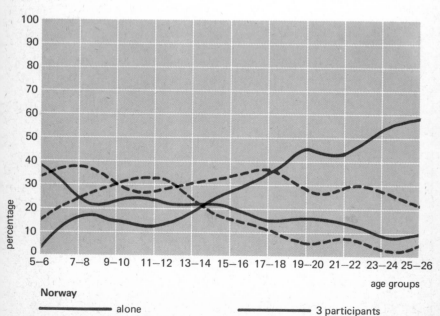

Norway

——— alone		——— 3 participants
- - - 2 participants		– – – 4 or more participants

Figure 3:1 Percentage of boys in various age groups who commit crime alone or in groups of varying size: **a (top left)** shows known offenders in two East London (UK) boroughs who have committed all types of offence; **b (bottom left)** shows known offenders found guilty of theft in Norway.

Probably the issue most debated is the organisational structure and membership of the gang. A number of studies has questioned the traditional picture based on Thrasher's study of over a thousand groups in Chicago in the twenties. Thrasher described the gang as having 'tradition, unreflective internal structure, *esprit de corps*, solidarity, group awareness and attachment to local territory'. There were known leaders, a recognised membership and clearly defined roles such as war counsellor, armourer and treasurer. As Yablonsky[20] points out, the descriptions of New York gangs given in the early fifties by the New York Youth Board supported this picture. It is also supported by other studies. A detailed investigation of gang leaders in Los Angeles revealed that many of the gangs had an area tradition going back thirty to fifty years. They were organised on an age-graded basis into 'babes', 'midgets', 'juniors' and 'seniors', all relatively autonomous groups, but firm allies.

This picture is not supported, however, by Yablonsky's detailed study of a conflict gang, 'the Balkans' in central New York. He concluded:

Today's violent gang is characterised by flux. It lacks features of an organised group, having neither a definite number of members, specific membership roles, a consensus of expected norms, nor a leader who supplies logical directions for action. It is a moblike collectivity that forms around violence in a spontaneous fashion, moving into action – often on the spur of an evening's boredom – in search of kicks.

Despite claims that they had hundreds of members, and numerous alliances, Yablonsky only discovered about 20 to 30 boys who seemed firm members. The core members were even fewer. There were separate formal roles of president, war counsellor and armourer but, as Klein has also pointed out from studies of gangs in California, there were frequent changes of members filling these roles. Most studies, in fact, seem to support the view that although a potentially large 'membership' may be mobilised at times of external threats from other groups, gangs usually only have a relatively small core.

In Thrasher's study, over three quarters of the gangs had no more than 25 members. Similarly, Short and Strodtbeck[21] in their recent detailed survey of 16 Chicago gangs rarely found more than 20 members gathered together – even though formal membership was as high as 68. Again Gannon,[22] who gathered material from New York Youth Board social workers, points out that although average gang membership may be 35, the group is held together by a small clique of six to 15 boys, although two thirds of the groups had no formal leadership. Klein and Crawford, in Los Angeles, also claim that although gang membership may be as high as 200, there were usually fewer than 30 to 40 active members.[23] Turnover is high, with many members 'joining' for only a few weeks or months. Apparently gangs observed as far apart as Argentina[24] and Paris[25] only have, at the core, a fairly small group of permanent members, between about eight and 20. Thus the large gang, although it may exist on certain occasions of stress, is not a permanent and solidary group: as in Short's and Strodtbeck's words 'the gang is not the close-knit highly cohesive entity which one might expect'. It seems that it is in the situation of impending conflict that the gang attempts to increase its hold over peripheral members in order to help in defence. In this situation members have no conception of the size of their organisation. Yablonsky found that although he could only trace 51 possible members, their estimates of the size of the 'team' varied enormously, 20 guessing at between four and six hundred. Duke, the leader, explains this by saying:

Each guy wasn't sure of his own membership or who else was in the team, so they naturally weren't sure of their alliances. Each one had a different idea as to the organisation of the Balkans.[26]

Yablonsky calls this kind of group a 'near-group', meaning that it is midway between an organised group, such as a social club, and a mob involved in a riot (see figure 3:2). He admits there are organised social gangs whose activities are mainly athletic, and that there are delinquent gangs which are small cliques of boys engaged in semi-professional theft. But membership of such a group, he contends, is not easily achieved, for such boys must have the ability to relate to each other in a consistent, constructive and loyal manner.

Yablonsky's picture of the 'Balkans' as a loose-knit collectivity of violently aggressive adolescents has been queried at two levels. First, some studies have questioned the extent of violence in gangs (see page 97); others have suggested that groups are more cohesive. Jansyn[27] analysed the records kept by group 'detached' workers of the activities of a gang called the 'Dons'. Records were kept over a two

90

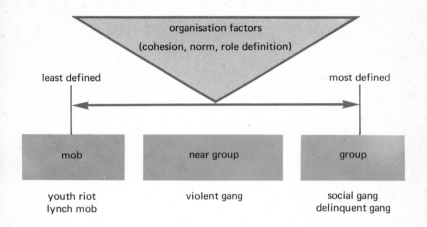

Figure 3:2 The concept of the 'near group'.

organisation factors
(cohesion, norm, role definition)

least defined   most defined

mob	near group	group

youth riot   violent gang   social gang
lynch mob   delinquent gang

and a half year period and an attempt was made to measure the stability of the group by recording whether members were with the group on a number of different occasions. He found that taking two days, a year apart, two thirds of the membership was constant: for the nine 'core' gang members it was as high as 76 per cent. Seven of the nine core members seemed to be almost constant attenders. Klein and Crawford, in Los Angeles, made a rather similar kind of analysis. Observers recorded which boys contacted each other over a period of six months. The number of 'interactions' are shown for 32 members in figure 3:3. It can be seen that in over two-thirds of the 992 (32 × 31) possible relationships no contacts took place, and in three quarters there was either none or only one contact. In other words only 25 per cent of the possible combinations of contacts were made. There were, in fact, two main cliques accounting for 14 of the members (see figure 3:4). Using this method Klein and Crawford analysed the contacts into four 'clusters' of gang boys – those labelled A and B with relatively high amounts of delinquency, and those labelled C and D, with low amounts. Cohesiveness in each group was measured in four ways: the proportion of gang members who were 'clique members': the proportion of mutual contacts of all possible contacts; the proportion of only single contacts of all contacts, and the proportion of contacts

91

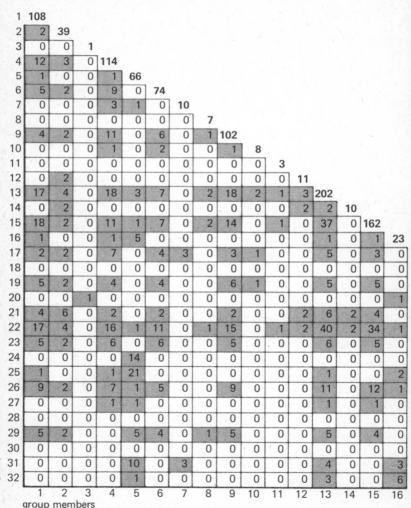

Figure 3:3 The number of observed contacts made by each of 32 gang members over a six month period in Los Angeles, USA.

Figure 3:4 Two cliques shown by the interaction of group members within figure 3:3. Derived from figure 3:3 by factor analysis. Only those who had ten or more contacts with at least one person were included in the analysis.

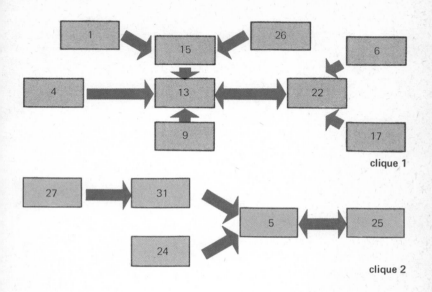

clique 1

clique 2

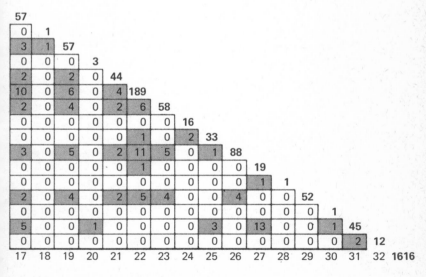

Table 3:1 A percentage comparison of the types of group contacts of boys in four groups with different rates of delinquency.

	Higher delinquency		Lower delinquency	
	A	B	C	D
Percentage who were members of the cliques	42	43	16	15
Percentage of all contacts which were *mutual* contacts between members of the clusters.	81	72	20	32
Percentage of all contacts which were once-only (single) contacts.	54	35	73	77
Percentage of all contacts made by members of the clique which were contacts *within* the clique.	82	73	47	40

It can be seen from this table that the higher delinquency groups were more likely to be clique members and have more of their contacts within the clique.

which were between clique members of all contacts made by clique members. The results, shown in table 3:1 clearly demonstrate that the 'clusters' with high delinquency are more 'cohesive' – have more mutual contacts, than low delinquency 'clusters' (groups). Methods of this kind are clearly providing a more detailed picture of the structure of peer group relationships.

Outside the United States there is less evidence of gang activity either of a cohesive or disorganised kind. Scott studied the records of 151 boys in a London remand home and came to the conclusion that there were three categories of group: adolescent street groups, structured gangs and loosely diffuse groups. Only 12 per cent of the sample could be said to be members of a 'gang' and then this consisted only of a clique of two or three. Most were involved only in 'fleeting casual delinquent associations' among friends and siblings whose activity was not normally delinquent.[28] Similarly, Downes, in informal observations in London's East End, failed to find delinquent gangs. 'The dominant pattern [was the] street corner group of four or five with a few individuals on the periphery. While they persisted over time and invariably possessed a dominant personality, all the other features of the delinquent gang were absent'.[29] They were in fact friendship groups of a fairly permanent nature.

Vaz has reported that 'the usual view [is that] Paris gangs range from five to eight members, while others, it is said, vary between ten and twenty boys'.[30] One such gang, 'Le Bande de la Place N', described by Jean Monod[31] appeared to have been a cohesive group centred around a style of life which emphasised 'bourgeois' leisure pursuits and clothes: they were attempting to transform themselves into the 'secret thief' and the 'irresponsible fool' pursuing the leisure ethic emphasised by Matza.

In summary, then, the literature on the structure, size and cohesion of the gang is extremely variable. There is obviously a need to study this area in detail, and construct theories which can be applied to different forms of delinquent groups. It seems, however, that most delinquency is carried out in small cliques, and that the larger group forms a focus of interest and sometimes of loyalty when its members are threatened by outside groups. There is a core of serious delinquents and a fringe of 'drifting' delinquents who attach themselves to this core at times of crisis or stress.

Patterns of delinquency

What forms does subcultural and gang delinquency take? Is there evidence for Cloward and Ohlin's (and Cohen's and Short's) distinction between different types of subculture?

The only study to find differentiated subcultures was Spergel's inquiry in New York.[32] In this very small-scale study, he interviewed ten delinquents, ten non-delinquents and ten drug users in each of three areas of a large eastern American City. He also observed behaviour in each area: 'Racketville' – a stable working-class area with adult rackets (professional and organised crime), 'Slumtown' – a socially disorganised area of new immigrants, and 'Haulberg' – a traditional lower-class area with no rackets. Boys were asked to say

95

whether they were likely or not to participate in a number of delinquent ('illegitimate') activities. In Racketville, 71 per cent of the delinquents' responses were 'illegitimate', compared with 47 per cent in Slumtown and Haulberg. But Spergel claimed that the *form* of delinquency was different in each area. The boys in Racketville were concerned with graduating to adult rackets, and their groups were stable. In Slumtown, the major activity was conflict and groups were fluid, as Yablonsky has described. The activity in Haulberg was mainly planned theft for immediate gain carried out largely 'for fun' by casual street-corner friendship groups. There was no separate drug subculture. Chein also found in New York[33] that drug use was largely the activity of the older adolescent who has 'grown out of' violence and gang activity and has not yet made stable adult relationships, a finding which supports Cloward and Ohlin.

This picture of well-defined subcultures has not been found elsewhere. In fact, the picture is quite the opposite. Most delinquency is described as being versatile and non-specialised.

In Short and Strodtbeck's detailed analysis of the patterns of delinquent behaviour of sixteen Chicago gangs, observers noted over a period whether members had been involved in any one of a long list of legitimate and illegal activities. Through the use of factor analysis, the authors were able to see in what ways these types of behaviour were grouped. The analysis distinguished five different groupings, which were named:

1 *conflict* activities, being mainly individual and group fighting, carrying concealed weapons and assault
2 *stable 'corner boy'* activities, in which the main items were individual and team sports, social activities and gambling
3 *a stable sex* pattern, with intercourse, statutory rape, 'signifying' (a form of teasing) and use of alcohol
4 *a retreatist* pattern, with homosexuality, fathering an illegitimate child and drug use
5 *an authority protest*, including auto theft, drinking alcohol, running away from home, joyriding and truancy.

There was no evidence of a 'criminal' subculture in the sense that theft for gain was a dominant activity. Gambling and theft were more part of a recreational rather than a criminal pattern. Despite help from social workers and the police they failed to find in Chicago any gang 'whose primary activities and norms were orientated around drug use or rational, systematic, economically motivated criminal activity'. There were, however, some criminal cliques:

No clear separation between criminal and conflict emphasis is apparent from the factor analysis or from observational data. The latter suggest, however, that various criminal activities may characterise *cliques* of *conflict* gangs. Data from a large white street corner group *without discernable delinquency specialisation* also suggest that criminal cliques may develop within such groups ... [our data] are consistent with descriptions of 'semi-professional' theft as an emphasis of individuals and cliques developed within the context of a 'parent delinquent subculture', rather than a fully developed delinquent subculture as described by Cloward and Ohlin ... On the basis of our experience in Chicago ... we are sceptical of the existence in this city of gangs of this type.[34]

This picture of a mixture of theft and violent activity, rather than a commitment to either, is supported by the detailed observational studies of gangs in Boston by Walter Miller.[35] In this study Miller found little evidence of serious aggression. Twenty-one gangs were chosen for study, because of their 'rep' for toughness. 'Assault orientated' behaviour was relatively common in these gangs but most of it involved words rather than deeds. There were individual assaults but few large-scale collective ones. On average, there was only one assault for every two boys in a ten-month period. Of all illegal involvements, assaults made up 17 per cent and property damage seven: theft was far more common, accounting for 35 per cent of all offences – and 54 per cent of the major ones. (It appeared to be 'normal and purposeful' theft carried out in order to gain money to spend and goods to use; it was not 'non-utilitarian' as Cohen has claimed.) The picture of continual and uncontrolled aggression described by Yablonsky was also not supported. Although just over a quarter of members were known to have taken part in assaults only four per cent were 'heavy participants' in four or more violent crimes. Over half the assaults were simple fights between two antagonists, and in as many as 40 per cent of incidents gang members acted alone. As in the gang observed by Yablonsky, much time was spent *planning* fights: out of fifteen plans for gang wars only one came off. Miller concluded that 'a major objective of gang members is to put themselves in the posture of fighting without actually having to fight'.

Nearly all other studies have had similar findings – a general pattern (outside of very occasional mob-like fights) of fighting, rowdyism and petty thievery. Gerald Robin, in a study of the criminal records of Philadelphia gang boys[36] noted that a quarter of the offences were against property, 13 per cent violent, 37 per cent general disorderly conduct and the remainder juvenile offences such as incorrigibility, running away and truancy. Nevertheless, over two thirds had committed at least one assault, and a third a severe physical attack. However, there was no stable pattern in their conduct. Only one fifth of these offenders had as many as 75 per cent of their offences of the same broad type, and only six per cent had 90 per cent the same. In other words there was little evidence of specialisation. Jansyn also pointed out that the Dons' behaviour was a mixture of fighting and stealing, there being no clear conflict or criminal subculture. Much the same pattern was found in Argentina, Paris and London. Downes concludes that his boys in no way aspired to professional crime: 'the self-image of the Poplar boy ... was that of the hooligan not the criminal'. Most of the offences were petty theft and rowdyism connected with recreation.

In summary, the evidence seems to point towards the 'parent-male-subculture' suggested by Cohen and Short. In areas of transition, with new immigrant populations and little social cohesion groups tend to be more violent; but violence, although discussed a great deal, does not seem to be the only, or even primary, goal of the group members. In fact, it appears that when it is violent the group acts more as a defensive collectivity than as an arm of aggression. Nevertheless, at the core there may be cliques who are especially involved in planned and persistent theft.

Group solidarity

This theme of defensiveness is an important one, for a number of writers have suggested that the internal cohesion or solidarity of the gang depends on external forces rather than on the mutual attraction of the members. Furthermore, they have claimed that the dominant factor leading to delinquent activities is concern of the members over their status either as a total group or as particular individuals within the group.

Jansyn, Short and others support Cohen and Matza in noting that delinquents appear to depend heavily on their peers for status. As the Sherifs state,[37] the 'sense of excitement and thrills is related to the fact that other adolescents are the ones who *count,* whose actions make a difference, whose support enhances a feeling of belonging and unity ... in disadvantaged areas the adolescent group becomes the almost exclusive source of personal satisfaction. . .' Strodtbeck and Short's observational study of Chicago gangs supported the view that the gang provided an alternative status system for youths who were alienated from conventional society; fights and other delinquencies occurred when the leaders or the group as a whole felt their status to be threatened. They give an example from the observations of a detached worker's report:

I was sitting talking to the Knights, re-emphasizing my stand on guns, because they told me they had collected quite a few and were waiting for the Vice Kings to start trouble. I told them flatly that it was better that I got the gun than the police. They repeated that they were tired of running from the Vice Kings and that if they gave them trouble they were fighting back.

I looked out of the car and noticed two Vice Kings and two girls walking down the street. William then turned around and made the observation that there were about fifteen or twenty Vice Kings across the street in the alley, wandering up the street in ones or twos.

The Vice Kings encountered Commando (the leader) Jones, and a couple of other Knights coming around the corner. The Vice Kings yelled across to Commando and his boys, and Commando yelled back. I got out to cool Commando down, since he was halfway across the street daring them to do something. I grabbed him and began to pull him back.

But the Vice Kings were in a rage, and three came across the street yelling that they were mighty Vice Kings. At this point, along came Henry Brown with a revolver, shooting. Everybody ducked and the Vice Kings ran. I began to throw Knights into my car because I knew that the area was 'hot'.

In the car the boys were extremely elated. 'Baby, did you see the way I swung on that kid?' 'Man, did we tell them off?' 'Did you see them take off when I leveled my gun?' 'You were great, baby ...' The tension was relieved. They had performed well and could be proud ...

From this incident Short and Strodtbeck conclude:

No doubt the Vice Kings too felt the thrill of having faced conflict and come off well. They had met great danger bravely, and had a good alibi for not having won unquestioned victory – the enemy had a gun. The Knights, on their part also had an alibi – the worker had intervened. Both sides therefore won, and could mutually share satisfaction and enhanced reputation.[38]

But Short and Strodtbeck do not support Cohen in regarding this status-rewarding behaviour as an example of 'short-run hedonism' or immediate gratification. They claim that the delinquent leader is taking a conscious 'chance', where the rewards of gaining and keeping status are higher than the possibilities of arrest or injury (they suggest the possibility of arrest for the skilful Negro gang boy is no higher than ·02!). Faced with the fact that 'all boys are in jeopardy of radically changing their standing if they elect to stand aloof', it obviously makes sense to 'join the action'.

Similarly, the 'Dons', according to Jansyn, became more involved in delinquent activities as the gang became more disorganised: 'Apparently as an attempt to enhance their position, several of the lower status members actively participated in a growing conflict with another group'. In Jansyn's view a decline in group solidarity is threatening to members, and 'they respond to this threat by group action which arouses interest and attracts and involves members'. Short's evidence certainly suggests that threats to status and membership are important catalysts, for it appears of paramount importance to the gang boy to gain status in the eyes of his peers.

But threats from other groups are not the only external forces welding the group together. Members are likely to be subject to criticism, and even ostracised, by teachers, community workers, parents and others in authority. Besides this they are (see chapter 2) more open to harrassment by the police and to arrest than other boys.[39] It seems a plausible argument that this 'labelling' of the gang boy as 'difficult' or 'intransigent' will reinforce his self-image as a 'bad' person and lead to behaviour that produces further hostility and rejection from adults. It is this process, by which law enforcement leads to a reaction of more deviant behaviour from the delinquent group, that Wilkins[40] has called 'deviance amplification', and Lemert[41] 'secondary deviance'. We have at present almost no empirical data on how this process actually works.

There has been a great deal of discussion among criminologists about the extent to which the norms (or behaviour expected of members by others in the group backed by sanctions) of the delinquent group are binding on members. Short supports Matza by suggesting that boys are not committed through gang membership to delinquency, as Cloward and Ohlin claim. Instead, the group tends to discourage conventional middle-class behaviour by derision, rather than by outright rejection. The boy on the corner is not unaware or even unsympathetic towards middle-class standards, but his own situation within the group, his need for membership and status, successfully isolate him and make him open to group pressures in which 'gang norms such as sexual prowess and toughness, or alternatively coolness, lead to situational involvements which require delinquency'.[42] But in Short's view no gang norms require fighting or delinquency by all boys, even under the most provocative circumstances. Klein and Crawford go further and suggest that group norms as such are relatively non-existent in the delinquent gang world, except as myths which are exploded upon

100

test. They assert that norms such as 'not informing' or 'coming to the aid of others' are frequently not upheld. Exactly what the norms *are*, and in what situations they are likely to control the behaviour of gang boys, has certainly not been adequately investigated.

Some light on delinquent boys' attitudes to committing offences has been shed by a novel piece of research by Schwendinger and Schwendinger.[43] 54 delinquent and non-delinquent boys were asked to play roles as 'objectors' or 'proponents' for a delinquent action; one example was:

I want you to act out this story: teenagers are arguing over whether they should beat up an Outsider who insulted their club. An Outsider is someone outside their circle of friends. Those who are in favour of beating him up argue with the others about it. The others are finally *convinced* that the Outsider should be beaten up by the *entire* group.

The results showed that the 'objectors' among the non-delinquents raised moral issues, such as the harm to be done and the rights of the victim. But among the delinquents there was 'little moral ambivalence'; the 'objectors' among the delinquents were concerned mainly with *tactical* issues such as the danger of being caught. There seems from this study to have been a big difference between the outlooks of delinquents and non-delinquents, and little evidence for Matza and Sykes' view that delinquents feel guilty about delinquent acts and have to find *moral* justifications for them. The Schwendingers make the interesting suggestion that delinquents may privately have moral qualms, but that *publicly* they are constrained to put forward their amoral views, and it is this 'public vocabulary' which they act on; and in this sense they certainly support Matza's thesis of mutual misunderstandings.

Core members and leaders

Most observers agree that there is a difference between the core and casual members of the gang. But there is some dispute over what kinds of boys become the leaders and central characters of the groups. Yablonsky's view is that they are 'sociopathic' individuals who use the gang as a vehicle for acting out *personal* hostility and aggression. They are unable, he claims, to fulfill the demands required for participation in more normal groups, and their main role is to serve as a 'symbol of idealised violence': the personification of the masculine lower-class hero.

Malcolm Klein asked 'detached' gang workers to describe the core members. When these descriptions were analysed two main 'factors' appeared, one describing a 'deficient aggressive' component and the other 'group involvement'.[44] These factors are also mentioned by Nathan Gerrard,[45] who typifies the core member as a person cut off from conventional society through inability to make personal relationships, and who is attempting to gain prestige within the gang through aggressive behaviour. These writers appear to give the impression that core members are unable to make relations, yet other observers, such as Miller, have emphasised that ability to relate to others in the group is important. The Los Angeles gang leaders also emphasised smartness and intelligence, rather than simple toughness, as being more important characteristics of leaders.[46] It may be that the social disabilities and aggressiveness of the core member are not distinctly psychological problems but are part of the role behaviour *expected* of the leaders in the delinquent group. If they did not exemplify the life of the subculture it would atrophy, for many other members are, as we have seen, only marginally involved in delinquent activity. The point seems to be that to play the leader role demands that the person should cut himself off, more than any other members, from conventional standards of behaviour. It is probable that only those who do not have the constraints of school, home and kinship ties become available for leadership roles. Short and Strodtbeck's description of 'Duke', a Negro gang leader who shot three people in a group skirmish, supports this view. He was able to handle relations within the group so as not 'to needlessly cause other boys to lose face', and he exemplified all that was expected of a leader:

Fearless and effective, [he could] dance well enough to 'turn out' almost anyone in the neighbourhood ... other dancers typically cleared an area for him and his partner. He dressed 'sharp' and 'made out' with the girls.

In the shooting incident, the gun was passed to Duke, for as leader he was expected to be prepared to use it. If he had not done so, his status would have been threatened. As the authors suggest, his actions arose not from any 'sociopathic' disturbance but 'in line of duty as part of the leadership role'.

Delinquent versus middle-class values

While it may be that core members exemplify the 'animosity towards teachers, police, certain ethnic groups, people from other neighbourhoods and even some from their own neighbourhood', that Jansyn reports, to what extent are the other members really involved in a value and normative system that is rebellious and rejecting of middle-class styles of life? This is a central issue in Cohen's and Cloward's and Ohlin's theories and so has attracted more investigation than almost any other aspect of delinquent subcultural life.

The most ambitious enquiry so far carried out is Short and Strodtbeck's Chicago study. They asked members of both Negro and white gangs to compare (in a semantic differential test) different 'images' of conduct, ranging from ones approved by the middle class such as graduating from school, saving and reading, to those assumed to appeal to the gang boy such as pimping and having good connections with criminals. The findings of many comparisons showed, in general, that delinquent boys rated the middle-class images higher than the delinquent ones: 'theoretical formulations failed to make sufficient allowance for the meaningfulness of middle-class values for gangs'. On the other hand gang boys also evaluated behaviour such as making out with girls, pimping, fighting, and having good criminal connections higher than did lower-class non-gang boys and middle-class boys. It seems that while approving the kinds of behaviour typical of the delinquent subculture they rated them lower in prestige than middle-class behaviour. On the other hand, Spiller's study in Roxbury, Mass.[47] produced rather different results. Gang boys were asked to rate kinds of behaviour which were 'middle-class', 'lower-class' and 'adolescent' concerns. The results showed that a third of observed behaviour was 'lower-class', two thirds 'adolescent' and only four per cent 'middle-class' in its orientation, and Spiller concluded that:

Lower class gang members are motivated more by attempts to achieve standards and measure up to the qualities valued within their own subculture milieu, than by efforts to achieve culturally distant and or ill-understood values.

Similarly, Miller and his colleagues, also working in Boston, claim that the picture of the gang boy as angry, frustrated and anti-adult authority is not substantiated by their research. Instead, the most important motivating factor appears to be the desire of boys to gain prestige in each other's eyes – a finding which again supports both Cohen and Matza. But there are a number of difficulties within this kind of study. First, what individuals tell interviewers may not be what they really think. Second, and probably more important, what they think as individuals may be no reflection of what they say or do when in association with others. In fact, Short and Strodtbeck provide a very good example of this. When asked individually about sexual behaviour boys approved of conventional views, but when asked in the group, the same boys derided these views. As the Sherifs have pointed out:

If 'delinquent subculture' has any meaning it must refer to the *norms* shared by group members. The question of whether or not such norms exist in a particular group can be resolved only by observing inter-action over time under conditions in which the group pursues its activities without 'putting on a face' for adult outsiders ... Direct questions to group members about their values or rating scales designed to obtain indicators of values are not valid predictors of what members do under the changing circumstances of group interaction.[48] (our italics).

But there are of course enormous difficulties in carrying out this kind of 'participant observation'. In fact no one has yet managed to do it successfully and one of the main drawbacks of all the 'observational' studies quoted in this chapter is that material has been collected by social and community workers whose prime job is to change gradually the behaviour of delinquent groups.

Short may be correct in suggesting there is no evidence for personal rejection of, or 'reaction formation' against, middle-class values: they are still recognised as being 'correct', but they are not seen as appropriate guides to behaviour *in the group*. Cloward and Ohlin recognise this point, for they admit that delinquents may recognise the moral validity of the middle-class value system while still not giving it legitimacy as a guide to their actual behaviour. To do this successfully, Cloward and Ohlin suggest that the delinquent will need a means of coping with the strain of feeling guilty and that this will be achieved by defining delinquency 'as a response to an amoral situation'. This is precisely what Matza and Sykes mean by techniques of neutralisation.

Along similar lines, some attempts have been made to test whether or not delinquent boys have blocked aspirations as both Cohen and Cloward and Ohlin have claimed. Short[49] asked gang and non-gang boys about the occupations to which they aspired, and the occupations which they expected to gain. He found that non-gang boys had the highest aspirations, but that gang boys had the greatest *discrepancy* between what they aspired to and what they felt they would achieve. The boys who were most delinquent felt that educational opportunities were completely closed to them. Clark and Wenninger[50] in a study of a number of different types of community also concluded that what mattered was not aspiration to high or low goals, but the perceived chance of reaching whatever was desired without resorting to illegal means.

There is, however, one major theoretical problem with this type of research. It is not at all clear (because the writers are themselves unclear) whether Cohen or Cloward and Ohlin expect delinquents to actually *feel* frustrated, *feel* their aspirations to be blocked, personally experience a 'reaction-formation' in the face of status frustration or consciously decide to withdraw legitimacy from middle-class values and norms. Both theorists are basically concerned with analysing why the subculture exists as a collective form of behaviour, rather than the motivations or personal feelings of members of the subculture. In other words, through a theoretical model, they are trying to explain why delinquent subcultures are more meaningful and appropriate forms of behaviour for many lower-class males than the behaviour emphasised by the school and other agencies of social control. They both admit that the subculture, once in existence, is *learned* like other behaviour. Each individual does not have to go through the crisis of solving a problem of adjustment. Cloward and Ohlin specifically say: 'Each generation does not solve anew the problems of class structure barriers to opportunity but begins with the solution of its forebears'.

The theory is probably not therefore testable by asking each delinquent about his motives. These theories, like many others which attempt to explain the existence of particular cultures, are functional theories aimed at describing why the subculture serves a function for its members. They imply that without the subcultural solution lower-class boys *would* feel status deprived.

These theories need to be tested in relation to the facts they purport to explain. For example, Cohen and Cloward and Ohlin both agree that the subculture exists primarily in the lower class among adolescent males. They disagree with each other (as does Matza with both) on what the norms and values of the subculture are, and what the strength of the norms are: Cohen sees them as requiring behaviour which is oppositional, deliberately malicious, negativistic and flouting middle-class society; Cloward and Ohlin as requiring more instrumental behaviour aimed at getting the lower-class goal of money through illegitimate routes and if these too are blocked, gaining prestige through violence. If it is shown that the behaviour takes neither of these forms then some other explanation is needed, for Cohen's thesis *rests* upon the need to explain the oppositional nature of the norms.

Some support for Cohen's thesis comes from a few studies of the educational performance of delinquent boys. One fact which stands out is their low level of educational achievement. Opportunities for educational and vocational advancement along legitimate lines really *are* blocked. Of course it is difficult to know whether poor educational performance is a result of delinquency, or vice versa; but David Hargreaves' study of an English secondary school suggests that poor school performance may come first.[51] Hargreaves noted enormous differences between the conduct, attitudes and peer group relations of boys in the upper academic stream and those in the lowest streams. Those in the upper stream shared similar values to the middle-class teachers, and the boys with good academic records had high status among their peers, being at the centre of group relations. Among the lowest streams the opposite was the case: those who most devalued school had the highest status, and the values and norms were in general anti-school and authority. Hargreaves suggests that this division between an academic and a delinquent subculture does not exist when boys first enter the school, but that the behaviour of the lower streams is a response to the low aspirations teachers have for these pupils. In fact the negative expectations of the teachers went to reinforce the negative behaviour and attitudes of the low-stream boys. For these boys, Hargreaves suggests, the group rewards became more attractive than those offered by the teachers. The school accentuated a sense of failure, deprivation and alienation, and boys were forced to accept low aspirations and seek a substitute system to replace the values of the school. They emphasised masculinity and fighting prowess, and those forms of dress and behaviour – long hair, jeans, pop music and street corner activity – which were the antithesis of those expected by the school. Another English sociologist, Barry Sugarman, has noted a similar anti-school phenomenon.[52] Those with poor performance and conduct ratings at school are most involved in what he calls a 'youth culture' in which:

the role of a 'teenager' ... is, roughly, an inversion of the official 'pupil' role. In place of ... deferred gratification it puts an emphasis on spontaneous gratification or hedonism. Similarly it repudiates the idea of youth being subordinate to adults ... In conflict with the school is a rival view of life which is held fairly self-consciously but not very explicitly by a fair number of pupils in common.

This youth culture, he claims, is essentially 'the culture of the non-mobile working class, the downwardly mobile and of those who cherish mobility along channels where the criteria of school do not apply'. It is no accident, he claims, that their idols are the pop stars, for this culture 'is the opium of the (teenage) masses ... they want to forget ... the futility and failure of school days, the frustrations of being a sub-adult ... and the dullness of adult life lying ahead'. It is this disenchantment with school which Downes aptly terms 'dissociation'. There seems less evidence of thwarted aspirations than of the inability of the school to engage delinquent boys in activities which are both meaningful to them and provide them with an opportunity of achieving status within their own peer group. Dissociated from school and work, the delinquent boy, Downes suggests, turns to leisure for his excitement and interest, and even here he is ill prepared to participate in conventional leisure activities. All that is open for him is the street and the seeking of excitement and status through delinquency.

Lower and middle-class delinquency

There can be no doubt that the sub-culture of the gang which has been described in the studies so far reviewed is a lower-class pheno-menon. To what extent do groupings and behaviour differ from those found in so-called middle-class gangs?

Cohen and Short[53] hypothesised that middle-class delinquency would be more a 'playboy' activity than the more serious delin-quency of the lower class:

It seems probable that the qualities of malice, bellicosity and violence will be underplayed in the middle-class subcultures and that these subcultures will emphasise more the deliberate courting of danger ... and a sophisticated, irresponsible, 'playboy' approach to activities symbolic, in our culture, of adult roles and centering largely around sex, liquor, and automobiles.

There are no detailed studies of middle-class groupings, but the Myerhoffs in their two-week 'field observations' in California[54] showed there was little serious delinquency in the group. There was little violence or defiance of authority and most anti-social acts were connected with leisure activities – the use of cars and alcohol. There were however some thefts of articles from employers, which seemed to be considered acceptable behaviour by the group. What differentiated these youths from the lower-class gangs was their lack of anti-authority activity and their self-perception as non-delinquent. This picture is supported by Vaz[55] who claims that most delinquency is carried out in groups in the pursuit of leisure as the 'unanticipated consequence of conformity in social affairs'. There is clearly a great need for more investigation of the delinquency revealed in self-report studies.

Conclusions

To what extent do these studies shed light on the theoretical debate outlined at the beginning of the chapter? All have suggested, first, that while gangs exist they are not usually highly organised around one dominant activity, but that delinquency is versatile and largely carried out in small groups. Although there are many 'hangers-on' to the gang, it is only a small number of core members who are persistent in serious delinquency and who maintain the norms for the group. The vast majority are peripheral members whose commitment to the subculture is relatively weak.

These criticisms obviously damage subcultural theory in two respects. First, they challenge the notion that the delinquent subculture demands delinquency and so *commits* the delinquent: few appear to be completely involved in the demands of peer group relations. Secondly, they clearly contradict Cloward and Ohlin's formulation of different subcultures pursuing quite separate styles of life. But the fact that gangs appear less cohesive and less demanding than originally thought does little injury to the concept of subculture itself. As Downes has pointed out, a subculture is like other 'cultures': it is a shared system of values and ways of behaving that influence people *in their interactions with others*. A set of ideas and prescriptions governing behaviour can certainly bind people together without there being a formal gang. All the evidence points to delinquency being mainly the product of the interaction between members of groups. It seems that what is often important is the significance of the delinquent act for the relationship between members – reflecting status or membership concerns – rather than as an end in itself.

There seems, therefore, to be much support for theories which emphasise the importance of status and membership of groups for adolescents. There also seems to be a good deal of evidence to support Matza's contention that few adolescents are 'committed' to delinquency and that this activity is mainly episodic. On the other hand the lower-class subculture does seem different from middle-class forms of behaviour. There is ample evidence to suggest that although boys may not personally feel frustrated or reject middle-class values, the norms of the subculture reflect the objective fact that school and work fail to provide a framework for social relationships for those in the lower social classes, and that the delinquent subculture does provide an alternative system of values and norms which enable the boy to achieve membership of, and status within, a meaningful group.

Yet, it must be admitted, even this is still largely speculation. We certainly need more theories which will guide empirical research designed to explore the structure, values, norms and the social dynamics of the group relationships which produce delinquency. Without this research and the development of new hypotheses on a limited scale, more 'grand generalisations' will largely be a waste of effort.

4 The classification of crimes and criminals

Criminologists have almost always agreed that there is no such thing as *the* cause of crime, but they have tended to use two very different arguments in support of this contention. The first of these is based on the fact that numerous comparisons of groups of criminals with groups of non-criminals have failed to produce any single characteristic or 'factor' (such as coming from a broken home, being illegitimate, or suffering from some psychological abnormality) which absolutely distinguishes the two groups. Some such factors may be associated with criminality, in the sense that they are more frequent among offenders than among non-offenders; but even these factors are invariably found to be absent in the case of some who have broken the law, and present in the case of some who have not. Thus – the argument runs – crime must have many 'causes'. The second argument is based on the observation that the concepts of crime, delinquency, deviant behaviour, etc., apply to a very wide range of different kinds of behaviour – burglary, tax fraud, truancy, incest, bootlegging, assassination – having in common only the fact that they have been declared to be contrary to legal or moral rules in various times and places. No single causal explanation, it is suggested, can possibly cover such heterogeneous phenomena; they *must* have different causes, just because they are so different.

Whatever the merits of these arguments, they are independent of one another: and some writers have vehemently asserted one while ignoring, or even appearing to deny, the other. For example, Professor Sheldon Glueck – one of the most ardent advocates of the 'multiple factor theory' of crime causation – has claimed to have shown, by the research that he and his wife have carried out, that delinquents are distinguished from non-delinquents by a wide range of biological, psychological and sociological factors, which combine in a number of different ways to produce delinquency. Yet this research (reported in the Gluecks' book *Unraveling Juvenile Delinquency*[1]) was based on a sample of 500 boys who had committed a fairly wide variety of kinds of delinquent acts, probably under an even wider range of circumstances. Given the heterogeneity of their delinquent behaviour, it may be thought scarcely surprising that no single 'factor' distinguished these 500 boys from the 500 'truly non-delinquent' boys with whom they were compared.

There is a third argument to the effect that crime has many causes, which still crops up occasionally in criminological writings. This is the argument that every single crime is a product of an absolutely unique combination of individual and social factors – that every crime has its own 'causes', irreducibly different from those of every other crime. In one sense, this is perhaps true. What we identify as the 'cause' or 'causes' of an event depends in part on our purposes: and when we are ascribing responsibility to a man for a crime, for example, we may identify certain things which are unique to the particular case as 'things which made him do it'. But it is different when our purpose is scientific explanation, since for this purpose we are interested in *generalisations* – preferably ones as wide as possible – and we seek as causes things which apply to all instances of the thing or event we are trying to explain, and not just to one particular case. Now, there is no absurdity or inconsistency in searching for a single theoretical explanation of all criminal, delinquent or deviant behaviour. Such a theory – which would consist of a number of logically connected and empirically verified general statements specifying the conditions in which crime occurs – should aim to integrate all the different factors which are shown to distinguish offenders from non-offenders, and should aim to explain *how* these factors 'produce' delinquent behaviour. This is precisely what one of the best-known criminological theories – the differential association theory, propounded by Edwin Sutherland – sets out to do, and is what the usual form of 'multiple causation' approach utterly fails to do. But viable general theories of this kind, applicable to all crime or delinquency, seem to us to be a long way off; and there is unfortunately no guarantee that any such general theory will ever be shown empirically to be correct. The known facts about crime – which any such theory would have to fit – are complicated; and one important reason for this is that the concept of crime covers such a wide and heterogeneous range of behaviour.

To overcome this problem, many criminologists in recent years have concentrated on studying particular *types* of crime, in the hope of producing theories (so-called 'theories of the middle range') which, though applying to a restricted range of illegal behaviour, nonetheless go beyond the explanation of particular illegal acts. Sociological examples from the United States of this kind of theory and research on specific types of crime are Lemert's studies of

111

Figure 4:1 Possible relationships between different types of crime.

professional theft

property crime

professional crime

theft

'naive' and 'systematic' cheque forgery;[2] Sutherland's studies of professional theft[3] and 'white-collar' crime;[4] Cressey's research on the criminal violation of financial trust;[5] Wattenberg's and Balistrieri's study of car theft;[6] and Clinard's and Wade's study of vandalism.[7] The studies of subcultural delinquency discussed in the last chapter are another example of this approach: they focus on a single kind of delinquent behaviour, and aim to produce valid theories which fully explain the origins, distribution and frequency of this kind of behaviour even if they do not apply to other types.

It is not necessary that the types of crime or delinquency isolated and explained in this way by different researchers should be in any way comparable with each other; nor is there any reason to think that they would be comparable, since researchers should be free to choose to study whatever types of behaviour happen to interest them. Moreover, it would be perfectly possible for criminologists to develop a respectable body of empirically verified theories by formulating and testing explanations for different types of crime, on an *ad hoc* basis. The different types of crime which different theorists choose to study do not need to be mutually exclusive, nor even compatible; and the theories developed for these different types of crime need not be related logically – or even capable of being related – to each other.

Figure 4:1 shows one way in which three different types of crime, studied by three different researchers, might be related. In this case the first researcher might formulate and test a sociological theory of professional crime; the second might develop a psychological theory concerning theft; while the third might develop a social-psychological theory relating to the broader category of 'property offences'. It will be seen that all three of these type-categories overlap, and that 'professional theft' is a sub-type of all three. But provided they are logically compatible, all three of these researchers' theories *may* be equally valid for professional theft: that is, they may all three provide correct predictions and equally plausible explanations of the frequency, distribution, etc., of professional theft. (Of course, this is rather a long shot. More probably, if the three theories were all valid for a single type of crime, they would simply be concerned with different questions about it. Or they might just be alternative descriptions of exactly the same set of facts – as, for example, psychoanalytic theory and learning theory sometimes seem to be.)

In other words, an anarchic approach to the study of different types of crime – which is the one that criminologists have mainly followed so far – is not necessarily self-defeating. Nonetheless, many criminologists take the view that it is desirable to relate different types of crime or criminal systematically to one another: that is, to try to combine them, according to some consistent principle of classification, into a *typology* rather than settling for a collection of disparate types. There are some obvious advantages in doing this. For one thing, it makes the subject neater, and thus easier to study. At a descriptive level, a great deal of empirical information about crime and criminals has been amassed in the past 150 years or so; a systematic method of classification helps to put this information into usable order to show the relations within it, and makes it easier to see what further information is needed. For another thing, if the explanation of criminal behaviour is one's object, it is better if the types studied are mutually exclusive. The possibility just mentioned – that three different theories may each be valid for a particular type of crime, such as professional theft – is in fact remote; moreover, a researcher who is studying crime from a single theoretical point of view – say, a sociological one – will naturally wish to classify his subject into types which do not overlap.

In addition, it is often assumed that the development of a typology of offences or offenders will actually improve the chances of developing a general causal theory. Cloward and Quinney (whose recent typology of 'criminal behaviour systems' is discussed on pages 126-7) go so far as to assert that a system of classification 'is a necessary preliminary to the development of a general theory'. It is not clear, however, why this should be thought to be so; in fact, the matter is not as simple as this. A typology which accords with a general criminological theory can only be constructed if it is known which attributes of offenders (or their behaviour) are relevant to that theory. In other words, the typology *presupposes* the theory, for without the theory there is no way of knowing which types should be included in the typology. Typology construction thus goes hand-in-hand with the development of theory, and is not a 'necessary preliminary' to it.

Nonetheless, typologies can have heuristic value in criminology. They can make it easier for the theorist to see analogies between different kinds of criminal behaviour, or similarities between different kinds of offender, and thus make it easier for him to trace the causal processes which apply to them. Systematic classification can help to reveal empirical relationships between different factors (for example, offenders' personality types, social backgrounds and offences), and may suggest hypotheses to account for these relationships. A great many typologies of offences and offenders have been devised by criminologists over the past hundred years for the purpose of aetiological research. We shall discuss some (though by no means all) of these in this chapter. We shall also outline the more important properties which, in our opinion, a criminological typology ought to have if it is to be useful for research purposes; and we shall review briefly some empirical research relevant to one particular group of offender typologies – namely, those based on the concept of a criminal career. In chapter 7 we shall consider the use of offender typologies in relation to the choice of treatment or punishment.

Typologies and criminological theory

The word 'typology' is used in a number of different ways – not all of them clear – by different writers on this subject. In particular, some writers distinguish between a *system of classification* and a *typology*. Usually the first of these expressions is taken to refer to a method of

114

grouping individuals into classes which are defined by one or more variables, and which may include all the actual or possible combinations of those variables. The second is often used to refer to any set of mutually exclusive types, each of which may be defined or identified by different kinds of criteria; in addition, it is sometimes specified that the variables defining the types are 'empirically interconnected'. For reasons which will become clear below, we do not draw this distinction; and we use the term 'typology' to include any system of classification which results in groups defined so as to be mutually exclusive.

It is important to note, however, that these intermediate 'types' in this sense do not merely represent quantitative differences along a *single* dimension – like the divisions of intelligence levels according to IQ test scores. Many classifications of delinquents are in fact of this kind; a well-known example is the seven-fold classification according to interpersonal maturity ('I-level') propounded by Sullivan, Grant and Grant,[8] discussed in chapter 7, pages 198-9. It seems misleading to call classifications of this kind 'typologies' at all – at least unless there is good reason to think that the cutting points defining each 'type' are not simply arbitrary.

What is meant by a 'type' of offender, or a 'type' of criminal behaviour? It seems that if we divide any set of things of the same kind – that is, things describable by the same general term, such as 'criminal' – into sub-sets, by reference to one or more of the attributes of those things, then each of the sub-sets exemplifies a 'type' of the thing in question. Of course, the attributes used to divide up the set must themselves be general, and not merely the identifying characteristics of particular individuals. For instance, if we took a group of 100 criminals and 'classified' them by their full names, places and dates of birth, we would probably divide the group into 100 sub-sets, each consisting of one criminal; but this would not mean we had identified 100 'types' of criminal. But subject to that reservation, it seems that pretty well any attribute, or set of attributes, will serve as a basis for type-classification of offenders or offences, though of course some will seem more useful than others, depending on the purpose of the classification. There is no 'natural' or uniquely correct classification of offences or offenders.

Most of the typologies devised by criminologists have in fact been very simple ones, using only a few variables as type-criteria and containing only a few broad types. Classifications of criminals and delinquents have been based on such things as age, sex, current offence (in legal terms), personality type, marital status, social class, and criminal record as type-criteria; classifications of offences have used such things as the motive of the offender, type of norm violated, circumstances of the act, relationship with the victim, and frequency with which the behaviour is performed.

The type-distinction which has probably been made most often by criminologists is that between *individual* criminals on the one hand, and *social* criminals on the other. This kind of classification was made, more or less clearly, by the Italian 'positivist' criminologists Lombroso and Ferri, in the late nineteenth century; and it has been restated by many other writers since then, notably by two American sociologists, Lindesmith and Dunham,[9] in 1941. The distinction between 'individual' and 'social' criminals is usually treated as both a descriptive and an aetiological one. Thus, according to Lindesmith and Dunham, the crimes of the 'social criminal' are

supported and prescribed by a culture, and the person committing such crimes achieves status and recognition within a certain minority group by skilfully and daringly carrying out the criminal activity which, in that group, is customary and definitely designated. This type of criminal acts in close collaboration with other persons without whose direct or indirect co-operation his career would be virtually impossible.

The crimes of the 'individualised criminal', by contrast

are not prescribed forms of behaviour in his cultural milieu nor does he gain prestige or recognition in his social world by committing them. They are committed for diverse ends which are personal and private rather than common and socially accepted ... The 'individualised criminal' commits his crimes alone, and, ideally conceived, is a stranger to others who commit similar crimes.

The 'individual' and 'social' criminals are thus polar opposites, and are to some extent pure or 'ideal' types; it is possible to identify a number of less extreme variants of either, ranged on a continuum between these extremes. Lindesmith and Dunham, for example, regarded insane criminals as epitomising the 'individual' type, but also included under this heading 'situational' offenders – such as those committing crimes of passion, or offending because of dire economic need: they pointed out that 'although this behaviour is not definitely prescribed by the mores it may be and usually is encouraged or facilitated by prevailing ideas of conduct'. These further distinctions obviously make the 'individual' – 'social' distinction more useful.

116

Another factor frequently used in typologies of criminals is the *frequency* with which offences are committed: the main distinction here being between the 'occasional' or 'once-only' offender, and the persistent offender, 'habitual offender' or 'career criminal'. This distinction – first made, it seems, by the nineteenth-century writer Henry Mayhew[10] – has been regarded as fundamental by criminologists of almost all schools; we ourselves shall argue later that it is of primary importance in the classification of criminals for the purpose of aetiological research.

It is difficult to generalise about more detailed kinds of classification of crimes and criminals. But many – perhaps the majority – have been based in one way or another on the offender's *motivation*. An example is Rich's classification of juvenile theft,[11] illustrated in figure 4:2.

There seem to be two broadly different approaches to the creation of typologies in this field, which are related to different ways of formulating criminological theories. Let us call these the 'empirical' and 'theoretical' approaches respectively. The first proceeds simply by grouping together individuals or patterns of behaviour according to their most obvious apparently relevant features, so that each group contains members which are as similar as possible to each other and as different as possible from all other groups. This classificatory procedure is rather like that used by a man sorting a basket of fruit, who puts the apples, oranges and lemons into different piles because they *look* different; we might call it the 'look and see' method of classification.

Of course, one usually has some vague *a priori* idea of which features are or might be relevant when using this method; e.g. when classifying offenders one will usually only consider features having some conceivable relation with criminal behaviour, and not such things as colour of eyes. It is often supposed that the types picked out by this empirical method *must* have different explanations. But the choice of type-criteria is not dictated (at least at a conscious level) by any particular theory of criminal behaviour, and in practice the primary basis of classification is usually some readily ascertainable first-order facts about the offenders (such as their ages, or current offences, or whatever else happens to be contained in their records) rather than abstract theoretical variables. An example of this kind of classification of offenders is the criminal career typology devised by Roebuck (discussed on pages 129-31) which is based primarily on the type of offence most frequently committed by the offender.

Figure 4:2 A classification of juvenile theft according to motivation.

type	motivation	description of offence
proving	Attempts to prove own manhood or toughness. Self-re-assurance, rather than attempts to achieve status with peers	Theft or burglary carried out alone; taking motor car.
marauding	Excitement: the offence often involves considerable and deliberately chosen risk.	Unplanned or 'semi-planned' crimes, carried out in groups of three or more
comforting	A substitute for affection of which the boy is deprived; or an aggressive act of resentment arising from such deprivation.	Stealing from parents; impulsive pilfering, either alone or with one other.
secondary	Rational	Planned theft of any sort, with a definite idea of what can be stolen and reasonable precautions against detection.
other	(Various)	Offences not classifiable under above headings: examples include stealing under instruction from parent, or stealing food after having run away from home.

It is basically this method of grouping which is reproduced by statistical methods of taxonomy such as 'association analysis', which was developed by Williams and Lambert[12] for use in plant ecology, and which was first applied to offenders by Wilkins and MacNaughton-Smith.[13] Statistical methods of this kind are intended to show which attributes of a group of individuals tend to be clustered together; *any* attributes can be used, provided they are logically independent. The advantage of these techniques is that they make possible much more complicated analyses than could be done by simple inspection of the data; and because they use a precise statistical definition of 'similarity' they are more objective than intuitive methods of classification. But they are still very much in the experimental stage, and their utility is uncertain even in the biological sciences; it has been shown, for example, by Lange *et al.*[14] that association analysis will group data known to be random. This is an especially serious problem in the social sciences, where there are few hypotheses or theories which can indicate the significance of observed groupings. We refer to these techniques here, therefore, merely to illustrate in its most extreme form the 'empirical' approach to typology construction.

Goodman and Price[15] have experimentally applied a variant of this technique ('dissimilarity analysis', invented by MacNaughton-Smith[16]), to girls sent to borstal institutions. For a group of 129 girls, the presence or absence of 18 attributes was recorded. Each girl was compared with all of the others in respect of these 18 attributes and the one most unlike the rest identified; this girl was then paired with each of the 128 others, and the pair most unlike the remaining 127 identified; and so on, until a group was formed such that if any further girl was considered, she was less similar to this group (in terms of these 18 attributes) than to the remainder. This process was then repeated for each of the two groups thus formed, until no further sub-groups could be formed. Four groups – consisting of 46, 8, 37, and 38 girls respectively – were thus formed; the pattern of subdivision, and the significant features of each group, are shown in figure 4:3.

Another example of an empirically-derived typology is Hewitt's and Jenkins's classification of 'problem behaviour' syndromes among maladjusted children.[17] In the records of a sample of 500 boys referred to a Michigan child guidance clinic, Hewitt and Jenkins found a total of 94 different kinds of 'problem behaviour' displayed by the boys. Three groups of these were found to be intercorrelated (that is, displayed by more or less the same boys). These three 'behaviour syndromes' were called by Hewitt and Jenkins 'unsocialized aggressive behaviour', 'socialized delinquency' and 'overinhibited behaviour'; the items which comprised each are shown in figure 4:4.

This study also illustrates the way in which empirically-derived typologies may be related to criminological theories. After identifying the three 'behaviour syndromes', Hewitt and Jenkins examined the home backgrounds of the children in their sample, and found that certain kinds of early upbringing were correlated, to some extent, with each of the syndromes. For example, the 'unsocialized aggressive' children tended to have experienced parental rejection, whereas the 'overinhibited' children tended to come from homes described as 'repressive', or to suffer from physical defects. Psychological theory – of a rather eclectic kind – was then invoked by the authors to explain these correlations. Several replications of Hewitt's and Jenkins's study have been carried out, the most recent of these being done in England by Field,[18] who used a group of boys admitted to approved schools. She found a number of boys displaying the 'unsocialized aggressive' and 'overinhibited' syndromes (but none displaying 'socialized delinquency'); however, she found no evidence of the correlations reported by Hewitt and Jenkins between these syndromes and any aspects of early upbringing or home background.

The second ('theoretical') approach, by contrast, starts off with a specific theory, from which a relatively specific basis for classification is deduced; descriptive criteria are then found for grouping individuals in accordance with this theoretical scheme. The best examples – and by far the commonest ones – of this approach to typology construction are those derived from psychiatric or psychological theory. For example, Freudian theory (in one of its many forms) states that the various experiences of early childhood lead the id, ego and superego to develop (or fail to develop) in certain ways; and that under certain conditions the resulting psychological states may precipitate abnormal behaviour, including illegal behaviour. Using this theoretical framework, Friedlander[19] classifies delinquents according to whether they suffer from 'antisocial character formation', organic disturbances, or psychotic ego-disturbances; and she further sub-divides the first group according to whether environmental or emotional stress or neurotic conflicts are present, giving descriptive criteria (of a fairly vague kind) for identifying each type. A similar classification of delinquents has been suggested by Argyle,[20] who derived his typology in a very different way. Instead of proceeding (as Friedlander did) on the basis of clinical impressions, Argyle reviewed the results of studies of personality tests, in order to discover the personality traits (or, more precisely, the tests which purported to measure the traits) which distinguished delinquents from non-delinquents. Having found a number which did this, Argyle estimated the extent to which these were intercorrelated, and could be grouped into 'types' exhibiting a number of traits. He identified four such delinquent types – those with 'inadequate super-ego', 'deviant identifications' (i.e. gang members), 'weak ego-control' and 'lack of sympathy'. The theoretical basis of this typology lies both in the tests which Argyle considered, and the conceptual framework which he used to group them.

Each of these two methods of typology construction has its strengths as well as its weaknesses. The 'theoretical' approach is guaranteed to distinguish types of crime or criminal behaviour in a way which is theoretically relevant – provided that the theory in question is a coherent one. It may well be, however, that some of the types logically deducible from the theory simply do not exist in reality. For example, even if Freudian theory were shown to be correct, there still might not happen to be any 'criminals from a sense of guilt' of the kind which that theory describes. An empirical typology, on the other hand, must include a certain proportion of the crimes and/or criminals which actually exist. But it may be far from clear *why* those characteristics are grouped together; and the characteristics themselves may not be of any use in explaining why the behaviour in question occurs.

In practice, neither the 'theoretical' nor the 'empirical' approach, as we have described them, is often found in pure form in criminology. Most existing typologies of offences or offenders are the result of an uneasy compromise between the two. Since there are at present very few well-established theories in any of the behavioural sciences from which criminological typologies can be derived, the majority of typologies are predominantly 'empirical' in character; at the same time, most imply some sort of commitment to a particular psychological or sociological theory. Because these theories may be found, on further research, to be invalid, existing classifications of offences or offenders must be regarded as provisional. But the development and testing of new theories depends, to some extent, on

121

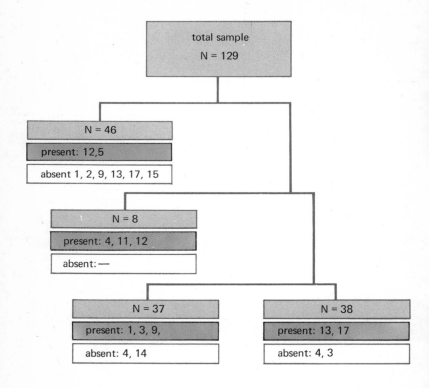

Figure 4:3 (below) Classification of borstal girls by means of MacNaughton-Smith's 'dissimilarity analysis'. The attributes shown by each group tended to distinguish that group, either by their presence or their absence, to a statistically significant extent from the other three groups.

Figure 4:4 (right) The three delinquent 'behaviour syndromes' identified by Hewitt and Jenkins. These three groups of traits (based on ratings and reports in case histories) were found to be intercorrelated among the cases in Hewitt and Jenkins' sample of 500 children seen in a child-guidance clinic. Numbers beside the trait names indicate the percentage of those displaying that trait who were in the 'syndrome' group characterised by that trait. Thus, for example, 70 per cent of *all* gang members in the sample of 500 were in the 'socialised delinquency' group.

unsocialised aggressive behaviour (52 cases)

- assaultive tendencies
- 'initiatory' fighting
- cruelty
- open defiance of authority
- malicious mischief
- inadequate guilt feelings

socialised delinquency (70 cases)

- association with un-desirable companions
- membership in delinquent gang
- co-operative stealing
- furtive stealing
- habitual school truancy
- running away from home
- staying out late at nights

overinhibited behaviour (73 cases)

- seclusiveness
- shyness
- apathy
- worrying
- sensitiveness
- submissiveness

0 10 20 30 40 50 60 70 80 90 100

percentage of all cases with each trait
found within the three 'behaviour
syndromes'

the systematic study of different types of crime and/or criminal, and the analysis of similarities between them. *Some* sort of typology must be chosen, therefore, to serve as a starting-point for future aetiological research and theory. What features should this typology ideally possess?

Requirements of a good typology

Classification always reflects some purpose, and one method of classification is 'better' than another only in respect of some particular purpose or purposes. Moreover, a typology which is good for one purpose is not necessarily good for another. Gibbons[21] has suggested that a single offender typology might be developed which would be useful both in aetiological research and in the treatment of offenders; he remarks that:

It seems but a small jump from the view that the causes of illegal behaviour vary among types of delinquent or criminal careers, to the conclusion that efficacious therapy procedures similarly vary with the kind of behaviour to be treated or changed.

This seems to us, however, to be a fairly large jump, in the present state of criminology. It is by no means clear, at the present, that knowledge of the causes of an offender's delinquency is of any use at all in getting him to stop breaking the law. Of course, one reason for speculating about the causes of crime is to try to find ways of controlling it; and aetiological research may in time suggest new and useful ways of dealing with delinquents. But – even if we ignore the fact that no criminological theory has yet been adequately tested and confirmed, for any type or types of crime – it simply does not follow that typologies which are useful in aetiological research will necessarily be of any value at all when it comes to the choice of treatment or punishment. What is wanted for that purpose (as we shall see in chapter 7) is a typology which separates offenders whose treatment needs are different; and such a typology may be utterly useless for explanatory purposes, just as an aetiological typology may turn out to be useless for treatment purposes.

What, then, are the requirements of a good typology for the purpose of aetiological research? The ultimate object, of course, is that it should separate offenders or kinds of behaviour into types which have different theoretical explanations appropriate to them. A typology which does this may be said to be *valid*; and it is this which one tries to establish by research. But there are some other properties – which may be called *formal* properties – which a good typology ought to have. First, it is generally agreed that the *scope* of the typology should be as wide as possible: all other things being equal, the best typology is the one which includes the greatest number of offenders. It is easy to make too much of this requirement; and it is surely unrealistic to expect that (as is sometimes suggested) a criminological typology should include all offences or offenders. But many of the typologies described in the literature are fairly limited in this respect. For example, Hewitt and Jenkins could manage to include within their three 'behaviour syndromes' only 39 per cent of their sample of 500 cases; Field, in her replication of their work, obtained exactly the same figure. In other words, three out of every five delinquents could *not* be fitted clearly into one of Hewitt's and Jenkins's three categories. Field's replication illustrates a second requirement of a good typology: namely, its types should so far as possible be mutually exclusive. The Hewitt-Jenkins typology appears not to meet this requirement; Field (who used slightly different, though more precise, criteria than Hewitt and Jenkins) found that 51 per cent of her sample were 'mixed' cases falling under two or more types. The remaining 10 per cent could not be classified at all.

Thirdly, it is important that the types specified by a typology should be easily and reliably identified. If the type-definitions include theoretical variables (such as 'weak super-ego' or 'anti-social reference group'), adequate operational definitions of these should be available; and type-criteria should be as unambiguous and objective as possible. Here, typologies which are based on such things as criminal career and work record should generally be superior to typologies based on psychiatric diagnosis or psychological assessments; but in practice, given the inadequacies of official records relating to offenders in most countries, there is probably not much difference. Finally, there is the question how many types the typology should contain. Clearly, a typology which is being used for treatment purposes should be as rich in types as possible, and should include at least as many types as there are possible kinds of treatment or punishment; any type which is shown by research to be unrelated to the outcome of treatment can then be discarded. But in the case of typologies for aetiological research, the position is rather different. An empirically-derived typology, which is not based on any particular theory, should probably also contain a fairly large number of types; the trouble is that there is no real way of knowing how rich in types, or how detailed, it should be. The number of types in a typology which is derived from a theory, on the other hand, will obviously depend on the range of behaviour which the theory aims to explain.

Types of offender versus types of offence

A typology which is used for aetiological research in criminology may either be a classification of *offences* or a classification of *offenders*. Sociologically-orientated criminologists tend to concentrate on offences, whereas psychologists tend to focus on people who commit offences; but either kind of theory can be attached to either kind of typology. For example, as we have seen, Hewitt and Jenkins began by identifying three different patterns of behaviour; but they attempted to explain these by means of a psychological theory based on the characteristics of offenders.

A recent sociological example of a typology of offences is Clinard's and Quinney's analysis[22] of 'criminal behaviour systems'. Clinard and Quinney use as defining characteristics in this typology four variables – the criminal career of the offender, the extent to which the behaviour has group support, correspondence between criminal behaviour and legitimate behaviour patterns, and societal reaction. Each of these four variables is allowed to take three values (high, medium, or low). The authors then characterise eight different 'criminal behaviour systems' – violent personal crime, occasional property crime, occupational crime, political crime, order crime, conventional crime, organised crime, and professional crime – in terms of the four defining variables. (Two of these types are illustrated in figure 4:5.) It is not actually clear whether Clinard and Quinney regard the four variables as defining criteria of the eight types, or whether they regard them merely as features which just happen to distinguish between these eight 'criminal behaviour systems'. Either way, the four variables would presumably figure in any theory which was valid for all eight 'behaviour systems'. But four variables, each permitted to take three values, have 64 possible combinations, not just eight. Any theory about the causes and distribution of crime which was based on these four factors should also explain why only eight combinations of these factors actually occur – if indeed that is the case.

Historically, most of the typologies propounded by criminologists

Figure 4:5 Two of the eight 'criminal behaviour systems' of Clinard and Quinney.

	Professional crime	Occasional property crime
Criminal career of offender	HIGH Crime pursued as a livelihood; criminal self-concept; status in the world of crime; commitment to world of professional criminals	LOW Little or no criminal self-concept; does not identify with crime
Group support of criminal behaviour	HIGH Associations primarily with other offenders; status gained in criminal offences: behaviour prescribed by group norms	LOW Little group support; individual offences
Correspondence between criminal and legitimate behaviour	MEDIUM Engaged in an occupation; skill respected; survival because of co-operation from legitimate society; law-abiding persons often accomplices	LOW Violation of value on private property
Societal reaction	MEDIUM Rarely strong societal reaction, most cases 'fixed'	MEDIUM Arrest; jail; short imprisonment, probation
Legal categories of crime	Shoplifting, pickpocketing, forgery, counterfeiting, fraud	Some auto theft, shoplifting, cheque forgery, vandalism

have been typologies of *offenders*. This is probably because of the clinical approach of psychiatrists and psychologists to criminology, and because criminologists' main concern with classification has been in relation to treatment and the control of crime. Now, there is nothing wrong with this general approach. But the majority of typologies of this kind have not been related to any kind of criminological theory. Moreover, on closer examination many of them are incomplete, because they are not really related to *criminal* or *deviant* behaviour. Instead, they are what might be called typologies of *persons* – they classify human beings according to attributes such as personality or character traits or social background, which apply to human beings generally and not just to offenders. Friedlander's typology, which we have already cited, is an example of this. 'Antisocial character formation', 'organic disturbances' and 'psychotic ego-disturbances' may all be displayed by persons who are not in the least criminal, delinquent, or deviant; and (as Friedlander herself admits) they are not displayed by all criminals.

Of course, in one sense typologies like Friedlander's are 'about' criminal behaviour, since they are derived from studies of groups of persons who have broken the law. But they take no account of different forms of criminal or deviant behaviour – as opposed to symptomatic or 'abnormal' behaviour – with the result that they cannot explain why certain personal characteristics lead to violent crime in some cases and purposive theft in others. Yet in many cases this is plainly not just a matter of chance. Moreover, they cannot explain why those personal characteristics should lead to *any* kind of crime in some cases, but not in others. Why should some persons suffering from 'antisocial character formation' commit thefts, while others develop neurotic symptoms? It seems to us to be important that, as criminologists, we should seek to develop theories which completely explain *criminal* behaviour – not just 'aggressive' behaviour, or 'abnormal' behaviour, or behaviour in general. Crime is, after all, what criminology is supposed to be about. But it is just this which theories based on typologies like Friedlander's cannot possibly do, no matter how far they may be confirmed by empirical research. Of course, there may be room for disagreement about the *definition* of 'criminal behaviour', and about whether it should cover borderline cases such as 'white-collar crime'; many sociologists would prefer to study the broader phenomenon of 'deviant behaviour', of which crime (in the sense of acts contrary to the criminal law) is only one part. There is none-

128

theless a distinction between behaviour of this kind – which is contrary to legal or moral norms of conduct – and much of the behaviour characteristic of psychological abnormality.

Classifying offenders by their criminal behaviour

How, then, should we classify offenders in a way which is relevant to the type of criminal behaviour which they commit? A first suggestion is to use the legal category of the offender's current, or most recent, crime. Popularly, a man who kills is called a 'murderer'; one who breaks into dwelling-houses in the night a 'burglar', and so on. But there is an absurdity in ascribing certain characteristics to a *person,* on the basis of a single *act* which that person commits – just as it would be absurd to describe a man as a 'golfer' if he once played nine holes and then never went near a golf course again. If offenders are to be classified in terms of their criminal behaviour, it seems that this must be done by reference to a criminal *career* – that is, the relatively persistent, regular or frequent committing of a certain type of offence.

One interesting attempt to develop a typology of this kind empirically has been made by Julian Roebuck.[23] Using the arrest records of four hundred offenders selected at random from receptions into a reformatory in Virginia, Roebuck identified thirteen different patterns of criminal behaviour, of which eight were 'single patterns' showing a relatively high frequency of one type of criminal charge. To qualify as a 'single pattern' type, the offender's record had to show at least three arrests, all for the same charge, or – if he had been arrested on other charges as well – at least four arrests for the same charge, with at least one of these occurring in the most recent third of the arrest history. Careers were classified as 'double pattern' or 'triple pattern' if these criteria were met for two or three types of crime.

The thirteen criminal types identified by Roebuck, and their frequencies in his sample, are shown in table 4:1. Roebuck analysed the social and personal backgrounds of these different types, and found that certain characteristics were associated to some extent with the different patterns of criminal behaviour: for example, the armed robbers tended to be comparatively young, to have been reared in unsatisfactory homes in slum conditions, and to have been members of juvenile gangs.

This method of offender classification is open to certain objec-

Table 4:1 Frequencies of criminal career types in a sample of 400 adult prisoners.

	Number	Per cent
Single Pattern types		
Narcotic drug offences	50	12·5
Robbery	32	8·0
Gambling	16	4·0
Burglary	15	3·8
Sex offences	15	3·8
Fraud	10	2·5
Car theft	8	2·0
Forgery and counterfeiting	4	1·0
Total, single pattern types	**150**	**37·5**
Double pattern types		
Larceny and burglary	64	16·0
Drunkenness and assault	40	10·0
Total, double pattern types	**104**	**26·0**
Triple pattern type		
Drunkenness, assault and larceny	43	10·8
Mixed pattern ('Jack-of-all-Trades')	71	17·8
No pattern (less than three arrests)	32	8·0
Total	**400**	**100·0**

tions. To begin with, it has often been pointed out that legal definitions of crimes are often arbitrary, and do not indicate important behavioural differences; for example, until recently the distinction in English law between larceny by a trick and obtaining by false pretences was often a highly artificial one. But as Roebuck has argued, it is easy to make too much of this point; the major legal categories – burglary, assault, robbery, etc. – certainly do mark off significant behavioural differences. What is true is that legal categories by themselves are too crude for research purposes, and need to be further subdivided by taking into account individual or social factors relating to the offences. A domestic quarrel between husband and wife, a fight between two strangers in a public bar and an attempted armed robbery may all result in the offence of malicious wounding, but it is probably not useful, for criminological purposes, to classify these three acts as instances of the same offence. The extent to which legal categories should be subdivided or grouped together, and the factors used to do this, will of course depend on the researcher's interests and point of view.

An interesting example of one such classification is that used by McClintock and Gibson, in their study[24] of robbery in London. This classification is based principally on the circumstances in which the victim was attacked, with each main type subdivided according to other situational factors such as the type of victim, method of attack, or relationship between attacker and victim. This classification cuts across a number of legal definitions, and groups together acts on the basis of behavioural similarities.

Such a classification overcomes another criticism of Roebuck's method, which is that a homogeneous criminal record (in legal terms) does not necessarily indicate *systematic* criminal behaviour, though this is obviously an important distinction for theoretical purposes. An offender may have a dozen arrests or convictions, all for the same type of offence in legal terms, but his behaviour may still not be at all systematic in the sense of displaying specialised techniques, consistent relations with victims, etc. This is especially true in the case of offences of burglary and larceny. In any case, Roebuck's rather arbitrary criteria of a 'single pattern' type are inadequate, since they take no account of the fact that offences against property – and in particular larceny – account for the great majority of arrests and convictions, in most jurisdictions. Thus a man whose criminal record included ten offences of which six were larceny could be a 'single pattern' type by Roebuck's criteria, even though his criminal career did not in fact show particular concentration on this type of offence; on the other hand, a man who had seven convictions of which three were for sexual offences would have a *relatively* 'specialised' career – with a greater-than-average number of sexual offences – even though he did not meet Roebuck's criteria.

A typology which goes some way to meeting these criticisms has been proposed by Gibbons.[25] This typology, which makes use of the notion of a criminal 'role-career', is based on a number of assumptions and hypotheses of contemporary sociological theory, about the learning of different social roles (i.e. socially prescribed patterns of behaviour, which may or may not involve criminal or deviant behaviour). Gibbons argues that many offenders display stable patterns of delinquent or criminal 'role-playing'; and he hypothesises that different role-careers are caused by different combinations of social and personal factors. From this perspective, Gibbons proceeds to develop a typology of juvenile delinquents, and one of adult criminals. The fifteen adult criminal types he uses are as follows:

1 Professional thief
2 Professional 'heavy' criminal
3 Semiprofessional property criminal
4 Property offender – 'one-time loser'
5 Automobile thief – 'joyrider'
6 Naive cheque forger
7 White-collar criminal
8 Professional 'fringe' violator
9 Embezzler
10 Personal offender – 'one-time loser'
11 'Psychopathic' assaultist
12 Violent sex offender
13 Non-violent sex offender – 'rape'
14 Non-violent sex offender – statutory rape
15 Narcotic addict – heroin.

These fifteen types are defined, or rather described, in terms of four variables which serve as type-criteria: offence behaviour, 'interactional setting', self-image, and attitudes. (Two of these 15 types are illustrated in table 4:2.) In addition, for each type Gibbons describes what he assumes to be a typical role-career or pattern of criminal behaviour over time; he then hypothesises that certain 'background dimensions' – such as social class, family background, peer group associations, and contact with law-enforcement agencies – are correlated with each type. For example, according to Gibbons

132

Table 4:2 Two adult criminal 'role-careers'.

Definitional dimensions	1 Personal Offender 'one-time loser'	2 Professional 'heavy' criminal
Offence behaviour	Usually a major crime of violence – murder, manslaughter or serious assault (not, however, a sexual crime).	Armed robbery, burglary, and other direct assaults on property. Crimes involve detailed planning and high degree of skill, with actual violence seldom used.
Interactional setting	Normally the victim is well known to the offender, e.g. killing of spouse or other family member. Crime may be outcome of a long history of wife-beating or other family violence.	Crimes usually carried out as team or 'mob' operations, with each member having a specialised role, e.g. driver of getaway car.
Self-image	Non-criminal self-image; often reports offence to police, and is contrite, guilty and repentant.	Defines himself as a criminal; exhibits pride in specialised skills and views crime as a lucrative and satisfying way of life. Draws a clear distinction between himself and other 'amateur' criminals.
Attitudes	Pro-social attitudes generally; has conventional occupation before arrest and plans to return to conventional work. Usually married and has conventional marital and family life.	Scorn for inept policemen, but respect for competent ones; no great hostility to police, who are regarded as necessary persons who have a job to do. Negative attitudes to conventional work roles.
Role-career	Usually no previous criminal record, except possibly drunkenness or wife-beating. Usually receives long prison sentence, and makes satisfactory parole adjustment.	Normally urban, lower-class background; begins career as predatory gang delinquent; tends to continue in crime until middle age, when may 'retire' into non-criminal occupation.

the 'role-career' of the professional 'heavy' criminal usually begins with membership in a delinquent gang, is characterised by increasing involvement with older professionals from whom necessary skills are learned, and often terminates with 'retirement' into a non-criminal occupation in middle age. The background dimensions of this type, Gibbons suggests, generally include an urban, lower-class background; neglectful upbringing and/or criminal siblings or parents; differential association with delinquent or criminal peers; and involvement with the police as a juvenile, though little contact with them (because of his criminal skill) as an adult.

Gibbons admits that this typology is not intended to include all forms of criminal behaviour; he describes it as 'a reasonable middle ground between gross systems of differentiation among offenders, such as "property" and "personal" criminals, and categorical systems which employ an extremely large number of types, such as a scheme based on specific offence labels'. While many of the descriptions which Gibbons gives of his offender types are very similar to those given by other writers, he himself points out that there has not yet been much empirical research which could show the typology's validity either for aetiological or treatment purposes. As we have already indicated, we think it is unlikely that a single typology will be adequate for both of these purposes. Nonetheless, Gibbons's work is an extremely interesting example of offender type-classification which, though basically empirically derived, is still guided by a more or less systematic theoretical approach.

How common are homogeneous careers?

As we have seen, Gibbons's offender typology, like that of Roebuck and a number of other writers, makes use of the notion of a criminal career. It is true that some of Gibbons's types have 'careers' consisting of only one offence; but others are described as persistent offenders whose offence behaviour is more frequent, and relatively homogeneous. But how common, in fact, are homogeneous careers of this kind?

The available evidence suggests that unfortunately they are not in fact very common. In any year, the majority of offenders convicted and sentenced by most courts are first offenders, the majority of whom are not subsequently reconvicted; of those who are reconvicted, a substantial proportion have committed different types of crime from that which led to their first appearance in court. The matrix in table 4:3a was prepared by the Institute for Defence Analyses for the President's Crime Commission;[26] it shows the probability of a man whose last arrest was for a crime of one type being re-arrested for a crime of that type or a different one. The figures on the principal diagonal of this matrix (printed in bold face) show the probabilities of offenders' being re-arrested for the same type of crime as that for which they were last arrested: and it will be seen that the highest of these – for burglary – is ·459. In other words, the probability that a man arrested for burglary will have his next arrest for this type of crime is less than one in two; and the chances of 'repeating' in this way are even lower for the other types of crime shown in this table. Moreover, what this matrix shows are the probabilities that an offender, *if re-arrested,* will be re-arrested for the seven types of offence. It must thus be multiplied by the *overall* re-arrest rates for these types of offence, to take into account the fact that some offenders are not re-arrested at all. Table 4:3b shows the results of this analysis, using estimated overall re-arrest rates based on a study of criminal careers carried out in the United States by the Federal Bureau of Investigation.[27]

If we make the assumption (which may not, in fact, be correct) that the matrix in table 4:3b is valid for all arrests in an offender's career, it can be estimated that of all those arrested once for any of the seven offences and subsequently re-arrested five or more times, about 16 per cent will have half or more of their arrests for burglary. On the same assumption, the chance of six or more arrests, at least half of which are for larceny, is only about one in thirty. This finding is of interest, since larceny accounts for about 45 per cent of all arrests for Part I offences in the United States each year, whereas burglary accounts for only about one-quarter. The probability of a homogeneous career involving other types of offence is even smaller; on the same assumption as above, the probability of an offender eventually having a career of five or more arrests with even one-third of them being for aggravated assault is less than three per cent.

The crime-switch matrix (table 4:3a) does suggest some degree of homogeneity in the careers of persons committing serious offences against property (robbery, burglary, and larceny of property worth over $50). The probability that an offender, arrested for any one of these three offences and subsequently re-arrested, will have his second arrest for one of these types of crime is about 80 per cent; whereas the probability of his second arrest being for a serious offence of per-

Table 4:3a The 'crime-switch' matrix.

Last arrest for an Index crime	If arrested again for Index crime (see left), probability that it will be for						
	1	2	3	4	5	6	7
1 Murder, non-negligent manslaughter*	**0·025**	0·025	0·150	0·400	0·200	0·100	0·100
2 Forcible rape*	·020	**·150**	·110	·260	·200	·140	·120
3 Robbery	·015	·010	**·350**	·060	·350	·115	·100
4 Aggravated assault*	·025	·040	·150	**·300**	·085	·200	·200
5 Burglary	·010	·020	·135	·063	**·459**	·282	·031
6 Larceny ($50 and over)	·010	·020	·140	·025	·400	**·275**	·130
7 Car theft	·010	·027	·045	·028	·390	·222	**·278**

* Best estimates on inadequate data.

sonal violence (homicide, rape or aggravated assault) is less than one in ten. By contrast, for those arrested for one of these three violent crimes, the probability of re-arrest being for another violent crime is about four in ten. A study confirming this conclusion was carried out by Peterson et al.[28] in St Louis, Missouri. They found that in a sample of 88 men, aged forty and over on arrest, a high proportion had stable careers consisting either of two or more arrests exclusively for violent crime (33 cases) or of two or more arrests for non-violent property crime (18 cases); only eight men in this group had mixed arrest records for both violent and property crimes.

Table 4:3b The 'crime-switch' matrix with non-re-arrest rates taken into account.

Last arrest	Not re-arrested	Next arrest Re-arrested for crime of type						
		1	2	3	4	5	6	7
1 Murder, non-negligent man-slaughter	·600	**·010**	·010	·060	·160	·080	·040	·040
2 Forcible rape	·500	·010	**·075**	·055	·130	·100	·070	·060
3 Robbery	·400	·009	·006	**·210**	·036	·210	·069	·060
4 Aggravated assault	·260	·019	·029	·112	**·222**	·063	·148	·148
5 Burglary	·230	·007	·015	·104	·049	**·354**	·217	·024
6 Larceny ($50 and over)	·410	·006	·012	·083	·015	·236	**·162**	·077
7 Car theft	·200	·008	·022	·036	·022	·312	·178	**·222**

The figures in the left-hand column of this matrix are estimates based on a study of criminal careers carried out by the US Federal Bureau of Investigation and published in the *Uniform Crime Reports* for 1968. The remaining seven columns of the matrix are the result of multiplying each row of the 'crime-switch' matrix (see **table 4:3a**) by the overall re-arrest rate for that type of crime (i.e. 1·0 minus the entry in the left-hand column). Thus, for example, of those arrested for burglary, an estimated 23 per cent are not re-arrested at all; but 35·4 per cent (·77 × ·459) are re-arrested for burglary.

However, 'violent crime' and 'non-violent property crime' are both very broad categories, and both include a number of different, more specific, patterns of criminal behaviour. It should also be noted that these studies, like Roebuck's (see page 129) are based on *arrest* records, rather than on *convictions*. Arrest records may give a more accurate estimate of the total amount of an offender's criminality, but they may exaggerate its homogeneity, since many police forces make a practice of arresting suspects on the basis of the nature of their previous arrests or *modus operandi*.

When more stringent criteria are used, the degree of homogeneity is reduced. Thus, Robin[29] made a study of the delinquent and later criminal careers of members of 27 gangs in Philadelphia in 1962. He found that while there was a tendency for these offenders' crimes to get more serious as they got older, there was little evidence of stable patterns of a single type of offence. Only a fifth of the 395 gang members with at least five police contacts had as many as three-fourths of those contacts within any one of three broad offence categories (offences against the person, offences against property, or disorderly conduct).

Several English studies also support the general conclusion that homogeneous criminal careers are rare. In the Cambridge study of sexual offences,[30] based on a sample of 1,985 men convicted in 1947, it was found that only 17 per cent had any previous convictions for sexual crimes of any kind, and that only two per cent had four or more convictions of the same kind (most of these being persons who committed homosexual offences or indecent exposure). Moreover, nearly half of those with more than one conviction for a sexual offence had also been convicted of three or more *non*-sexual offences. In his study of crimes of violence committed in London, McClintock[31] found that only one-fifth of the offenders could be classified as 'violent recidivists' with one or more previous convictions for a violent offence; only about three to four per cent had previously been convicted three or more times for violent crimes, though about 15 per cent had three or more previous convictions for *non*-violent crimes. In another study, of robbers convicted in London in 1950–7, McClintock and Gibson found that while the majority had previous convictions, these were mostly for larceny and other non-violent property crimes; only 16 per cent could be classified as 'robbers' who concentrated mainly on this type of offence. Similarly, research by Hadden,[32] on offenders convicted of fraud, found only about one-sixth had specialised in fraud; another 12 per cent had begun their criminal careers by committing other offences (mostly larceny) and had tended in later years to specialise in frauds.

Conclusion

It seems clear, then, that homogeneous criminal careers are not common, and that offender typologies based on this notion will consequently be very limited in scope. A typology based on criminal careers may well be useful as a starting-point for aetiological research; but – if 'mixed' careers are excluded – it is bound to leave the great bulk of criminal behaviour unexplained.

It seems to us, therefore, that any offender typology which is intended to distinguish different causal processes should begin by explicitly distinguishing between 'occasional' or 'once-only' offenders on the one hand, and 'habitual' or persistent offenders on the other; and by further sub-dividing the latter group into those who display homogeneous criminal careers and those who do not. The distinction between 'occasional' and persistent offenders has been ignored by most contemporary criminologists – with the conspicuous exception of Gibbons, whose typology was discussed above. But Gibbons errs, in our view, in regarding the 'once-only' offender as having a 'role-career'. A man who commits only one isolated offence does not have *any* criminal career – even a very short one; and we suggest that the *kind* of explanation appropriate to his behaviour is likely to be very different from the kind of explanation applying to the man who persists in crime. The self-report studies described in chapter 2 of this book have shown that most persons commit some kind of offence at some time or another in their lives. In the absence of evidence to the contrary, it seems reasonable to regard these isolated acts as normal events, the occurrence and distribution of which – if it is not completely random – is best explained, at least in most cases, by relatively simple situational factors (such as opportunities to commit crime).

The crimes of persistent offenders are different; and a man who is repeatedly arrested for serious offences certainly cannot be regarded as completely normal, in the statistical sense. (We do not mean, of course, that he has to be thought of as ill.) Even a mild degree of persistence in crime suggests a degree of personal involvement – reflected, perhaps, in self-concept, attitudes and social relationships – which the 'once-only' offender is unlikely to possess: and the notion of a criminal career accordingly becomes more appropriate. In other words, it seems likely that the cause of the persistent offender's crimes is not just the more frequent occurrence of the same thing which causes the occasional offender's crime.

Of course, it is possible that a dichotomous classification of 'occasional' and 'persistent' offenders is far too crude, and that several degrees of involvement in crime need to be distinguished for explanatory purposes. For instance, it may be that, as Glaser[33] has suggested, many offenders' careers take the form of a 'crime-noncrime' cycle, in which the offender alternates between periods of legitimate work and periods of criminal behaviour. Again, as

Polsky[34] has recently pointed out, many kinds of property crime lend themselves admirably to 'moonlighting' – that is, they may be undertaken to provide a second source of income, either part-time or full-time, by one who continues to hold down a regular, legitimate job at the same time. The precise delineation of these 'intermediate career' groups must, in our opinion, be based on self-reported crime as well as arrests or convictions. Indeed, when the undetected offences of persistent offenders are considered, a somewhat greater degree of homogeneity of behaviour may be found than is suggested by official records.

The only firm conclusion that we can draw, then, is that frequency or intensity of criminal behaviour must be taken into account by any valid aetiological typology of offenders. In addition, such a typology should probably distinguish those offenders with relatively homogeneous criminal careers, even if they are not very numerous. We recognise that this does not take us very far, and it is a dispiriting result after so much effort has been put into this subject. It may well be that the empirical or descriptive approach to this problem, which has been the basis of most research so far, is fundamentally the wrong one and that more attention should be paid in future to the development of theories from which classifications can be deduced.

5 Understanding the sentencing process

Criminologists have paid scant attention to the sentencing process. Their major concern has been with the effects of sentences on offenders. The shortness of this chapter compared with the next two testifies to the relative amounts of empirical work in these two related areas. Yet research on the decision-making process involved in sentencing is essential; for it is, after all, mainly the decisions made by judges and magistrates that determine which types of offender undergo which various punishments and treatments.

Most studies of sentencing have been concerned with what appear to be inexplicable disparities between sentences passed on similar cases. Researchers have in general attempted to see whether these disparities can be explained by the peculiar nature of the cases coming before different judges or courts. The method has been to correlate various facts about the offence and the offender with the severity of the sentence imposed. This method has obviously produced useful information about what factors are given most weight in the sentencing process. At the same time it has drawn attention to the importance of information about the offence and the offender on sentencing and led to a critical analysis of the role of those who provide information, such as the prosecutor and probation officer. In addition to this empirical approach, studies have been made of judicial rules and conventions for sentencing, especially those embodied in judgments of the courts of appeal. In England, for example, D. A. Thomas[1] has contributed much to the understanding of sentencing through a critical analysis of the principles and practical directions laid down for sentencing in the Court of Appeal, Criminal Division. But in this chapter we shall be concerned entirely with the contribution of empirical research to the understanding of the sentencing process.

Studies of sentencing disparities

In the studies so far reported of sentencing disparities, three different methods have been used. At the crudest level are comparisons between the proportions of offenders receiving various sentences in different courts, with no attempt being made to assess the extent to which the courts receive similar cases. A second method has been to take very large numbers of cases and assume that the different types are distributed at random between the judges, so that each has a similar proportion of trivial or serious cases to deal with. The third method has attempted to control for different offenders coming before different judges by matching or prediction techniques. The results of studies using these methods will be reviewed in turn, and their conclusions subjected to critical analysis. We shall show that a new model is necessary if sentencing research is to answer some of the major questions about how judicial decisions are reached.

Crude comparisons between courts The evidence pointing to disparities in sentencing among the judiciary at all levels is overwhelming. As a paper prepared by the United Nations Secretariat in 1965 stressed:

In most countries there is, admittedly, a varying degree of disparity and inconsistency in the sentencing process, and this tends to engender disrespect and even contempt for the law.[2]

In the United States Federal courts in 1962 the average sentences of imprisonment for all cases ranged from 12·1 months in the northern circuit of New York (65 cases) to 57·6 months in the southern district of Iowa (41 cases). For forgery, average sentences ranged from 7·2 months in Mississippi to 54 months in Northern Indiana. And as Judge Youngdahl pointed out[3] these averages themselves concealed large variations: a defendant who robbed seven banks received three years while others convicted of a single robbery received as much as twenty and twenty-five years. Similarly, in income tax cases Judge Youngdahl claimed:

They are embarrassing in their revelation of sharp variations in practice and opinion among the courts dealing with this crime.

In England in the early 1950s Grünhut found very large variations in the use made of fines and probation in juvenile courts throughout England and Wales. In the courts of two neighbouring northern towns, Rotherham and Halifax, the proportion of young persons put on probation was 12 and 79 per cent respectively.[4] Patchett and McClean have shown that these variations are still with us. In Barnsley (in 1962–3) '73 per cent of boys under fourteen and 65 per cent of those between fourteen and seventeen are fined. The corresponding national figures are 17 per cent and 28 per cent.'[5] While these studies have not controlled for the type of offender coming before the courts it is hard to disagree with Patchett and McClean's conclusion: 'There must be a difference of a fundamental nature between the approach of the Barnsley bench and that of most other benches'.

'Random sample' studies The most influential of early studies was by Frederick Gaudet and others,[6] who investigated the sentences imposed on 7,638 cases over ten years by six separate judges in a New Jersey county court. Gaudet noted that the cases were assigned to the judges by the prosecutor on a rotational basis and therefore concluded that different types of offence and offender would be randomly distributed between them. In general, judges A and F are more lenient than the others: they imprisoned about a third of offenders, whereas the others imprisoned half or more. The relative severity also changed depending on the type of offence (see figure 5:1). The judges also differed as much in the length of prison sentences they gave as they did in the frequency with which they used imprisonment. Edward Green has severely criticised Gaudet's conclusions on the grounds that the hypothesis that judges received similar cases was not proven.[7] It is true that the attempts made by Gaudet to compare cases given different judges were inconclusive, and that the numbers for three types of offences – sex crimes, stealing with violence and liquor offences – were small, but on the other hand larcenies made up 80 per cent of the cases and it seems plausible that, with such large numbers, cases were distributed reasonably evenly between judges. Green notes also that the cases studied by Gaudet were all 'high misdemeanors' (felonies) for which there was great scope for discretion in the choice of sentence and hence, even if the randomness is assumed, it was not surprising that disparity occurred.

A similar method to Gaudet's was used by Shoham in a study of 566 cases dealt with by eight judges of the three district courts of Israel (Jerusalem, Tel-Aviv and Haifa).[8] Shoham confined his analysis to offences against property and the person, and found considerable variations in the severity of the sentences imposed. Table 5:1 shows that only three judges – those labelled R, S and G – imposed sentences around the average and that the others vary according to the type of offence. Judge N, who is in general the most severe, was least severe for offences against the person; Judge A is by contrast relatively lenient with property offences and severe with those against the person. Overall the punishments given by the

143

Figure 5:1 (right) A comparison between the proportion of property and sex offenders given various sentences by six New Jersey judges.

Table 5:1 Relative severity scores of eight Israeli district court judges

Judge	All offences		Offences against the person		Offences against property	
	Per cent	Rank	Per cent	Rank	Per cent	Rank
N	71	1	10	8	59	2
A	62	2	88	2	48	7
L	62	3	90	1	55	3
R	50	4	49	4	48	6
S	49	5	50	3	52	5
G	46	6	46	5	55	3
J	40	7	46	5	33	8
D	30	8	15	7	72	1

The relative severity of penalties is measured in relation to the *median* severity of 50 per cent. It can be seen that the variation in severity is greatest for offences against the person, and that Judges A, N and D, in particular, have different policies for offences against property and against the person, relative to other judges.

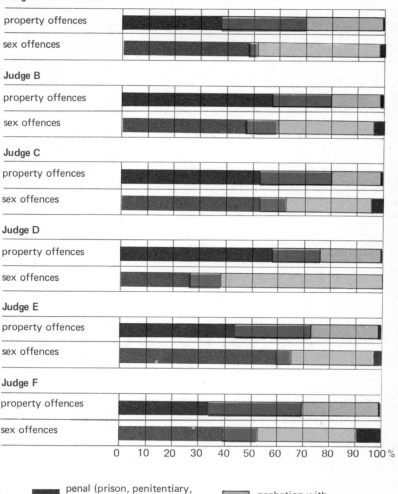

Judge A

property offences

sex offences

Judge B

property offences

sex offences

Judge C

property offences

sex offences

Judge D

property offences

sex offences

Judge E

property offences

sex offences

Judge F

property offences

sex offences

0   10   20   30   40   50   60   70   80   90   100 %

penal (prison, penitentiary, reformatory or correctional house) sentences.

suspended sentence without supervision

probation with supervision

fines

judges varied considerably (see figure 5:2). It should be noted, however, that Shoham only quotes percentages in the article. Apparently three of the eight judges received only about thirty cases each, and it therefore seems hard to justify the assumption that offenders of different types were evenly distributed between them.

Matching studies Edward Green's study of 1,437 cases dealt with by eighteen judges in the Philadelphia court of Quarter Sessions during 1956–7 is the most sophisticated sentencing enquiry yet completed. Green examines the influence of both legal and non-legal factors on the sentences passed. By 'legal' factors Green meant: **a** the type of crime committed, **b** the number of bills of indictment on which the defendant is convicted, **c** the prior criminal record of the offender, and **d** the recommendations of auxiliary agencies of the courts contained in reports of pre-sentence investigations and neuropsychiatric examinations. The non-legal or 'legally irrelevant' factors were sex, age, race and place of birth. In addition Green also took into account the influence of the prosecutor and the type of plea – guilty or not guilty – made by the defendant. He comes to the conclusion that the legal factors explain most of the disparities apparent in a crude look at the decisions of the court. The most important factors were the seriousness of the offence and the previous convictions of the offender. Judges reflected to some extent the scale of seriousness defined by the statutory maxima, with the exception that they tended to punish more severely those offences involving bodily harm to specific persons (see figure 5:3). When these legal factors were held constant, non-legal factors such as sex, age, race and place of birth were seen to be of little influence in sentencing. In other words, this court was acting on a 'tariff' basis in fixing sentences. Green used the legal factors, in combination, to predict the likelihood of a defendant being sent to the penitentiary, or to prison for a short sentence, or receiving a non-institutional sentence. Table 5:2 shows that there are considerable differences in the sentencing patterns of cases falling into the three score categories. Those with a high score on Green's prediction table (i.e. those who have committed a more serious crime and have a longer record) are much more likely to go to the penitentiary than those with a low score. Using this table Green is able to compare the sentences imposed by different judges on offenders falling into the same 'risk category'. His analysis shows that in those sentencing the low score group (23 to 35) there

Table 5:2 Percentage of offenders receiving penitentiary sentence in three prediction categories.

	Grave offence	Offence of intermediate gravity	Minor offence
Prediction scores:	45—58	36—44	23—35
Penitentiary : 12 months and over	69·5	30·3	7·2
Prison: 3–11½ months	19·7	45·3	26·5
Non-imprisonment	10·8	24·4	66·3

were two groups of judges: twelve imposing prison sentences in between 60 and 82 per cent of cases and six imposing such sentences in only 30 to 50 per cent. Within each of these two groups of judges there was a high degree of consistency; for example, in the high score group only four judges stood out from the other fourteen in imposing penitentiary sentences in under half the cases. Again, in neither group were there statistically significant differences between judges. Where serious and minor cases are concerned, in other words, there seems to be a reasonable amount of consistency within the Philadelphia Bench. But there is not complete uniformity. And in the middle score group there is much more variation: there are three distinct sub-groups of judges (see table 5:3). The evidence seems clear, as Green concludes:

As cases move from the extreme of gravity or mildness towards intermediacy, judicial standards tend to become less stable and sentencing increasingly reflects the individuality of the judge.[9]

Considering that the judges in Green's study all sat in the same court, and had an opportunity to meet and be aware of each other's decisions, these findings are all the more important.

In England, Mannheim, Spencer and Lynch[10] studied the sentences imposed on four hundred boys aged 14 to 17 found guilty of larceny in eight London juvenile courts in 1951. The aim of the

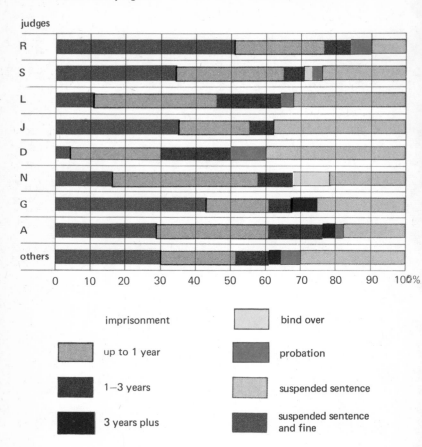

Figure 5:2 Percentage of various types of sentence given by eight Israeli district court judges.

judges

R

S

L

J

D

N

G

A

others

0 10 20 30 40 50 60 70 80 90 100%

imprisonment

bind over

up to 1 year

probation

1—3 years

suspended sentence

3 years plus

suspended sentence and fine

enquiry was to attempt to explain marked variations in the sentencing practices of these courts. The analysis showed that the proportion of boys put on probation ranged from 18 to 66 per cent and those discharged from 18 to 48 per cent. They looked at all the information available in the files of the police and probation service, at social indices of the areas served by the courts, and took into account the sex of the chairman at each court. None of these factors, by itself, explained the different sentencing patterns of the courts. It may be

148

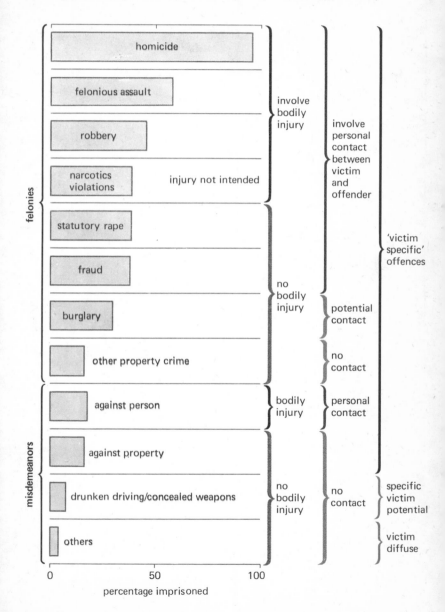

Figure 5:3 Offence categories scaled according to the percentage of cases receiving penitentiary sentences and the degree of *'violation of personality'*.

Table 5·3 Sentencing of cases of 'intermediate gravity' by 18 Philadelphia judges.

Judge	Prison: 12 mths and up		Prison: 3-11½ mths		Non-imprison-ment		Total
	No.	%	No.	%	No.	%	No.
1* Judges ranking 1-3†							
D	0	**0·0**	7	**77·8**	2	**22·2**	9
E	2	**8·0**	18	**72·0**	5	**20·0**	25
P	8	**11·8**	38	**55·9**	22	**32·3**	68
Total	10		63		29		102
2 Judges ranking 4-11†							
C	7	**18·4**	24	**63·2**	7	**18·4**	38
F	4	**20·0**	16	**80·0**	0	**0·0**	20
A	6	**21·4**	7	**50·0**	4	**28·6**	14
Q	3	**21·4**	7	**50·0**	4	**28·6**	14
L	4	**22·2**	8	**44·4**	6	**33·4**	18
K	4	**25·0**	12	**75·0**	0	**0·0**	16
N	4	**30·8**	5	**38·4**	4	**30·8**	13
G	41	**34·2**	36	**30·0**	43	**35·8**	120
Total	73		115		68		253
3 Judges ranking 12-18†							
H	7	**38·9**	8	**44·4**	3	**16·7**	18
M	8	**42·1**	7	**36·8**	4	**21·1**	19
O	23	**41·2**	17	**32·7**	12	**23·1**	52
J	13	**44·8**	14	**48·3**	2	**6·9**	29
B	5	**50·0**	2	**20·0**	3	**30·0**	10
I	20	**57·1**	9	**25·7**	6	**17·1**	35
R	4	**80·0**	1	**20·0**	0	**0·0**	5
Total	80		58		30		168

* differences within each of the three groups were not statistically significant.

† in the proportion of prison sentences of a minimum of 12 months and up which were imposed.

that a more sophisticated attempt to combine the items into a prediction equation as Green later did would have produced a different picture, but the authors concluded:

The classification of data which were used for the purpose of comparison was thought to cover most of the possible variations which could relate to the individual case. It appeared to include those aspects of cases which experts were likely to report on or courts to enquire about. However, if consistency exists in the treatment policies of these courts, it seems that the factors producing such uniformity are not derived from the data examined in this study nor recorded in the files.

In adult magistrates' courts similar conditions seem to prevail. In the years 1951–4, one of us (Hood) found that the proportion of men aged 21 and over sentenced to imprisonment for an indictable offence varied between 8 and 47 per cent in the 119 police districts (courts or groups of courts) then existing in England and Wales: but the majority imprisoned between 15 and 27 per cent.[11] Twelve courts, representing those with high, medium and low imprisonment rates, were studied. Information relevant to the offences committed, and to the background of the offenders was recorded and correlated with the proportion receiving a sentence of imprisonment. None of these factors by themselves accounted for the disparities in sentencing practice, and it is debatable whether any combination of them would have done so: the severe courts were more severe in relation to every factor studied. Clearly, offenders were being imprisoned by some courts who most likely would have received fines if they had appeared at others. Not only did the use of imprisonment vary, but also probation and fining (see figure 5:4).

A study has been made by Hall Williams of men sentenced for breaking and entering at English courts of quarter sessions.[12] Here there were 'considerable differences ... between the sentencing policies of small courts with low case-loads, mostly held in rural areas, and the large courts with heavy case-loads, sitting in metropolitan areas'. The former courts tended to rely far more on previous records, whereas the larger courts seemed also to take into account

such factors as the length of time at risk since any previous sentence, the number of current offences and offences taken into consideration, and also the question of whether there were any co-defendants ... the larger courts appear to adopt a more balanced sentencing policy in the sense of giving equal weight to factors relating to previous record and factors relating to the current indictment.

Explanations

The studies summarised above nearly all give individual differences of approach between judges as the main reason for disparities in sentencing. Yet they attach rather different meanings to the concept of the 'individual factor'. Gaudet attributes the variation to the 'human equation', or the 'personality of the judge', using this term in its widest sense to include the influences of social background, education, religion, experience on the bench, temperament and social attitudes. Mannheim, Spencer and Lynch conclude that their results suggest 'the subjective or intuitive assessment of the individual case does, in the main, prevail'. Shoham also states that:

The personal attitude of the trial judge and his individual sentencing habits have in fact a marked influence on the severity of punishment ... in a great many cases this *indefinable element* [our italics] may play a more important role in determining the type and severity of sentence than the nature of the offence and the personality of the offender.

Green defines in more detail what he means by 'the individuality of the judge'. He suggests two reasons for disparities being especially prevalent in cases of intermediate gravity. First, they may be due to differences in the scales of 'penal values' being used. He does not amplify this, but obviously in these cases the question of the right balance between punishment and treatment will be at its most problematic. Secondly, he suggests judges have different 'impressions of the seriousness of cases':

In cases that are patently mild or grave, the defendant can be clearly perceived with respect to the nature of criminality which is measured by the criteria for sentencing. Hence there is a relatively high degree of concord among the judges. Conversely, in cases of intermediate gravity, ambiguity is more apt to characterise the judge's perception of the defendant with resulting increase in disparity.[13]

Similarly, Hood attributed disparities between the magistrates' courts in his study to disagreements on the objects or philosophy of sentencing and to differences of opinion about the actual effectiveness of alternative sentences open to magistrates. The analysis also suggested that there may be different traditions on benches passed on by learning through the experience of older members of the bench, and that the most severe benches were composed of middle-class magistrates sitting in small non-industrial communities.

Most of these studies have two things in common:

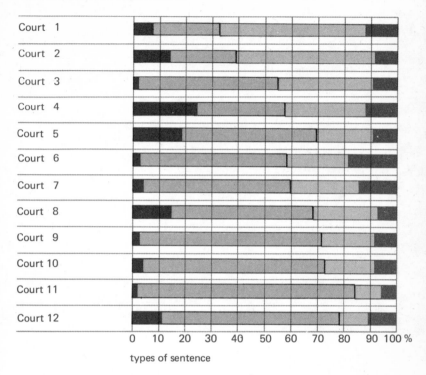

Figure 5:4 The proportion of adult male offenders receiving various sentences at twelve English courts.

types of sentence

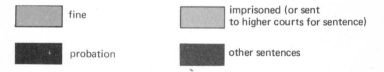

fine

imprisoned (or sent to higher courts for sentence)

probation

other sentences

1 With the exception of Green and Hood they are vague about what they mean by the 'personal factor', the 'indefinable element', or 'individuality of the judge'.

2 More important, they provide no material about the judges themselves to show how these 'individual differences' are related to decision-making in the courts. None of these studies has been designed to do this.

Sometimes it even appears to be assumed that the facts of the case – the offence and the offender – no longer play a part in the sentencing process, but that some hidden 'irrational' element takes over. Shoham, for example, even suggests that the 'personal element' is *more* important than the facts of the case! But to explain sentencing disparities in terms of a 'subjective' or 'indefinable' element is really to give no explanation at all – at least until it is shown just what this 'element' is, what its causes are and how it enters into sentencing decisions.

What those writers who refer to the 'personal equation' (and similar things) may mean is that judges do not follow any single consistent policy, or policies, in sentencing: and that the choice of sentence is made in a completely arbitrary way, as it were by tossing a coin. Alternatively, they may mean that individual judges are influenced, either consciously or unconsciously, by factors (such as race or class prejudice) which ought to be irrelevant to the choice of sentence. Either way, the implication often is that the sentencing process is unjust, or inefficacious, or both. Now, this *may* be the case; but it cannot simply be assumed that it is. There are at least three other possibilities:

1 Individual judges may be following substantially different sentencing policies, which make different sentences appropriate for the same type of case; alternatively or additionally
2 Different judges may be receiving different kinds of information about the offenders whom they sentence; or
3 They may be *classifying* offenders and/or offences in different ways, even though they receive the same kinds of information about them and have the same general aims in sentencing.

If any of these things is happening, disparities in sentencing may result, even though each individual judge may consistently be following a policy of rational decision-making.

It is obvious that none of these possibilities can be investigated merely by showing that judges with different backgrounds tend to pass different sentences on comparable groups of offenders. What is needed is a model of judicial decision-making that will help us to understand how the personal background of the judge and other factors affect what he does, and thus help us to explain observed differences in sentencing practice.

Legal rules and sentencing principles

We suspect that much criticism of disparities in sentencing is based on the belief that the choice of sentence can and should be nothing more than the mechanical application of a set of legal rules to the facts of particular cases – that, as Blackstone said, 'the judgment though pronounced and awarded by the judges is not their determination or sentence, but the determination and sentence of the law'. In the same way, it has sometimes been assumed that other kinds of judicial decisions – concerning, for example, the interpretation of a statute or the choice between two precedents – are just a matter of the mechanical application of pre-existing rules; Blackstone can also be quoted for the view that judges never make new laws, but merely deduce their conclusions from a pre-existing set of rules. In reaction to this oversimplified doctrine, certain legal theorists – in particular, those known as 'legal realists' – have argued that judicial decisions on questions of law are not rational at all, but are just a product of the judge's background, prejudices or digestion. This view is also too simple. It is true that rules cannot determine their own application; and that even if the rule is a fairly explicit one – for example, a rule attaching a penalty to certain facts defined as 'larceny' – the judge must still decide whether or not the rule applies to the particular facts before him, and this is not simply a 'mechanical' process of deduction. But it is not necessarily arbitrary – like tossing a coin – either; as Levi,[14] Hart[15] and other legal theorists have shown, judicial decisions on questions of law *can* (logically) be both rational and consistent, even though certain judges' decisions may in fact occasionally be neither.

The same thing is true for sentencing decisions; and we suggest that an adequate model of the decision-making process in the case of sentencing must be based on the rational application of rules to particular cases. In other words, sentencing must be studied as a kind of judicial activity. But the rule-application involved in sentencing is a much more complicated matter than that of ordinary judicial decisions. To begin with, in many jurisdictions – especially in magistrates' or other inferior courts – there are no explicit legal rules indicating the kinds of sentence appropriate to different types of case (apart, of course, from statutory maximum penalties). There may not even be a generally agreed judicial practice, or set of objectives. Moreover, even where there are fairly explicit legal rules or conventions relating to sentencing, these are typically not

155

strictly binding on judges, in the way that ordinary rules of law are. They are usually intended to *guide* judges' decisions, but are not meant to be followed as if they were binding precedents. Thus, even where these rules and precedents are fairly clearly spelled out (as they are, for example, by the Court of Appeal in England), judges are still left with a considerable amount of discretion in the choice of sentence. There may therefore be room for legitimate disagreement among judges, both as to the general aims of sentencing, and the way in which these aims should be realised in concrete cases.

In particular, it seems clear to us that in many legal systems there is no general agreement on the principles which should govern sentencing decisions, or on what the balance between competing aims should be – not even at a general level, let alone in relation to specific types of case. Even where lip-service is paid to vague objectives like 'reform' or 'deterrence', there is little agreement as to how these objectives can best be achieved. It follows from this that there is little agreement as to what information about offence and offender is relevant to the choice of sentence, and even less on the relative weights to be given to different items of information, in deciding upon the appropriate sentence. Nor is there agreement as to what categories should be used to classify offences and offenders in relation to sentencing. For example, in cases of drunken driving there is no consensus on whether the degree of drunkenness is relevant to the sentence, or, if an accident has occurred whether injury to a 'victim' should be taken into account. Similarly there is little agreement about whether previous convictions for non-motoring offences are relevant to a motoring case. Thus it could easily be that each of two judges was consistently following a rational decision-making policy, and yet that they would impose very different sentences on the same offender. Equally, they might both impose the same sentence, but for very different reasons: for example, the one might see a lengthy criminal record as a sign of wickedness calling for a long 'retributive' prison sentence, while the other might see the same record as a sign of incorrigibility, calling for a long 'preventive' prison sentence.

A model of the sentencing process

Figure 5:5 (see pages 168–9) illustrates a model of the sentencing process which takes into account the factors we have mentioned. This model represents the *structure* of the sentencing process in typical common-law jurisdictions. It includes not only the important part played by legal rules and conventions, but also the part played by those who provide information for the courts, such as the prosecution and the probation service. It also links together factors relating to the judge, the offence and the offender; and it shows, we think, the part which all of these factors may play in the choice of sentence. Of course, the exact values of the variables in this model will vary from judge to judge (or rather, from court to court). But to the extent that each court is consistent – to the extent that the judge 'treats like cases alike' – it should be possible to predict the sentence that will be imposed in a given type of case, if the other information required by the model is known.

Let us look more closely at the various components of the model, beginning with the judge himself. The judge can be described in two related ways: by personal variables such as his age, social class, political affiliations, personality, social attitudes, etc., and by role variables relating to his office as a judge – his length of experience, status on the bench, type of previous legal experience (whether for prosecution or defence), his manner of handling the court procedure, etc. Presumably these factors will determine his general view of his work, and especially mould his attitudes towards the aims of punishment, whether they be mainly retributive or orientated towards deterrence or reformation. His social background, and especially the extent to which he views himself as a 'professional' and reads assiduously about the problems of dealing with offenders, will also affect his opinions and knowledge about the effectiveness of the alternative punishments and treatments available to him.

Thus the judge will sit with a general *'set'* of attitudes towards the problems of sentencing. He will then be confronted with a case. This case will contain information about the offence and information specifically about the offender. The information will be supplied by the prosecution, the defence and by specialist agencies, such as probation officers and psychiatrists. The judge will directly control what information is heard about the case through legal rules, particularly the rules of evidence. He may also indirectly affect what is heard because (for example) those who provide information will probably, if they know the judge, select information which they think he wants and disregard items which he never appears to use.

The judge, then, hears information about the offence and the offender: and he has to use this information to reach a judgment on the nature of the case as a whole. To do this he has to assess how serious the case is, and what sort of person the offender is. However, there are several possible categories for classifying both offence and offender. The diagram shows some of them. The information which the judge regards as *relevant* will depend on which categories he uses. For example, the judge who is concerned with the inherent wickedness of the case may pay particular attention to public opinion, one who is concerned with its potential danger will look at the prevalence of the offence, and so on. The same is true for categorising the offender. The categories the judge will use will depend upon his general aims of punishment. Those aiming at retribution will be most concerned with information about the offence; those who wish to rehabilitate will look mainly at the offender. But the retributionist is most likely to be concerned with categories such as degree of harm done, and inherent wickedness, whereas the judge aiming at generally deterring others from the offence will categorise seriousness by its potential danger. Thus views on the aims of punishment will control what information is thought relevant to the sentence.

But information is not perceived in the same way by everyone. Facts are what one perceives them to be, and judges with different backgrounds and experience may perceive the same facts differently. What, for example, is a serious offence? There are at least three different levels at which judges might disagree.

First, they may rank offences in general in a different way: for example, some judges may consider income tax evasion as serious as breaking and entering, while others think it less serious. Obviously, different opinions would rest on different criteria of seriousness being emphasised. The judge who thinks income tax fraud is more serious, will emphasise the amount of monetary loss to the state, the calculated intent of the offence and the position of trust of the offender: on the other hand, the judge who ranks breaking and entering more seriously will emphasise the invasion of privacy, the physical damage to property and shock to householders. Secondly, even within one general type of offence, such as larceny, there may be differences of opinion on the relative seriousness of different forms of the crime – such as between shoplifting and larceny by a servant from an employer. Similarly, with motoring offences there may be variations in the relative severity attributed to failure to insure a motor car and the offence of failing to stop after an accident. Again it depends on the criteria used. Thirdly, there can also be variations in the perception of what is or is not a serious, average, or trivial example of some specific type of offence. Particularly important here would be the weight given to such factors as the actual harm done, the potential harm, the degree of intent, the prevalence of the offence and the relationship between the offender and the victim. But even if they use the same criteria, two judges may still disagree. For example, if faced with the same case of wounding, they may perceive it as more or less serious depending on their own knowledge of fights or the number of similar cases they have dealt with in court. Similarly, there are no objective measures for stating what constitutes a 'bad home'. What appals one judge may be commonplace to another. Again, one may perceive a guilty plea as evidence that the offender is truly trying to help the court, another that it is only proof that he was caught red-handed.

We suggest that it is primarily differences in the way in which information is categorised and perceived, especially in cases of intermediate gravity where there is obviously most room for disagreement, which explain disparity in sentencing. Obviously, the more sophisticated attempts to 'individualise' treatment become, the greater are the possibilities of variations in judicial practice.

The kinds of categories the judge uses and his perception of the facts about the cases he hears will all be part of what he calls 'his experience' and may be 'fed back', to some extent, to reinforce his set of attitudes towards sentencing. For example, the judge who deals with serious crimes of robbery may feed back information that will reinforce a retributive and deterrent viewpoint. The judge who looks for mental abnormality in the cases he deals with will feed back information that may reinforce a preventive and rehabilitative set of attitudes.

But it can be seen from figure 5:5 that there are other factors at work. Once the judge has considered all the information about the 'case as a whole', he has three decisions to reach. First, what specific aim does he want to achieve, or what balance of aims? To decide this he will have to reconsider the information in the light of his general aims and his knowledge of the effectiveness of punishments. In addition, if he allows it, he may be advised by a probation or medical report and may receive strong pleas from the prosecution or defence for a particular kind of sentence. His second decision will be to decide on the general type of penalty, whether it be incarceration, supervision in the community, a fine or a discharge. Again he will have to reconsider the information and reports. In this decision, however, he will be to some extent controlled and certainly guided, first by legislative restraints which either prohibit certain penalties for particular types of offender or limit the range of discretion, second by judicial conventions or rules laid down by courts of appeal which again limit the range of discretion. Thirdly, after again reconsidering information, recommendations, and conventions he will place the offender at an appropriate point within the range of the penalty upon which he has decided.

Though it may be difficult in practice to find adequate operational definitions for some of the things included in this model, there seems to be no reason, in principle, why this cannot be done. It should be possible to discover something about the objectives which judges are trying to accomplish, the information which they consider relevant to sentencing, and so on, by means of attitude testing or quasi-experimental sentencing exercises; these things can then be related to the sentences which the judges impose in different types of case. Of course, it may be argued that the model which we have presented here does not accurately represent the logical structure of rational sentencing decisions. It is, after all, a first attempt; and (like any theoretical construction) it may be shown to be wrong in some detail. Our point is that *some* such structure must be assumed, if worthwhile research on the decision-making process is to be carried out. It may also be shown that some judges' sentencing decisions really are arbitrary or irrational or that they do not consistently follow any kind of rules or policies. But to say this is to say that those judges' decisions are not in accordance with any model such as the one which we have described here; that is a hypothesis, and a model of this kind is needed to test it.

Some research findings pertinent to this sentencing model

There have been no detailed studies of the way in which personal attributes of judges affect their sentencing practices, although one of the authors (Hood) is currently completing such an enquiry dealing with the sentencing of serious motoring offenders at magistrates' courts in England, and a detailed study of Canadian magistrates is being carried out by John Hogarth.[16] In the United States a number of distinguished judges have claimed that personality plays an important part. They are quoted by Winick, Gerver and Blumberg:[17]

'a decision is the unconscious result of instinctive prejudices and inarticulate connections' [Judge Holmes]; forces which judges 'do not recognise and cannot name have been tugging at them ... and the result is an outlook on life' [Judge Cardozo]; 'much harm is done by the myth that merely by putting on the black robe, and taking the oath of office as a judge, a man ceases to be human ... If the judge did not form judgments of the actors in those court-room dramas called trials, he could never render decisions' [Judge Frank].

But whether these 'admissions' can be taken at their face value as representing what actually influences a judge is somewhat dubious.

Some commentators, especially in the United States, have suggested that the political party of the judge is an important consideration in sentencing. Blumberg[18], for example, suggests that judges in a 'metropolitan court' studied by him owe their posts mainly to political connections or as a reward for political work. He does not, however, give any evidence of the way this affects sentencing except to suggest that they are acutely aware of political considerations. At a more subtle level, it is often supposed that political attitudes are related to other social attitudes and that the authoritarian will be punitive and the liberal pragmatically concerned with rehabilitation. Stuart Nagel has shown that in reaching decisions in federal and state supreme courts in the United States, there are consistent differences between Republican and Democratic judges. He has also shown that 'liberal social attitudes' as measured by Hans Eysenck's question-naire are related to judicial decisions.[19] Democratic judges tend to favour the defence in criminal law cases and the constitutional claims of criminal defendants (but few differences were statistically significant). Liberalism and progressive welfare views on sentencing may well be closely related. Both political and social attitudes are being examined in Hood's study of motoring cases.

There appears to be considerable evidence that judges vary in the type of judicial role they play. In 'metropolitan court' Blumberg distinguished six types, all with strongly contrasting 'judicial personalities'. At one extreme, were two judges who did most of the work of the court – the 'Intellectual-Scholar' and the 'Routineer-Hack'. Other types were the 'Political-Adventurer-Careerist', the 'Judicial Pensioner', the 'Hatchet Man' – hard on everyone – and the 'Tyrant-Showboat-Benevolent Despot' who was an unreliable scourge at one moment and a beaming paternalist at another. Unfortunately, Blumberg does not show how those different back-grounds and roles affected sentencing decisions. The most interesting American study so far published is one carried out by Stanton Wheeler and his associates.[20] They compared juvenile court judges who wore robes and ran their court in a very formal manner with

Table 5:4 Correlation coefficients between various attributes of juvenile court judges and the percentage of offenders they committed to institutions.

Attributes of judges	Offenders committed (correlation coefficient)
Quality of reading	+ 0·33
Quantity of reading	+ 0·28
Attitudes stressing individual responsibility and toughness towards delinquency	− 0·26
Experience with delinquents	− 0·25
Age	− 0·23
Wearing a robe in court	− 0·23

Although the coefficients are low (and the numbers were small) it is clear that there is a positive relationship between such 'professional attributes' as wide reading and the use of institutions, and a negative relationship between severe attitudes and formality and the use of institutions.

those who followed a more informal procedure. The latter group were 'professional' in their outlook, reading far more about delinquency in professional journals. The former group were more punitive in their attitudes. Wheeler and his colleagues compared the proportions of offenders these two groups sent to institutions, and their general severity of punishments. This produced what they considered a surprising result (see table 5:4).

The judges who have taken the more severe sanctions are those who read more about delinquents, who read from professional journals, who do not wear their robes in court and who are more permissive in outlook ... Severity of the sanctions, therefore, appears to be positively related to the degree to which a judge uses a professional, humanistic, social welfare ideology in making his decisions.

The authors suggest that the explanation of their finding is that welfare-orientated judges see institutions either as therapeutic or as shelters from bad homes. They did not perceive their actions as severe, as an infringement on liberty, but as action in the best interests of the child. In other words, the 'formal' judges were using categories such as 'bad' and 'good' in classifying offenders because of their punitive approach, and were only using institutions where the child was extremely bad – and using them, of course, as a punishment. The 'professional' group was using another set of categories, namely, 'extent of need for treatment' – which derived from their rehabilitative set of attitudes. Both groups, given the same facts, were interpreting them differently. This is shown by the fact that the use of institutional sentences was not correlated with severe attitudes but was related to a readiness to see *'abnormality* in the background of delinquent acts' (our italics). These findings are easily explained by our model (see figure 5:5).

Some evidence on the different use of categories of information comes from Hood's ongoing study. 506 magistrates from three broad areas in England were asked to assess the relative seriousness of nineteen offences, including eight motoring offences. Preliminary analysis shows that the variation in the ranking of some of these offences is substantial, showing considerable disagreement about their relative severity. Similarly, there were disparities when magistrates were asked to rank exactly the same case in terms of its seriousness. Another test showed variations in magistrates' stereotypes of the kinds of person they were dealing with in the courts.

The study also aimed to see whether there was agreement on the relative weight to be attached to items of information in sentencing. A sentencing 'game' was carried out at six courts with twenty-five 'benches' each containing two or three magistrates. First the magistrates reached a decision on a hypothetical case; then one at a time, various items of information about the case were changed. For example, the magistrates were told: 'In this case no one was injured, but *if* all the facts had been the same *except* that a person in another car had been severely injured, what would your decision have been?' On some items there was considerable disagreement as to the effect it should have on the sentence.

In other words, this study aims to show how magistrates react differently to the same facts about an offence and an offender, and how this affects their sentence. The final analysis will relate personal background, and facts about the magisterial role, to sentencing practice.[21]

No other studies have been made of the way judges use information, but two studies using similar techniques, by Wilkins and Chandler[22] and Carter,[23] have examined the items of information which probation officers consider relevant in reaching a decision whether or not to recommend that the judge put the offender on probation.

Wilkins and Chandler carried out a small experiment by administering an 'information board' test to 17 probation officers with different qualifications and length of service. This board contained items of information taken from probation files about a case. The items were written on cards and so arranged that only a general heading describing each could be read. The officers were then asked to select items in order of importance, reading the details of each before proceeding to the next one. After turning over four cards they were each asked to reach a decision and say to what extent they had confidence in it and how hard it was to make. Wilkins found that there was no agreed pattern in the order with which officers looked for information:

It seems that the way in which probation officers seek and utilise information in the course of making decisions is more a characteristic of the officers rather than the nature of the information.

In discussing the impact of the 'important' or 'weighty' items which most often led to decision changes, Wilkins concluded:

It may be that such items of information are related by the decision maker to his background and the item makes an impact ... this phenomenon may be related to stereotypes and prejudices.

In this small study, using only one case, Wilkins was not able systematically to relate individual characteristics of probation officers to their use of information and decisions. But this was done by Carter who used a similar method in a study of 14 United States probation officers in California. They were asked to select items of information relevant to their decisions concerning probation in five different hypothetical cases. Of 24 items, only an average of 7·8 were used per case. As Wilkins had found, the officers could not handle a large amount of information. The items chosen are shown in table 5:5. Carter found that:

A brief examination of the 'decision making' of the probation officers indicates that each officer develops his own style. Four of the fourteen officers followed identical patterns of card selection for each of the five cases; the remainder were quite consistent in their choices of information in each of the five cases, although some minor variations were apparent. None of the officers

Table 5:5 Frequency with which various items were selected by probation officers for pre-sentence recommendations in 69 cases.

Item on information card	Percentage of times card was selected
Offence	100·0
Prior record	100·0
Psychological psychiatric	79·7
Defendant's statement	69·6
Defendant's attitude	62·3
Employment history	60·9
Age	53·6
Family history	52·2
Marital status	42·0
Medical history	29·0
Education	21·7
Military history	17·4
Alcoholic involvement	15·9
Homosexuality	15·9
Drug usage	13·0
Interests and activities	13·0
Family criminality	11·6
Plea	7·2
Confinement status	7·2
Residence data	4·3
Religion	4·3
Legal representation	0·0
Place of birth	0·0
Race	0·0

selected information at random; instead they followed a common basic pattern that was still somehow unique to the individual. ... The final recommendations made by the officers in these cases showed considerable divergence.

In three of the cases there was a split between those who recommended imprisonment and those who recommended probation. There was also considerable variation in the number of items of information chosen before the decision was reached. The fact that decisions were not changed after the first few items were chosen suggests, says Carter, that probation officers may seek confirmation of their early decisions in the later data they select.

Whether or not the results of both these studies mirror what a judge does in selecting information, they are still important to a full study of sentencing, for the probation officer in his own right plays an important part in the sentencing process. He provides the judge with information, and *his* selection is what the court gets.

Blumberg suggests that:

To a large extent probation and psychiatric reports reaffirm and re-circulate the same knowledge about the accused originally furnished by police and prosecutor – refurbished in the patois and argot of social work and psychiatry ... the importance of the pre-sentence investigation as a decision-making tool for the judge is over-rated.

What Blumberg assumes is that the reports' main function is to provide support for the lonely job of decision-making facing the judge:

Because he is ill-equipped to be a sophisticated decision-maker in a job that requires decision-making daily and routinely, and at the same time requires him to be an administrator, manager and overseer, the judge must lean heavily on the services of others ... they learn to accept and internalise the routineering and ritualism of their socialisers ... He will then deliberately involve probation and psychiatric reports or a district attorney's recommendations to diffuse responsibility or to mitigate his own anxieties. The group decision functions not only to conceal individual mediocrity but can also be pointed to as evidence of profound efforts to individualise and at the same time make the administration of justice more uniform and equitable.[24]

In other words, the probation officer and psychiatrists are acting in the supporting role of 'handmaidens of the court'. In this situation we should expect probation officers as members of the organisation simply to supply the recommendations the court wants: to 'second-guess' the judge's opinion.

The importance of the probation recommendation has been examined in detail in an excellent study in California by Carter and

166

Figure 5:5 (overleaf) A model of the sentencing process. Green area and lines indicate information about the offence and its perception and classification by the judge. Purple area and lines indicate relevant information about the offender. Black lines indicate decision-making, or controls on decision-making. Broken black lines indicate recommendations for decisions made by prosecution, defence and other specialists.

Wilkins[25] who discovered that when probation was recommended by an officer the judge nearly always gave probation. There were, however, quite marked variations in the proportion of offenders put on probation in different courts. This seemed to be due mostly to *variations among the probation officers* who controlled the number of recommendations for probation. Probation officers, even from the same district, did not view 'the correctional process from identical perspectives'. To some extent their use of probation seemed to be related to their training: those with

graduate training or graduate degrees in social work or social welfare recommended probation for 56·3 per cent of their cases; officers with graduate work or graduate degrees in criminology in 69·6 per cent ... officers with graduate work or graduate degrees in sociology in 67·7 per cent of their cases. Officers with the longest service recommended probation for 54·0 per cent ... while the 'newer' officers recommended probation for 68·4 per cent.

As, in this study, the judges seemed to *follow* probation officers' recommendations there is an obvious need to study all those involved in the sentencing process and not just the judge.

In some countries the prosecutor also plays an important role in the sentencing process, through making specific pleas for a certain type of sentence. Green's is the only research to study the prosecutor; he concluded that different prosecutors did not affect the sentencing practice of the Philadelphia Court. On the other hand, it should be remembered that the prosecutor does play a very influential role in jurisdictions where it is common for bargains to be made in exchange for a plea of guilty. Here it will usually be for the prosecutor to decide whether he will accept a plea of guilty to a lesser offence and to present the evidence to the court. He is thus in a position to control nearly all the information relating to the offence, and a good deal of that relating to the offender, especially in relation to his previous criminal record.

So far we have concentrated our attention on the judge, his background, aims in sentencing and perception of the case, and on the part played by those who provide information to the courts. Variations among these factors are likely to account for most of the

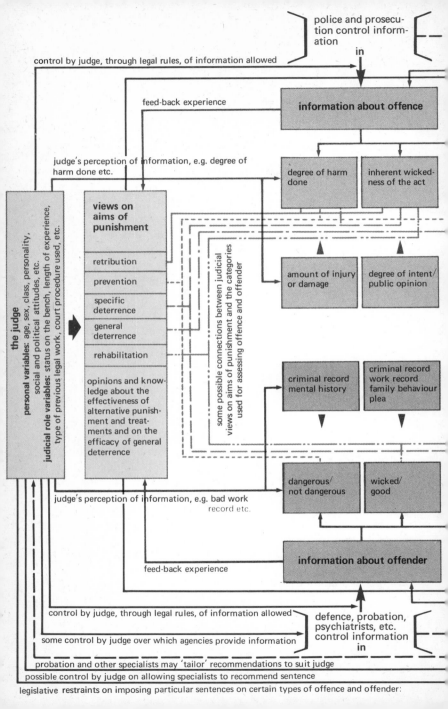

police and prosecution control information in

control by judge, through legal rules, of information allowed

feed-back experience

information about offence

judge's perception of information, e.g. degree of harm done etc.

views on aims of punishment

retribution

prevention

specific deterrence

general deterrence

rehabilitation

opinions and knowledge about the effectiveness of alternative punishment and treatments and on the efficacy of general deterrence

the judge

personal variables: age, sex, class, personality, social and political attitudes, etc.
judicial role variables: status on the bench, length of experience, type of previous legal work, court procedure used, etc.

degree of harm done

inherent wickedness of the act

amount of injury or damage

degree of intent/public opinion

some possible connections between judicial views on aims of punishment and the categories used for assessing offence and offender

criminal record mental history

criminal record work record family behaviour plea

dangerous/not dangerous

wicked/good

judge's perception of information, e.g. bad work record etc.

feed-back experience

information about offender

control by judge, through legal rules, of information allowed

defence, probation, psychiatrists, etc. control information in

some control by judge over which agencies provide information

probation and other specialists may 'tailor' recommendations to suit judge

possible control by judge on allowing specialists to recommend sentence

legislative restraints on imposing particular sentences on certain types of offence and offender:

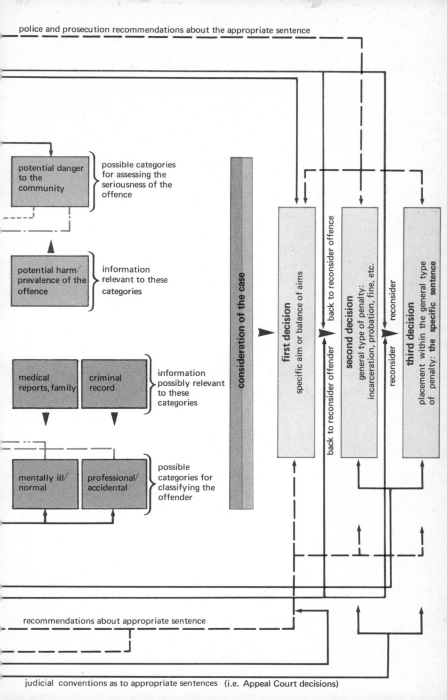

police and prosecution recommendations about the appropriate sentence

potential danger to the community

possible categories for assessing the seriousness of the offence

potential harm/prevalence of the offence

information relevant to these categories

medical reports, family

criminal record

information possibly relevant to these categories

mentally ill/normal

professional/accidental

possible categories for classifying the offender

consideration of the case

first decision

specific aim or balance of aims

back to reconsider offender

back to reconsider offence

second decision

general type of penalty: incarceration, probation, fine, etc.

reconsider

reconsider

third decision

placement within the general type of penalty: the specific sentence

recommendations about appropriate sentence

judicial conventions as to appropriate sentences (i.e. Appeal Court decisions) differences in approach to sentencing. But as we have said, sentencing is a *legal* process, and there are usually some legal rules limiting the discretion of the judge. Some of those rules, like the rules of evidence, affect the information which can be considered; others, like legislative restraints on discretion and the rulings of appellate courts, may directly affect the decision-making process.

In most countries, appellate courts will make some general pronouncements from time to time about the purposes of punishment; but in addition they may specify which category of offender should be considered appropriate for a certain aim. For example, D. A. Thomas has shown that the Court of Appeal in England has supported a general deterrent approach for robbers and for public officials and police officers convicted of fraud or dishonesty. On the other hand, rehabilitation has been supported as a 'last chance' approach for habitual petty criminals. In addition the court lays down certain rules as to what weight should be given to specific items of information. In other words, in our diagram (figure 5:5) these rules impinge on the process when the case is being weighed up as a whole. The English Court of Appeal has made judgments relating to the weight to be attached to the plea and attitude of the defendant, sentences on accomplices, giving evidence or assistance to the Crown, the effect on the offender's career of a conviction, his ignorance of the law, contributory negligence on the part of the victim, collusion by the victim, and other factors. Once the judge has placed the information he receives into a category or 'type of case' he is thus surrounded by legal conventions or even legislative rules limiting his discretion. (Of course, individual judges may not invariably follow these rules.) So far, lawyers have concentrated their attention on the use of these legal rules, regarding them as a means of gaining judicial assent to common practice. What we have tried to show is that, although these rules are an important part of the sentencing process, what needs to be studied now is the way in which judges, aided by the 'servants' of the court, process information in order to classify an offender as a 'certain type of case'.

6 Assessing the effectiveness of punishments and treatments

Increasingly, courts and correctional agencies expect criminologists to tell them how to control crime through the use of penal measures. Although sentencing practice in most countries may still reflect an emphasis (at least with adult offenders) on punishment according to the gravity of the current offence, there has nonetheless been a definite shift – at least at the level of official sentencing policy – away from a purely retributive or punitive approach. Instead of dealing simply with past misdeeds, courts are increasingly trying to deter potential offenders and to prevent recidivism as well. One consequence of this has been a demand for more (and more accurate) information about offenders' backgrounds and personalities, to help the courts to select the most effective sentences. But without empirical research into the effectiveness of punishments and treatments, there is no way of knowing what information about offenders is relevant to the choice of sentence.

A great deal of research in this field has been done in the past 25 years, in particular in England and the United States. Much of it has been of a relatively simple 'book-keeping' kind, involving little more than the counting of numbers reconvicted. But as new research techniques have become available, more sophisticated studies of existing forms of treatment have been carried out; and there have been several attempts to develop and test entirely new forms of treatment, for special groups of offenders. As we shall see in this chapter and the next, the results to date are by no means all negative; and in the next few years it may begin to be possible to provide the kind of information about the effects of punishments and treatments which the courts and correctional administrators want. But it should be borne in mind that for the moment, even despite this considerable progress, our knowledge is still limited and very rudimentary. It amounts in fact to a number of broad generalisations which, though better than nothing, should be treated as a basis for judicial or administrative decisions only with the greatest of care. We are still, as Leslie Wilkins has said, only at a stage where 'the nature of our ignorance is beginning to be revealed'.

There are methodological and practical problems raised by

research on the effectiveness of punishments and treatments. It is essential that judges, administrators, and students should be aware of these problems since (like all such problems) they affect the confidence that can be placed in the results of research. Understandably enough, consumers of penological research tend to want results which can be easily and mechanically applied, and they may be disillusioned by findings which are hedged about with many qualifications. But it is in just these circumstances that the danger is greatest, for the results of a badly designed research project or an unvalidated pilot study may easily take on the status of received truth, and become the basis for action. For this reason we discuss at length a few of the most important technical aspects of research in this area, before reviewing the results of this research to date.

Individual versus general prevention

It is important to note that almost all of the research done so far in this field has concentrated on only one of the objectives of sentencing: namely, the prevention of recidivism among offenders actually dealt with by the courts (sometimes called 'individual prevention'). Moreover, researchers have generally not distinguished between the deterrent and reformative aspects of individual prevention. There have been a few attempts (discussed in the next two chapters) to discover the extent to which penal measures have succeeded in changing the attitudes of offenders. But most researchers have been content merely to count the numbers of offenders who, having been dealt with by the penal system, have apparently succeeded in staying out of trouble for a fairly short period afterwards – without investigating the extent to which those offenders were actually 'reformed' by the treatment or punishment they received.

Meanwhile the effects of penal measures on the behaviour of those not actually subjected to them – potential offenders and the law-abiding public – have been almost completely ignored by researchers. This aspect of sentencing (sometimes called 'general prevention') is regarded by many judges and magistrates as being of primary importance; yet virtually nothing is known about the extent to which it is achieved in practice. This is probably due to a combination of things. The first is the inherent bias of most criminologists toward 'treating' or deterring the offender himself, and a concomitant scepticism about general deterrence: some argue, on theoretical or *a priori* grounds, that the threat of punishment does not deter

172

potential offenders, and so see no reason to investigate the question empirically. But deterrence (in the sense of a conscious or unconscious inhibition of criminal behaviour in order to avoid a penalty) is not the only aspect of general prevention. Both sociologists and jurists have often claimed that penal sentences have a general-preventive effect in reinforcing social values and strengthening what Durkheim called the 'common conscience', as well as alleviating fear and providing a sense of communal security. It is surely important to know how far this is true.

Unfortunately, it is extremely difficult to do empirical research on this question: and this is the second, and probably the more important, reason why so little has yet been done. There have been several inconclusive attempts to assess the deterrent effects of capital and corporal punishment – two little-used measures which are generally applied to very special types of offence and offender. It is also possible to point to a few instances in which changes in the law or its enforcement, or in the penalties provided, have been followed by sudden (though usually short-term) reductions in the offences concerned. Two recent examples in England are the heavy prison sentences imposed on a group of young men convicted in 1958 of assaulting coloured people in the Notting Hill area of London, and the 'exemplary' sentences imposed by another judge on persons convicted of stealing from public telephone kiosks in Birmingham, where this offence had become especially prevalent. In each case, the imposition of heavier sentences was well-publicised, and was followed by a decline in the type of crime in question. But there are almost invariably a number of other factors present in situations of this kind, which could explain the observed fall in crime rates. In the case of the Birmingham telephone kiosk thefts, for example, the reduction in crime appears to have been due at least in part to the installation of coin boxes of a kind which were less easy to break open, as well as to better policing; and there is some evidence that the racial violence in Notting Hill was declining even before the severe sentences were imposed.

As Andenaes[1] has pointed out, any research on this aspect of general prevention must make several distinctions between different kinds of crime and potential criminal. Offences of a kind which are typically impulsive, or are committed as a result of emotional stress or mental abnormality – including many murders, assaults and sexual offences – are presumably less likely to be deterred than rationally planned, purposive crimes against property. Some

173

account must also be taken of general moral and social attitudes towards different crimes; the threat of punishment is probably of little direct importance in inhibiting behaviour such as incest, which is widely felt to be repugnant or morally wrong; whereas it may be very important in the case of such things as parking offences or business regulations, for which such moral restraints are not usually present. Much depends, too, on the extent to which the law is enforced, and on the probability of detection and conviction. A dramatic illustration of this occurred in Denmark in 1944, when the Nazis arrested the country's entire police force: within a short time the crime rate rose sharply, despite the fact that severe penalties were still provided for offenders who were caught. (Of course, what matters here is the potential offender's belief in his chances of impunity, rather than his actual chances. A study recently carried out by the British Government Social Survey on deterrents and incentives to crime among 15 to 21 year-old boys found that many apparently *under*estimated substantially their chances of getting caught. But the boys' responses may merely have reflected the fact that they had no intention of committing crimes anyway.)

It is also important to distinguish between different types of potential offender, when assessing the deterrent effect of punishment. Opportunities to commit many types of crime are not randomly distributed among the general population. Moreover, the level of threatened penalties is only one element in general deterrence. For many middle-class persons the stigma and general social consequences of conviction (loss of job, status, and so forth) are undoubtedly more important than the sentence of the court; but for many lower-class or socially isolated persons this will not be true. Before we can even begin to measure the general-deterrent effect of specific penalties, we must thus identify with some precision the potential offenders to whom those threatened penalties apply.

This can in principle be done, even though it may be very difficult in practice. But it is even more difficult to see how the other aspects of 'general prevention' – the reinforcement, in different ways, of the moral values of the generally law-abiding – are to be assessed empirically. According to Durkheim,[2] the primary function of punishment is to reaffirm the values of 'upright people', by expressing aversion to the crime; without punishment, he thought, there would be an emotional breakdown of the 'common conscience' and of the social solidarity which depends on it. A blunter version of this theory was advanced by the Victorian jurist Sir James Stephen, who wrote that 'the fact that men are hung for murder is one great reason why murder is considered so dreadful a crime'. Recent English and American laws penalising various forms of racial discrimination may throw some light on the relations between punishment and social values. Of course it may never be possible, in practice, to test Durkheim's hypothesis in the case of 'ordinary' crimes like theft; but this is no reason to assume that such diffuse general-preventive effects do not exist where these crimes are concerned. Quantitatively, these effects may well be much more important in the long run than individual prevention. As the self-report studies discussed in chapter 2 have shown, almost everybody commits at least one (usually minor) crime at some time in his life. Nonetheless, the number of persons *frequently* committing serious offences is relatively low: the majority are generally law-abiding. A very slight change in the values and behaviour of this majority, through a change in the general preventive effect of punishment, could thus lead to a very large increase in crime.

Methodological problems of research on individual prevention

As we have said, the basic measure of the 'effectiveness' of punishments and treatments which is used by most researchers is the conduct of offenders in a period after the completion of their sentences. The treatment is presumed to have 'succeeded' in the case of those who are not convicted of further offences, and to have 'failed' in the case of those who have. But at once this raises a number of questions. Exactly what should the criteria of 'success' and 'failure' be? What length of follow-up period is appropriate? The fact that different researchers have taken different views on these questions makes it difficult, in many cases, to compare their results. But there are, in reality, no definite answers to these questions; what is needed is to be clear about the alternatives, and the main argument for each.

1 *Definitions of 'success' and 'failure'* All studies of the effectiveness of punishments and treatments use reconviction as a criterion of failure, whether or not they use other criteria as well. But there is much disagreement in practice about *what* reconvictions should be counted. Clearly there is a great deal of difference, for this purpose, between petty larceny and robbery with violence; between an offence committed under circumstances of exceptional deprivation and one carried out as a professional activity; between one unfortunate lapse of a 'situational' kind and a continued involvement in crime, especially of the same kind for which the offender was originally sentenced. A simple dichotomy of 'success' and 'failure' is obviously too crude to take all these important differences into account – even if there were agreement among researchers (or consumers of research) as to where the line should be drawn in each case.

A number of writers have used a three-fold classification, distinguishing between offenders not reconvicted at all, 'occasional' recidivists and habitual recidivists. Glaser, in his study[3] of federal prisoners in the United States, went further and distinguished between 'clear' and 'marginal' groups among both the successes and failures. The 'clear reformation' cases were those who had apparently committed no crimes (after being on parole for one year), had steady, honest jobs, and were avoiding criminal associates; 'marginal reformation' cases, though not returned to prison, had either failed to hold down legitimate jobs or had committed minor crimes or were associating with known criminals. 'Marginal failures' were those returned to prison (often, it seems, rather arbitrarily) for minor crimes or technical violations of parole rules; while 'clear recidivists' had been returned to prison after committing a major offence. Of course there are difficulties in using anything except one reconviction as a criterion of failure. Offenders who receive lengthy sentences when reconvicted will not be at risk to commit further offences; and success or failure after one reconviction may be due to the sentence given on *that* occasion, and not to the original treatment. Nonetheless, there seems to us to be a good case – especially for habitual criminals with a very high risk of reconviction – for describing as 'successful' those who are reconvicted only once during a follow-up period, so long as they do not commit major crimes.

What constitutes a 'major' crime, however, is itself a problem – again, one over which there is little consensus among researchers. One frequently used criterion of this is the severity of the sentence imposed on reconviction; only those offences resulting in imprisonment, for example, may be taken to show 'failure' after treatment. Disparities in the sentencing practices of judges may make this a misleading criterion, however. A more discriminating method is to use numerical scales for rating the gravity of different offences, like the scale recently developed by Sellin and Wolfgang.[4] Though this scale was originally developed for a different purpose – the construction of an index of delinquency which would reflect the seriousness of offences known to the police – it has been used by Scott,[5] in a study of the after-conduct of boys in English approved schools. Similar scales have been developed in California; one advantage of using them is that they make it possible to compare the seriousness of the offender's criminal behaviour before and after treatment.

There remains the perennial problem that offenders may commit crimes during the follow-up period but may never be caught. McClintock and Gibson, in their study of robbery in London,[6] noted that offenders who had carried out robberies on persons in charge of money or goods in transit had the lowest reconviction rate of any type (28 per cent, compared with the average of 45 per cent). But they concluded that 'these offenders' apparently greater success ... is illusory; they are merely better at escaping detection'. As we saw in chapter 2, official records do not necessarily give an accurate indication of the number of offences actually committed; and it cannot be assumed that undetected crimes are randomly distributed among offenders. It should be remembered, too, that criminal records are not necessarily complete, and that some offenders' convictions may not be traced. Thus the use of reconviction as a criterion of 'failure' tends to exaggerate the effectiveness, in absolute terms, of penal measures.

2 *Criteria other than reconviction* It has often been argued that penal measures aimed at reforming the offender are intended to do more than simply ensure the avoidance of reconviction. They are, for example, supposed to provide trade training, develop constructive uses of leisure, change attitudes towards authority, educate, improve personal relationships, make the inadequate more adequate. Probably very few would advocate that the 'success' of penal measures should be reckoned *entirely* in these terms, with reconviction being ignored. But in fact, these indicia of 'social stability' appear to be fairly highly correlated with the avoidance of reconviction, at least so far as objective measures – such as work habits, residential stability, and constructive use of leisure time – are concerned. Thus measurement of failure by the criterion of reconviction probably will, by and large, identify the failures by other criteria as well. Of course, a high correlation of this kind cannot be taken to show a causal relationship of any kind.

Some attempts have also been made to study changes in attitudes, values and other personality variables following treatment. In research in both England and California, extensive use has been made of two tests – the Jesness Inventory and the California Personality Inventory, in order to measure changes in attitudes supposedly related to delinquency. Both of these tests – which purport to measure such things as sociability, intellectual efficiency and value orientation – have been shown reliably to discriminate between delinquents and non-delinquents; but so far as the outcome of treatment is concerned, the results to date have not been clear.

3 *After what period should 'success' be judged?* Should the effectiveness of penal treatment be judged while the treatment is still in progress, or only after it has been terminated for a period of time? This question is not as simple as it may seem. No one would suggest that a prisoner's misbehaviour while inside the prison should be taken to show that imprisonment had 'failed' in his case, even if the misbehaviour amounted to a crime. But what about those measures involving an extended period of supervision and 'treatment' in the community, such as probation, parole, and (in some jurisdictions) the suspended sentence? There is clearly a case for not assessing the effectiveness of these forms of treatment until after they have been completed: that is, for ignoring reconvictions during the period of supervision, and beginning the 'follow-up' period only after the supervision is completed. This was done, for example, in the Cambridge studies of probation[7] and attendance centres.[8] But most studies of the effectiveness of probation have taken as the criterion of success the normal completion of the probation order, or its termination for good behaviour. In other words, they have counted as 'successes' those who managed to get through the treatment – never mind about a follow-up period afterwards! For this reason it is obviously very difficult to make straightforward comparisons between institutional and non-institutional forms of treatment. The problem is especially important in the case of parole and after-care, since there is some evidence[9, 10] that while these measures may postpone recidivism among certain types of offender, they do not really reduce it much over the long run.

On the other hand, a follow-up period cannot reasonably go on too long. Should a fine or a period on probation at age 20 keep a man law-abiding all his life, so that the measure is said to have 'failed' if he is convicted again at age 50? Fortunately, there is some empirical evidence which is helpful here. Several studies – e.g. by Mannheim and Wilkins,[11] McClintock,[12] and the President's Crime Commission[13] – have shown that almost all of those offenders who will ever be reconvicted after punishment or treatment are reconvicted within five years. In addition, there is some evidence – from Havel's study of the Special Intensive Parole Unit in California[14] – that the failure rate for offenders having a given risk of reconviction is roughly constant throughout the first year, and possibly longer. It has often been assumed that the first few months after an offender's conviction or release from prison are the time in which he is most likely to be reconvicted; but in fact this does not seem necessarily to be the case. Of course the *number* of offenders reconvicted, in a group released from prison, will be greatest in the very early part of the follow-up period, since the number at risk of their first reconviction will be greatest then. But the reconviction *rate* – that is, the number reconvicted for the first time in any period, divided by the number not yet reconvicted and thus still at risk in that period – appears from Havel's research to be no higher in the early part of the follow-up period than in later months. (Figure 6:1, from Havel,[14] illustrates this point.) Thus it is possible to estimate, with fair accuracy, the proportion of offenders who will be reconvicted within (say) five years, on the basis of a much shorter follow-up period. This makes it possible to compare studies of treatment which use different follow-up periods – a fortunate thing, since here too there is little consensus among researchers.

The problem of comparison Many follow-up studies have been concerned with a single form of punishment or treatment. Although these studies are unsophisticated, they do provide the courts and correctional administrators with basic data about the outcome of different forms of sentence. This is of value, for in many jurisdictions basic information about recidivism is not routinely collected, and there may thus be widespread misconceptions about the number of persons reconvicted. Even in the United States, statistics of the after-conduct of federal prisoners are not published. Thus, as Daniel Glaser has pointed out, the prisons 'must operate like businesses without book-keeping, in blissful ignorance of the extent of their profit or loss'. Glaser's own study of the federal prison system, based on over a thousand men released in 1956, exploded the 'myth' that over two-thirds of all prisoners return to prison: he found instead that in a follow-up period of four years only 31 per cent were re-imprisoned, and another four per cent were reconvicted but not re-imprisoned.

Studies of a single form of treatment or punishment may also

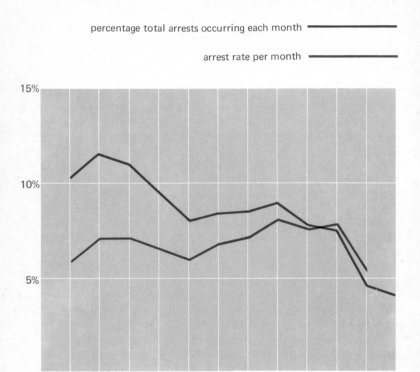

Figure 6:1 Percentage distribution of arrests per month, compared with monthly arrest rates for those 'at risk', in Special Intensive Parole Unit project.

percentage total arrests occurring each month ━━━━━━━

arrest rate per month ━━━━━━━

months on parole

throw light on the factors generally associated with reconviction. This is of value, for many of the factors which tend to distinguish delinquents from non-delinquents (such as coming from large families, or homes broken by divorce or separation) are not necessarily of value in predicting recidivism after treatment. Broadly speaking, most researchers have found that an offender's chances of recidivism are greater, the more previous convictions he has, the shorter the time since his last conviction, the younger he is, and the younger he was when first convicted; men have higher reconviction rates than women, and offenders against property generally have higher reconviction rates than those committing offences of violence. Nonetheless, the value of studies of a single form of treatment or punishment is very limited, since these studies cannot tell us what would have happened if the offenders in question had been dealt with in another way. Even a comparison of two such studies – of (say) imprisonment and probation – cannot tell us this, unless the offenders dealt with in the two ways are in other respects similar. But this is difficult to ensure; in particular, those put on probation, fined or discharged are generally much less criminal – and so less likely to be reconvicted after any kind of sentence – than those sent to prison. If we are interested in comparing the efficacies of different forms of treatment, this problem must somehow be taken into account. There are basically three methods of doing this:

1 *Random allocation* The random allocation of offenders to two or more types of treatment is the ideal method of making comparisons. Although it is still possible that two or more randomly allocated groups of offenders will differ in some relevant respect, the probability of this is calculable, and will be small if the numbers involved are fairly large. Random allocation has been used in several studies in the United States, in particular, studies of new and experimental forms of treatment; two examples, discussed in greater detail in the next chapter, are the Provo Experiment in Utah and the Community Treatment Project in California. This method is often difficult to arrange in practice, however; for example, there are obvious moral objections to random allocation at the sentencing stage, and considerations of 'security' usually make it impossible to allocate randomly to an open prison or probation those offenders with long criminal records, or who have been convicted of crimes of violence.

2 *Individual matching* One way of securing two or more comparable groups of offenders who have already been sentenced is to match them as far as possible, on an individual basis, in all respects which are thought to be relevant to the outcome of treatment. This method was used by Wilkins in a small study[15] of the results of probation: 50 offenders convicted at a court which made extensive use of probation were matched in respect of age, sex, current offence and previous convictions with 50 offenders convicted at another court which used probation much less frequently, and the after-conduct of the two groups was then compared. As Wilkins himself points out, however, this method is not entirely free from problems: apart from

181

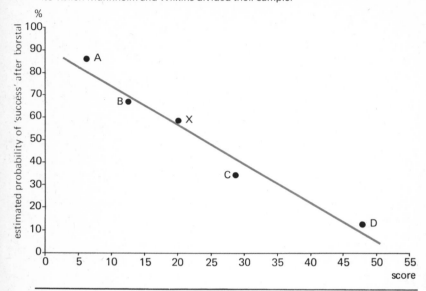

Figure 6:2 The Mannheim-Wilkins borstal prediction table. To find the estimated probability of boys' 'success' after borstal, Mannheim and Wilkins scored each boy on the factors shown in the table below. From the total score obtained in this way, the probability of 'success' can be determined from the graph. The points marked A, B, X, C and D on the graph show the mean scores, and corresponding probabilities of 'success', for the five 'risk groups' into which Mannheim and Wilkins divided their sample.

Factors	Add
If evidence of drunkenness	24
If any prior offence(s) resulted in fine	9
If any prior offence(s) resulted in committal to prison or to approved school	8
If any prior offence(s) resulted in a term on probation	4
If *not* living with parent or parents	7·5
If home is in industrial area	8
If longest period in any one job was:	
Less than 1 month	11·7
Over 4 weeks up to 6 weeks	10·4
,, 6 ,, ,, 8 ,,	9·1
,, 2 months ,, 3 months	7·8
,, 3 ,, ,, 4 ,,	6·5
,, 4 ,, ,, 6 ,,	5·2
,, 6 ,, ,, 9 ,,	3·9
,, 9 ,, ,, 12 ,,	2·6
,, 1 year ,, 18 ,,	1·3
,, 18 months	0

the difficulty of finding matching cases for unusual individuals, it is always possible that not all factors related to reconviction will be known, and that some relevant factor may be left uncontrolled.

3 *Statistical estimation of the risk of reconviction* To overcome these difficulties, the method most frequently used to estimate offenders' risk of reconviction is the statistical prediction table. Tables of this sort were first developed, about 40 years ago, in order to predict prisoners' success or failure on parole. They were first used to assess the effectiveness of treatment by Mannheim and Wilkins, in their study[16] of borstal training published in 1955. Subsequently, under the guidance of Wilkins, tables of this kind have been developed on a large scale by the California Department of Corrections, in whose publications they are referred to as 'base expectancy' tables.

Prediction tables are really 'experience tables'. They tell us, on the basis of the records of those who have undergone treatment, which factors in the backgrounds of offenders most sharply discriminate between those who have had a high rate of failure and those who have failed less frequently. The first step in constructing such a table is to examine the extent to which different factors – such as having a certain number of previous convictions, a particular work record or being of a certain age – are correlated with failure after treatment. Each factor that is positively correlated with failure is given a numerical score so that it is possible to discriminate between those with low scores (few adverse factors) who have low failure rates and those with high scores with high failure rates. The object of a prediction equation is thus to produce the maximum discrimination possible between success and failure on the basis of information in offenders' records. The scores which result from this analysis are usually conveniently classified into 'risk groups', each of which has a different probability of post-treatment failure. Usually the scores are weighted, according to the degree to which they are correlated with reconviction; though there are simpler methods, such as counting plus one for each adverse characteristic, which are in practice almost as efficient. (The original Mannheim-Wilkins table, and the scoring method on which it was based, are shown in figure 6:2; in this case the weights assigned to the five factors used were derived by the statistical method of multiple regression.)

Once a table of this kind has been constructed, offenders given different treatments can be matched in terms of the likelihood that they will be reconvicted (their 'base expectancy', as it is known in

Table 6:1 Comparison of closed and open borstals, using the Mannheim-Wilkins table.

Risk group	Open			Closed		
	No.	%	Percentage Success	No.	%	Percentage Success
Good (A, B)	94	43	**78**	33	20	**67**
Average (X)	90	40	**61**	69	43	**57**
Poor (C,D)	39	17	**38**	60	37	**28**
Total	223	100	**64**	162	100	**48**

The 'success rates' (figures in bold face) suggest that the open institutions may have been slightly more effective than the closed ones, even when the boys' risk of reconviction was taken into account.

California), and their reconviction rates compared to give an indication of the relative effectiveness of the different treatments. In this way, Mannheim and Wilkins compared open and closed borstal institutions, and concluded that the open institutions were more effective, even when the fact that they received more better-risk cases (those in categories A and B on their table) was taken into account. The actual figures they obtained are shown in table 6:1.

This procedure has been used by other researchers, and can be used to compare the effectiveness of any number of types of treatment. However, it has certain limitations. An overall comparison of a number of types of treatment may mask the fact that different factors are associated with success after different types of treatment. For example, it is possible that factors which were not predictive of success among borstal boys in general (according to the Mannheim-Wilkins table), were nonetheless predictive of success among those sent to open institutions. Moreover, even with a single type of treatment there may be factors associated with success for some offenders in a given 'risk group' but not for others. For example, Gibbens *et al.*,[17] in a follow-up study of criminal psychopaths in prison, found that an abnormal electroencephalogram (EEG) was not related to recidivism among the group as a whole. But when they distinguished between 'aggressive' and 'inadequate' psychopaths, they found that an abnormal EEG was related to a bad prognosis for the former group, but a *good* prognosis for the latter; the two opposing trends cancelled out for the group as a whole. Both Gibbens[18] and Hood[19] have shown that there are sub-groups of this kind in the borstal population, which cannot be identified by the Mannheim-Wilkins table. In these circumstances, comparison based on a prediction table of this kind will be relatively crude.

In an effort to overcome this problem, a number of researchers have experimented with recently developed statistical techniques such as 'association analysis' (described on page 119), and a similar method known variously as 'configural‑ analysis'[20] or 'predictive attribute analysis'.[21] The object of these methods is to classify offenders into groups which are more closely homogeneous with respect to the risk of reconviction. Unfortunately, as we noted earlier, these newer techniques are still in the experimental stage; and it is by no means clear that they are a real improvement, in practice, on the methods used by Mannheim and Wilkins.

In any case, the accuracy and reliability of prediction tables depend to a large extent on the identification of factors associated with reconviction. This in turn depends entirely on the quality of information which is available about offenders; and at the moment this is very low, wherever research is based on administrative records routinely kept by correctional agencies. Almost invariably, such personal and social data as are available in these records are haphazardly recorded, and are thus likely to be missing or inaccurate for a high proportion of cases; information on some topics (for example, relations with peer groups) is in our experience hardly ever recorded at all, even in probation officers' social inquiry reports. As a result, most of the prediction tables now in use are based on a fairly small number of factors, and for this reason studies of the effectiveness of treatment which are based on these tables may be erroneous. The courts may make allowance, in sentencing, for social factors related to reconviction which are not recorded in documents available to the researcher. If this happens, offenders dealt

185

with in different ways will not really be comparable, even though their 'expected' reconviction rates (according to a prediction table or other statistical analysis) are the same. Gaps of this kind in official records can be filled, to some extent, by *ad hoc* research projects in which information about offenders is collected from a number of sources (including interviews): Glaser's prison study is a notable example of what can be done in this way. But as the association between factors and reconviction may change over time (the original borstal prediction table is no longer valid) progress in the evaluation of punishments and treatments will not take place unless the records regularly kept by those who deal with offenders are greatly improved.

The results of research to date

Making due allowance for all of the methodological problems just mentioned, what conclusions can be drawn from research to date on the effectiveness of punishments and treatments? The following generalisations seem to us to be supported, to a greater or less extent, by the available evidence:

1 For many offenders, probation is likely to be at least as effective in preventing recidivism as an institutional sentence. Wilkins[15] found no significant difference in the reconviction rates (in a three year follow-up) of a group of 31 offenders placed on probation in an English higher court, and a group of 31 individually matched controls most of whom received institutional sentences (see table 6:2). Babst and Mannering[22] followed up 5,274 adult male offenders in Wisconsin, and compared the reconviction rates (in a two year period) of those placed on probation, with those put in prison and paroled. When type of current offence, criminal record and marital status (the factors most highly predictive of recidivism) were held constant, it was found that the success rate of probation was about the same as that of imprisonment for recidivists, and was significantly better for first offenders. According to Martin[23] a similar result was found in a demonstration project carried out in Saginaw, Michigan. In his study for the British Home Office Research Unit, Hammond[24] found that the reconviction rates of offenders placed on probation were broadly comparable to those of offenders given institutional treatment, when expected reconviction rates were taken into account. In a re-assessment of the earlier Cambridge study of probation, Hammond suggested that it showed that when expected

186

Table 6:2 Comparison of the effectiveness of probation and other measures for two individually-matched groups of offenders.

Court P (Probation)			Court Q (Matched control)		
	Success	Failure		Success	Failure
			Imprisonment	8	5
Probation	17	14	Fine, discharge	6	1
			Borstal, app. sch.	4	7
Total	17	14		18	13
Per cent success		54·8			58·1

reconviction rates were taken into account, the effectiveness of probation was about the same as that of other treatments for first offenders, but slightly better than expected for recidivists; in his own study, recidivists also did relatively better on probation than first offenders.

The general conclusion that probation is at least as effective in preventing recidivism as institutional treatment is also supported by two recent studies of receptions into Californian penal institutions.[25] In the first, Mueller estimated that 20 per cent of all new adult male admissions to the California Department of Corrections could have been recommended for probation instead of imprisonment, since the risk of their being reconvicted (as assessed by base expectancy tables) was comparable with that of probationers in California. In the second, Roberts and Seckle found evidence that about 40 per cent of California Youth Authority wards could be released immediately into the community without serious risk of reconviction, compared with the 16–17 per cent who are at present released immediately. In another study carried out in California, Davis[26] found evidence that probation could be more liberally used without producing an increase in recidivism: there was no correlation between the frequency with which probation was used (instead of imprisonment), and the rates of revocation of probation orders, in two different groups of counties.

It must be emphasised, however, that the research just discussed

Table 6:3 Reconviction rates as percentages of 'expected' reconviction rates, for a sample of 1,316 offenders convicted in London in 1957.

Previous convictions	Under 17		17–20		21–29		30 and over	
	None	1+	None	1+	None	1+	None	1+
Discharge	89	100	89	98	109	90	133	104
Fine	75	83	75	94	63	99	84	65
Probation	118	101	122	101	153	115	(150)	121
Approved school	138	102	—	—	—	—	—	—
Borstal training	—	101 ⎤		95	—	—	—	—
Detention centre	—	106 ⎬	150	110	—	—	—	—
Attendance centre	—	119 ⎦	—	—	—	—	—	—
Imprisonment	—	—	—	106*	146†	111*	(91†)	104*
Corrective training	—	—	—	—	—	104*	—	—

* The calculation was based on a three year follow-up and it was necessary to exclude sentences of over three years.
† Excluding six sentences of three years or longer.

(100=expected rate of reconviction within five years except where otherwise stated.) The number of juvenile first offenders committed to institutions other than approved schools was too small to provide a satisfactory result; similarly in the 17 to under 21 age group the results had to be combined into one figure for 'institutional treatments'. (Of the group, the borstal result was the best, being about average in effectiveness.)

cannot be interpreted as showing that probation is especially effective as a method of treatment.

2 The most important finding in Hammond's study is that fines and discharges are much more effective than either probation or imprisonment for first offenders and recidivists of all age groups. The main findings of this study are summarised in table 6:3 in which observed reconviction rates are expressed as percentages of the expected rates. It will be seen that the reconviction rates for the two 'nominal' measures not involving supervision are lowest for most groups of offenders in the table. (Further analysis suggested that fines were especially effective for those convicted of theft.)

It is important to note that the method of comparison used in this study is fairly crude, and may neglect factors relating to reconviction which were taken into account by the courts in sentencing. For example, McClintock found (in his study of crimes of violence in London[27]) that courts tended to use fines for 'situational' offences of violence, arising out of family disputes and the like, in which repetition of the offence seemed unlikely. If the courts which sentenced Hammond's offenders followed similar policies, this could explain the apparently greater effectiveness of the fine. Nonetheless, there is other evidence suggesting that many of these now placed on probation, in both England and the United States, could be dealt with by a nominal measure such as a fine or discharge without increasing the risk of reconviction. Several recent surveys have shown that in both countries a large proportion of those placed on probation now receive only nominal supervision and a minimum of 'treatment' of any kind. Lohman et al.,[28] in a large-scale study of US Federal probation and parole, found no significant difference in the success rates (no major violation) of offenders randomly allocated to 'intensive', 'ideal', 'normal' and 'minimum' supervision, though these ranged from case-loads of 25 and 6·71 contacts per month in the case of 'intensive' supervision, to case-loads of 125 and ·48 contacts a month for 'minimum' supervision.

It must be emphasised that this finding does *not necessarily* support the view that any offenders now sent to penal institutions should, as a matter of policy, be dealt with by non-institutional methods instead. Such a course could itself affect the recidivism rates of these and other offenders, as well as reducing the general-preventive effect of the penal system. Moreover, even if *recidivism* rates did not rise, a shift to non-institutional sentences would lead to an increased *crime* rate, since it would mean that some offenders now sent to institutions (and so not 'at risk') for a time would instead be at liberty in the community during that time. The social cost of these extra offences would have to be balanced, in any policy calculation, against the excess cost of keeping the offenders in institutions rather than leaving them in the community.

3 Longer institutional sentences are no more effective in preventing recidivism than shorter ones. Only a few studies have compared long and short sentences in the same type of institutional regime. Without exception, however, these show that in general, longer sentences – even of an avowedly reformative kind – do not produce lower reconviction rates. Mannheim and Wilkins found that above average periods of detention in borstal seemed to yield no better results than a period of about a year, for boys of all risk groups. Benson[29] and Banks[30] have also found no differences in reconviction rates among boys aged 17-21, as between imprisonment or detention lasting three or four months, and borstal training lasting on average over a year. Supportive evidence for this view also comes from Weeks's study[31] of the Highfields experiment in New Jersey, in which it was found that sentences of three to four months in an open institution, with a liberal regime and group counselling, produced about the same results as a two-year reformatory sentence. Several studies of adult prisoners have also shown that shorter institutional sentences do not lead to higher rates of recidivism. Hammond and Chayen found very little difference in the reconviction rates of persistent offenders given sentences of under four years, and those given preventive detention lasting in most cases seven or eight years; they also found that it made no difference whether the offenders were given five, six, seven or eight years' preventive detention, or were released after two-thirds or five-sixths of their sentences. An un-published study by Taylor, at the Prison Department in England, found that three-year sentences of corrective training produced results which were slightly (though not significantly) *worse* than two-year sentences. Finally, research by Johnson,[32] Mueller[33] and Havel[34] in California has shown that prisoners given an earlier-than-normal release on parole do not display higher failure rates than those released at the normal times. In some cases there was no difference in recidivism even when the time in prison was reduced by 20 per cent (an average of six months' reduction, on an average sentence of 30 months).

4 The offenders most likely to improve are the 'medium risks'. We have already noted that offenders who have relatively good chances, before treatment, of avoiding reconviction do not need – and are generally unlikely to benefit much from – intensive treatment. This

190

is also true of those persistent offenders who are very likely to be reconvicted whatever is done to them. These groups are fairly easily identified by the prediction methods now in use; when they are excluded, however, there remains a fairly large group of 'medium risk' cases for which the choice of sentence, and the development of new treatments, may yield substantial reductions in recidivism.

Two studies demonstrate this point empirically. Berntsen and Christiansen[35] carried out an experimental treatment programme on a random group of men serving short sentences of imprisonment in Denmark. This group, matched with controls who served ordinary sentences of imprisonment, was followed up for a period of five years. The authors found that the intensive treatment had the greatest effect (in terms of reduced recidivism) on an intermediate group whose previous career they describe as 'relatively crime-loaded'; neither the hard core of rapidly recidivating criminals, nor the first offenders, appeared to benefit from the experimental pro-gramme. Similarly, in the Special Intensive Parole Unit study in California, Havel[36] found that low case-loads and intensive super-vision on parole failed to improve the success rates of either 'good risk' or 'bad risk' offenders, though it did raise the success rate of those classified as 'medium good risks'.

Conclusions

There are a few other useful generalisations which can be derived from research in this area. For instance, there is some evidence – from the Mannheim-Wilkins study, and the Highfields experiment – suggesting that open institutions are at least as successful as closed ones. But at the moment the evidence for this proposition is very weak, and open to many methodological objections; and for the moment, it seems better to regard this point as 'not proven'.

It must also be admitted that a very large number of studies of the effectiveness of punishments and treatments have negative results: that is, they reveal no significant differences between the types of treatment investigated. But the picture is not as bleak as it may seem at first sight. To begin with, by no means all of the research in this area has produced negative results. In addition to the studies already cited, there have been some studies of particular forms of treatment (mostly of rather specialised individual or group therapy in institu-tions) which show overall differences in the reconviction rates of treatment and control groups. In a recent review of 100 evaluative studies of this kind Bailey[37] found a successful outcome reported in about one-half. It is true that a great many of these studies had serious methodological shortcomings, and that Bailey found that the more rigorous the research design, the higher the percentage reporting 'no change' or detrimental effects from the treatment. Nonetheless, of the 22 studies making use of a control group, nine reported a positive and statistically significant change in the outcome of treatment, and four more reported 'marked improvement' which was not statistically significant. These results are not spectacular, but they do not support the view that treatments are simply interchangeable, or that it makes no difference, so far as recidivism is concerned, which type of treatment an offender receives.

There is another possible reason why so many studies have shown little if any difference between the outcomes of different treatments. It is possible that where two types of treatment have the same *overall* results (as measured by reconviction rates), each is having different effects for different types of offender; what is effective in reducing the recidivism of one type of offender may actually increase the chances of recidivism for another type, and these differences may simply be cancelling each other out. It is true that the scope for this kind of interaction between type of treatment and type of offender is fairly limited where existing forms of treatment are concerned. All of the best and most reliable predictors of recidivism – age, previous convictions, type of current offence, age at first conviction – *antedate* the choice of sentence; knowledge of the treatment received by the offender does little, if anything, to increase the accuracy of predictions of his behaviour after treatment. Thus, even if all offenders could be allocated to the kinds of treatment most effective for them, the 'success rate' of the penal system as a whole would be very unlikely to reach 100 per cent.

Nonetheless, even a marginal improvement in the overall effectiveness of the system can have important social consequences. To raise the overall 'success rate' from 60 to 70 per cent, for example, would be to reduce recidivism by one-quarter; and this would be no mean achievement. Moreover, the limited effectiveness of the penal system in its present form merely reflects the limited effectiveness of existing forms of treatment; it is possible that new forms of treatment, for particular types of offenders, will make it possible to reduce recidivism still further. The relations between type of treatment and type of offender, and experiments with new forms of treatment, will be discussed in the next chapter.

7 Interaction between type of treatment and type of offender

So far, our discussion of research on the effectiveness of punishments and treatments has been concerned mainly with overall comparisons of the results of two or more types of treatment. In some of the studies described in the last chapter, offenders were classified into risk groups, according to base expectancy tables; and we noted that it is chiefly for the 'middle risk' group of offenders that the prospect of improving the effectiveness of penal measures seems greatest. But this is, of course, only a very crude way of classifying offenders. We must now take this process of taxonomy a step farther, and consider some ways of classifying offenders in ways relevant to the choice of treatment. Much of our discussion of typologies in chapter 4, where we were concerned with the explanation of criminal behaviour, is relevant here; but we must stress again that the problems of aetiology and the choice of treatment are quite distinct, and that a typology which is useful for either one of these problems is not necessarily valid or useful for the other.

The relation between types of treatment and types of offender is relatively new as a subject of criminological research; comparatively little research has been done on the problem, and the results to date cannot be said to be very encouraging. But the subject represents a natural development of the extensive research on the effectiveness of treatment which has been carried out over the past 25 years, and it seems likely that much more work will be done on it in the future.

In its most general form, the presupposition which underlies research on this problem can be stated as follows: for any type of offender, there is one type of treatment which is (in some sense) the most appropriate. In fact, researchers in this field to date have neglected general prevention and other possible aims of sentencing, and have concentrated on the objective of reducing recidivism. They have thus sought to show that different types of offender may respond differently to the same form of treatment; and that a measure which is effective in reducing the recidivism of one type of offender may actually increase the chances of recidivism of offenders of another type. There are many ways in which conceivably this

Table 7:1 Hypothetical outcome of follow-up study of three types of treatment and three types of offender.

| Type of offender | Number of successes and failures, for type of treatment | | | | | | | | |
| | X | | Y | | Z | | Total | | |
	S	F	S	F	S	F	S	F	%S
A(50)*	30	70	50	50	70	30	150	150	**50**
B (60)*	80	20	40	60	60	40	180	120	**60**
C (70)*	70	30	90	10	50	50	210	90	**70**
Total (60)*	180	120	180	120	180	120	540	360	**60**
Per cent success	**60**		**60**		**60**		**60**		

* per cent expected success rate.

Table 7:2 Hypothetical outcome of follow-up study: observed successes as percentages of expected successes.

| Type of offender | Type of treatment | | | |
	X	Y	Z	Total
A	60	100	140	100
B	133·3	66·7	100	100
C	100	128·5	71·5	100
Total	100	100	100	100

might come about. For instance, a long prison sentence might sever an offender's contacts with a criminal subculture, and thus make it less likely that he will return to crime when he leaves prison; but the same kind of sentence might isolate another type of offender from his family, legitimate job opportunities and so on, thus making him more likely to commit further offences after being discharged from prison. Or a type of psychotherapy which improves the mental state of one kind of offender may have an adverse effect on the mental state of another.

Let us illustrate this kind of situation with a hypothetical example. Table 7:1 presents the table of 'success rates' (in the sense of the proportions of offenders not reconvicted) which might be found in a large comparative follow-up study of three types of treatment – designated X, Y and Z – administered to three types of offender (designated A, B and C). A, B and C might refer, for example, to three different personality types; X, Y and Z might designate three different forms of sentence, or three different institutional regimes. The *expected* success rates of the three groups of offenders – based on their ages, previous criminality, and so on – are 50 per cent for type A, 60 per cent for type B, and 70 per cent for type C. For simplicity we have assumed that 100 offenders of each type are allocated to each of the treatments, so that the numbers not reconvicted in each case in the body of the table are also the percentages 'successful'.

It will be seen that treatment type X is apparently relatively effective for offenders of type B: the observed success rate of these offenders is higher than their expected rate. But this type of treatment may be said to be *ineffective* with offenders of type C, since the proportion successful in this case is just the same as would have been expected. And treatment X may be said to be not merely ineffective, but downright *detrimental,* for offenders of type A: since the success rate in this case is actually lower than knowledge of these offenders' previous criminality and other characteristics would have led us to expect. The same sort of thing is true, *mutatis mutandis,* for the other two types of treatment under consideration. Treatment Y is relatively effective for offenders of type C, ineffective for A's and detrimental for B's; treatment Z is effective for A's, ineffective for B's and detrimental for C's.

We must stress that the terms 'effective', 'ineffective' and 'detrimental' need to be carefully interpreted in this context, and must be understood here to refer to the relation between *observed* and

Table 7:3 Hypothetical outcome of follow-up study: optimum allocation for maximising success rates.

| Type of offender | Number of successes and failures, for type of treatment | | | | | | | | |
| | X | | Y | | Z | | Total | | |
	S	F	S	F	S	F	S	F	%S
A (50)*	—	—	—	—	210	90	210	90	**70**
B (60)*	240	60	—	—	—	—	240	60	**80**
C (70)*	—	—	270	30	—	—	270	30	**90**
Total (60)*	240	60	270	30	210	90	720	180	**80**
Per cent success	**80**		**90**		**70**		**80**		

* per cent expected success rate.

expected success rates. This relationship can be seen more clearly if we divide the 'success' categories in each line of table 7:1 by the numbers expected in each case, to succeed in avoiding reconviction. Table 7:2 shows the result of doing this. Where an entry in table 7:2 is less than 100, the treatment may be said to be detrimental; where it exceeds 100, the treatment may be described as effective; where it equals 100, the treatment is ineffective in the sense in which we are using that term.

In this hypothetical example, it may be said that there has been *interaction* between types of treatment and types of offender. From the point of view of maximising success rates, there has clearly been some misallocation of offenders to types of treatment. If all offenders in this study had been allocated to the treatments most effective for them, the outcome would have been that shown in table 7:3, and the observed success rate for the whole group of 900 offenders might in theory have been 80 per cent, rather than 60 per cent. (We say 'in theory' here because there are reasons why this may *not* happen in practice; see pages 212–13.) It can also be seen from our hypothetical example, that interaction effects of the kind illustrated may offset one another and be masked by similar overall outcomes for two or more types of treatment. Referring back to table 7:1, it will be seen that the overall success rates for treatments X, Y and Z are the same – 60 per cent – and that the overall success rates for each type of *offender* are the same as their expected success rates. From these overall comparisons, it might be concluded that there was no differences in effectiveness between X, Y and Z; and that they were all ineffective in the sense explained above. Only when the offenders are classified into types do differences in outcome appear.

We have assumed in this example that the expected success rates of the three types of offender are all different – 50 per cent, 60 per cent and 70 per cent, respectively – but this need not be the case. The reader may verify for himself that the relative differences shown in table 7:2 would still appear even if the expected success rate for each type of offenders were, say, 60 per cent. The optimum allocation policy, in order to maximise success rates, would still be the same. It should be noted, however, that even if interaction effects of this kind do occur, their potential effect on the overall success rate will depend in part on the number of offenders of each type who are dealt with, and their expected reconviction rates. For example, if most of the offenders in our hypothetical example (see table 7:1) were of type C, there would be less to be gained, in terms of increasing the overall success rates, by optimum allocation.

Finally, it must be borne in mind that in order to *demonstrate* the existence of interaction effects by means of a follow-up study, there must necessarily have been some degree of 'misallocation' of offenders in the first place. If each offender in our hypothetical example had originally received the type of treatment most effective for him – the case illustrated in table 7:3 – it would obviously never have been possible to detect the differences in effectiveness which are shown in table 7:1. Very little is now known about the relations between the sentencing policies of the courts, or the allocation policies in systems of prisons or reformatories, and the effectiveness of treatment. But there is some reason to think that the courts (and institutional allocation boards) are already taking into account, consciously or unconsciously, some factors which are related to the optimum treatment for different types of offenders.

The results of research to date

So far, it appears that fewer than a dozen research projects have been undertaken in English-language countries, of a kind which permit testing of hypotheses concerning interaction effects. Interim

Table 7:4 Results of the Camp Elliott study by Grant and Grant.

Type of offender	Type of supervision										
Maturity level	Predicted best			Predicted next best			Predicted worst			Total		
	S	F	% S	S	F	% S	S	F	% S	S	F	% S
High	49	21	**70**	47	18	**72**	37	24	**61**	133	63	**68**
Low	18	26	**41**	29	26	**55**	29	19	**60**	76	74	**51**
Total	67	47	**59**	76	44	**63**	66	43	**61**	209	137	**60**

This table shows the numbers and percentages of high-maturity and low-maturity offenders 'succeeding' (defined as returning satisfactorily to military duty) after three types of supervision at the Camp Elliott (California) Naval Retraining Barracks. For the 'predicted best' supervision, the difference in outcome between high-maturity and low-maturity subjects (shown in the left-hand column) is statistically significant; it could only have occurred by chance with a probability of less than ·01. But for high-maturity subjects the differences in outcome for the three types of treatment (shown in the top row of the table) is *not* statistically significant; such a difference might have occurred by chance with a probability of about ·85 ($\chi^2 = 2\cdot22$). The same is true for low-maturity subjects (second row of the table); in this case the observed difference might have occurred by chance with a probability of between ·50 and ·70 ($\chi^2 = 3\cdot53$).

or final results are now available for only a few of these. The main conclusions which can be drawn from these studies may be summarised as follows:

1 No research has yet produced clear evidence of full interaction, i.e. of treatment which is relatively successful for one type of offender being relatively detrimental when applied to another type of offen-

der. The research carried out by Grant and Grant[1] at Camp Elliott, a naval discipline barracks in California, is often said to have demonstrated interaction effects empirically; but the implications of this now famous study for the treatment of offenders are not, in fact, very clear. A total of 511 military 'delinquents' (most of them deserters from duty) were rated for 'interpersonal maturity' according to a seven-step scale originally propounded by Sullivan, Grant and Grant,[2] and were then classified as high-maturity (I-levels 4 and 5) or low-maturity (I-levels 2 and 3) for the purposes of the research. Briefly, the high-maturity subjects according to this classification were those who had internalised a set of standards by which they judged their own and others' behaviour; they were aware of the expectations of others and of the effects of their own behaviour on others; and they were capable of establishing and carrying through long-range plans. Low-maturity subjects, by contrast, were egocentric, impulsive, unaware of the effects of their behaviour on others, and tended to see other people only as objects to be manipulated in order to get what they wanted.

Groups of 20 high, low and mixed maturity level subjects each were randomly allocated to three types of training regimes – known as 'Living Groups' – each run by three supervisors, for periods of three to nine weeks. The three Living Groups were not described in detail in the original paper by Grant and Grant, who merely ranked them according to the predicted effectiveness of the supervisors. Other writers (including Glaser,[3] Wilkins[4] and Gottfredson and Ballard[5]) have suggested that the Living Group predicted 'most effective' involved intensive group counselling and group therapy, while that rated 'least effective' involved merely the traditional rigid disciplinary regime. But Grant and Grant did not say this; indeed, by ranking all three sets of supervisors they imply that all three Groups were carried on in more or less the same way, but that the supervisors predicted 'least effective' were simply less competent to carry out this type of treatment. It was found that the high-maturity subjects did significantly better overall than low-maturity ones; and the Grants concluded from their findings that ' ... military recidivism [sic] could be reduced by installing a closed Living Group program with effective supervision for high-maturity inmates'. Since the sample of offenders was somewhat selected and the criterion of 'success' was restoration to military duty (after an unspecified follow-up period), and since base expectancy data were not available, it is a little difficult to see how this claim can be supported:

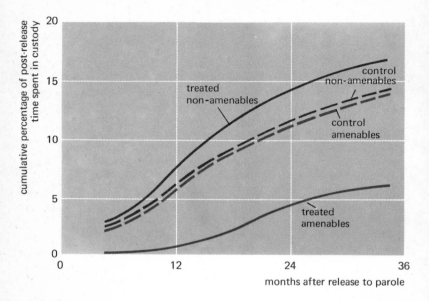

Figure 7:1 Comparison of the effectiveness of individual counselling for 'amenable' and 'non-amenable' subjects.

the overall 'success rate' for high and low-maturity subjects in the study was 62 per cent, whereas the overall rate of restoration to duty at Camp Elliott was said to be 'between 55 and 60 per cent'.

It was also found that among the inmates in the Living Group predicted to be most effective, there was a significant difference between the success rates of high-maturity and low-maturity subjects. There was a similar, though less marked, difference among those in the Group predicted 'next best'; but there was no difference in the success rates of the two types of offenders among those given the predicted 'least effective' supervision (see table 7:4). Commenting on these results in a later paper, M.Q. Grant has written that:

Not only were the treatment methods of some supervisory teams (psycho-dynamic oriented) effective in increasing the success rates of some kinds of delinquents (high maturity), but also they were markedly detrimental to the success chances of other kinds of delinquents (low maturity). Furthermore, the custody-oriented supervisory team had the reverse effect on high and low maturity subjects.[6]

Many other writers have echoed this conclusion; but it is, in fact, a *non sequitur,* and is not supported by the Grants' data. What the results actually showed was that for the predicted 'best' treatment, offenders' successful restoration to duty depended on their maturity levels, whereas for that predicted 'least effective', this was not so. But we cannot conclude from this finding that any of the three Living Groups was 'better' or 'worse' for either type of offender. In fact, high-maturity subjects did slightly worse after the predicted 'least effective' supervision, and low-maturity subjects did slightly less well after the predicted 'best' supervision. But in neither case were these results statistically significant; as the Grants themselves concluded in their original study, '... no significant differences were found which could be attributed to predicted supervisory effectiveness'.

A few other studies have produced results suggestive of full interaction between type of treatment and type of offender, though in no case is the evidence very strong. The best is probably Stuart Adams's[7] study of the Pilot Intensive Counselling Project reported in 1961. Adams compared the parole performance of 200 juvenile offenders given intensive individual counselling in a California institution, with that of 200 controls from the same institution. He found that of those rated as 'amenable' for this type of treatment, the after conduct of those given counselling was significantly better (in terms of being returned to the institution) than that of the controls. By contrast, the treated 'non-amenables' did slightly (though not significantly) *worse* than the 'non-amenable' controls (see figure 7:1).

2 Though a few studies have found types of treatment to have differential outcomes with different types of offenders, about an equal number have had negative results. One of the most interesting of these projects was carried out by Jesness[8] at Fricot Ranch, a California Youth Authority institution for 8 to 14 year-old delinquents. The project was intended to test the hypothesis that residence in a 20-boy lodge in the institution would increase the impact of staff-inmate interaction and peer-group influence, and thus provide more effective socialisation than residence in the normal 50-boy units. Jesness developed an offender typology based on 103 items drawn from test scores, behavioural ratings, and interview and social background data concerning the boys in the study. Statistical analysis of these data produced fifteen factors; an inverse analysis then classified the boys into eight groups, each representing a more

201

or less distinct delinquent type. For example, those in the first of the eight types – described as 'socialised, conforming thieves' – were rated high on conformity, school interest, and responsibility; they were of relatively high social status, were generally better than average on psychological tests, were older than average, less often came from 'problem families', always had delinquent companions and had long police records; they behaved well in the institution and generally stayed there only a short time. Type 4 – described as 'immature aggressive' – were generally the opposite of Type 1; and similar sets of criteria distinguished the other six types ('immature-passive', 'neurotic-anxious', 'cultural delinquent', 'manipulator', 'neurotic acting-out' and 'neurotic-depressed'). Though the numbers involved were small, the fifteen-month follow-up showed that boys of the three neurotic types did markedly better in the smaller experimental unit; only 14 per cent had their parole revoked, compared with 51 per cent of the neurotic boys housed in the normal 50-boy lodge. There were no significant differences between the revocation rates of treatment and control groups of all other five types. Moreover, the overall difference between the experimental and control groups tended to decrease the longer the follow-up was continued, and by the end of three years it was no longer significant; at that time almost 80 per cent of each group had been returned to the reformatory.

Other researchers have been even less successful in demonstrating differences in treatment outcome for different types of offender. Havel[9] classified parolees in the Special Intensive Parole Unit study (SIPU), into high-maturity and low-maturity groups (again following Sullivan, Grant and Grant). Parole officers were also classified, according to whether they adopted a primarily 'external' (situational) approach in dealing with the parolee, or an 'internal' (individual) one. It was hypothesised that low-maturity offenders would do better under 'external' supervision, and the high-maturity parolees better under 'internal' supervision. But neither hypothesis was confirmed; there were no significant differences in parole violation rates for either group, ('nor', according to Havel, 'can much comfort be taken by looking for trends').

Undoubtedly the most elaborate attempt to date to relate types of treatment to types of offenders is the Community Treatment Project, Phase One of which has been in progress under the direction of Marguerite Q. Warren since 1961. The subjects in this research project are delinquents committed for the first time to California

Youth Authority institutions by the juvenile courts of two cities (Sacramento and Stockton). These are randomly allocated to an experimental group, which receives immediate parole with intensive supervision in the community, and a control group which undergoes the normal institutional treatment. In addition to comparing treatment in the community with treatment in an institution, the programme is designed to discover and develop the most appropriate treatment methods for each of the different types of offender in the experimental group. The typology used in this project is based on the 'interpersonal maturity' levels proposed by Sullivan, Grant and Grant, with delinquents of each level of maturity then being further classified into sub-types said to represent their 'typical mode of interaction with the world'.[10] Thus low-maturity subjects (I-level 2) are further divided into 'unsocialised aggressive' and 'unsocialised passive' sub-types; middle-maturity subjects (I-level 3) into 'conformist immature', 'conformist cultural' and 'manipulator' sub-types; and high-maturity subjects (I-level 4) into 'neurotic acting-out', 'neurotic-anxious', 'cultural identifier' and 'situational emotional response' groups.

The latest published results of this research[11] show that the experimental group as a whole has had a much lower parole failure rate than the control group: of those at risk for 15 months prior to 15 June 1967, 30 per cent of the experimentals had had their parole revoked, against 51 per cent of the controls. A similar difference is present for the smaller numbers at risk for 24 months: 40 per cent of the experimentals had failed by this time, against 67 per cent of the controls. The results by sub-type, for the cohort at risk for 15 months in mid-1967, are shown in table 7:5.

It will be seen that there are several differences in the relative performances of these experimental and control subjects, in the eight sub-types which can be compared (there being no 'unsocialised aggressive' delinquents in the experimental group). In the two 'neurotic' sub-types the differences between experimental and control groups are statistically significant; and they approach significance for three other groups (the two 'conformist' groups and the 'asocial passive' group.) Three of these four differences also appear in the cohort at risk for 24 months by mid-June 1967. These differences have been fairly consistent since the first results were reported, though they have by no means been entirely so. Broadly speaking, it is in the two 'cultural' and two 'neurotic' sub-types that the differences between experimental and control subjects' after-

203

Table 7:5 Outcome of the Community Treatment Project (Sacramento and Stockton, California), for a cohort at risk for 15 months to March 1968.

I-level and sub-type	Experimentals		Controls	
	No.	Per cent Failure	No.	Per cent Failure
I–2 Unsocialised aggressive	0	—	4	50
Unsocialised passive	12	17	12	50
I–3 Conformist, immature	34	29	43	49
Conformist, cultural	24	25	30	43
Manipulator	35	31	37	46
I–4 Neurotic, acting-out	59	29	40	68
Neurotic, anxious	72	39	53	53
Situational emotional	8	13	7	14
Cultural identifier	14	43	14	36
Total	258	31	240	50

conduct have been the greatest. Unpublished results for a cohort at risk for three years at the beginning of 1968 also showed very similar results. Thus the project to date has clearly had differential outcomes, being markedly successful for some sub-types but not for others. There is no sub-type in which the experimental group has done significantly *worse* than its controls, though there has been a slight difference in this direction in the 'situational emotional reaction' group in all of the results reported to date.

These data are subject to two important reservations, however. The first concerns the sub-type classifications. Considerable research has been done to establish the reliability of ratings for the

I-level and sub-type classification used in the Community Treatment Project; Warren and her associates report inter-rater agreement, on average, in about 85 per cent of the cases.[12] But this result has been achieved by a small and highly experienced team of researchers who have worked together for several years; and according to Conrad it is 'prohibitively costly'.[13] Moreover, other researchers have not achieved the same level of reliability. Havel found agreement between two raters classifying offenders by level of interpersonal maturity (I-levels 2, 3 or 4) in 93 per cent of 138 cases when the classification was based on interviews; but in only 56 per cent of 566 cases when it was based on case records.

Three pencil-and-paper tests have been used in an effort to classify delinquents according to I-level. Gottfredson and Ballard,[14] using scales from the California Personality Inventory,[15] were able to classify correctly about 75 per cent of a sample of 302 offenders, with a 'middle group' of 48 cases left unclassified; if these latter cases had been randomly allocated, the total correctly classified would have been about 83 per cent, or five cases out of every six. Beverley[16] has developed two eighteen-item scales, one from the Jesness Inventory and one from the Beverley-Grant Opinion Scale, each of which correctly classified about three-quarters of a group of 280 boys (with no 'middle group' left unclassified). These are promising results – rather better, in fact, than those usually obtained with psychiatric diagnosis. But each of these tests classifies offenders into only two broad groups – high maturity or low maturity; Beverley was unable to distinguish I-level 2 cases from I-level 3, and difficulty on this point was also reported by Havel.

What is really important in this research project, however, is the classification of offenders according to sub-types ('asocial aggressive', etc.) *within* each broad level of 'interpersonal maturity' (see page 198). In the Community Treatment Project, this has so far been done by means of ratings based on interviews – a method with many drawbacks in practice. More recently, however, Jesness[17] has developed a scale for this purpose based on the Jesness Inventory; this has been used with considerable success both by him and by Davies[18] in England. The validity of the sub-types used by Warren and her associates is still a little suspect: in some cases, it is reported, an offender's maturity level has changed during treatment (from I-level 3 to 4, or 2 to 3), and he has not then fitted into any of the sub-types of the higher maturity level. But it is nonetheless extremely important to establish a reliable and objective means of classifying

205

Table 7:6 Offences leading to parole suspension and revocation in the community treatment project.

Offence	Revocation Experimental	Control	Suspension Experimental	Control
1 (Least serious)	3 ⎫	16 ⎫	275 ⎫	80 ⎫
2	4 ⎪	3 ⎪	101 ⎪	34 ⎪
3	3 ⎬ 44	17 ⎬ 87	88 ⎬ 596	47 ⎬ 277
4	11 ⎪	23 ⎪	58 ⎪	53 ⎪
5	23 ⎭	28 ⎭	74 ⎭	63 ⎭
6	14 ⎫	28 ⎫	36 ⎫	54 ⎫
7	7 ⎪	0 ⎪	18 ⎪	5 ⎪
8	1 ⎬ 34	1 ⎬ 34	3 ⎬ 82	2 ⎬ 78
9	11 ⎪	5 ⎪	24 ⎪	16 ⎪
10 (Most serious)	1 ⎭	0 ⎭	1 ⎭	1 ⎭
Total	78	121	678	355

Parole *revocation* (termination) is the criterion of 'failure' in the Community Treatment Project; parole *suspension* is a temporary consequence of a breach of parole (which may be a minor offence or technical breach of the parole rules) which is *not* counted as 'failure' in the Project. These figures suggest that different criteria of 'failure' have in practice been used for the two groups. (The numbers in the table refer to the numbers of offences committed.)

offenders in this more complex way, rather than merely splitting them into high and low-maturity groups. In fact, there are no statistically significant differences in the failure rates of high and low-maturity subjects, in either experimental or control groups in the Community Treatment Project, at either 15 or 24 months at risk.

This study illustrates an important methodological difference between treatment typologies and typologies used for aetiological research. As we argued in chapter 4, typologies used in treatment research should ideally be as *rich in types* as possible – otherwise differences in treatment outcome are likely to be obscured. If, in future, no differences appear in outcome of treatment for some of the sub-groups used in the Community Treatment Project, these can be ignored and the experimental programme reserved for those sub-types (the neurotic and conformist groups) which appear to benefit most from it. If reliable identification of these sub-types had not been possible, the only useful result of the project would have been the *overall* difference between experimental and control groups; and the point of the typologies would have been lost.

It must be added, however, that this overall difference between experimental and control groups is itself a little suspect. Apparently there have been marked differences in the strictness of supervision of experimental and control groups during the research. Warren[19] has noted that while teachers were at first sympathetic to the Community Treatment Project, they have since tended to become hostile to it (and thus perhaps to offenders involved in it). In addition she writes that:

It has proved impossible to operate the program without the experimental or control status of subjects being known, not only to decision-making personnel in the Youth Authority but also to school systems and to some extent law enforcement agencies.

In consequence, the experimental group as a whole has almost certainly been subject to more liberal criteria of 'success,' in comparison with the controls; and this difference may well have been even more marked, of course, in one or two of the sub-types. The figures in table 7:6, from an unpublished paper by Bottoms and McClintock, show clearly that there has been a considerable difference in the circumstances and offences leading to parole violation in the experimental and control groups.

Experiments in developing new forms of treatment

A typology of offenders may be used for the purpose of allocating the different types to existing forms of treatment; alternatively, it may be used to classify offenders according to their apparent treatment needs, with a view to devising entirely new methods of treatment which will meet those needs more effectively (or more economically) than existing methods. A number of the research projects discussed above have in fact had this objective. In particular, the development of specific methods of intensive treatment for different types of offender has been an integral part of the Community Treatment Project. For example, psychotherapy has been recommended for the 'neurotic-anxious' delinquents (I-level 4), but not for the low-maturity (I-level 2) group. Attempts have also been made to study the characteristics of caseworkers taking part in the project, and to relate these to the characteristics of the offenders in the experimental group.

Unfortunately it is difficult to evaluate this aspect of the Community Treatment Project, since the intensive treatment programmes for the different types of delinquents in the experimental group have apparently been modified somewhat since the project began. Moreover, in the early years of the research, the control subjects who were sent to institutions were not given comparable intensive treatment based on the theory of interpersonal maturity; instead, they merely received the ordinary training programme of California Youth Authority institutions. It is thus impossible to tell how much (if any) of the difference in the after-conduct of the experimental and control groups is due to the special types of intensive treatment, and how much is due to the fact that one group was treated in the community while the other was sent to institutions. However, since 1966, treatment methods based on the theory of interpersonal maturity have been introduced in a number of California Youth Authority institutions. Thus since 1966 the study has involved a comparison between intensive treatment in the community, and similar treatment in an institutional setting.

Another example of research aimed at developing a new method of treatment for a particular type of offender is the Provo (Utah) experiment carried out under the direction of L. T. Empey.[20] The subjects of this research were all persistent delinquents aged 15 to 17, who appeared to be involved in a delinquent subculture. The treatment was based on the assumption that the boys' commitment to the values of the delinquent group had to be modified, and the values of the group itself changed, if they were to be reformed. The treatment took the form of regular attendance, for a period of four to seven months, at a non-residential centre at which the offenders took part in a form of intensive group counselling known as 'guided group interaction'. After the judge had decided whether to sentence the offender to an institution or to probation, the offender was randomly allocated either to the experimental treatment or to the treatment chosen by the judge. It was found that the recidivism rates of the experimental and probation groups were identical, though they were lower than that of a similar group of habitual offenders sent to a reformatory. The treatment programme developed at Provo is being compared with treatment based on the concept of interpersonal maturity, in Phase II of the Community Treatment Project, now being carried out in San Francisco, California.[21]

This project incidentally illustrates two serious difficulties which may hinder research on experiments in new forms of treatment. First, while it was originally intended that offenders in the Provo project should also be randomly allocated to the experimental programme and to the reformatory, this was not possible in practice, because the judge sentenced too few offenders to the reformatory. Secondly, it was found that the success rate of the *control* group given ordinary probation was significantly higher than the success rate of probationers in the same area before the experiment was begun. This may have been attributable to something like the so-called 'Hawthorne effect'; that is, knowledge on the part of the probation officers who supervised the control subjects that they were taking part in an experiment may have motivated them to work harder or to introduce new and more effective techniques of their own. Evidence of similar effects has been found in a number of experimental studies in California penal institutions.

Such experiments illustrate the way in which attempts to distinguish types of offenders with different treatment needs may lead to the development of new and more effective forms of treatment. Valuable as these experiments are, however, their potential utility is somewhat limited. Even if a new form of treatment is found to be especially effective with a certain type of offender, it may not be feasible to provide that treatment in practice, on more than a limited scale. (This would be true of individual psychotherapy, which is extremely expensive.) It may also be that the type of offender shown to respond to a new form of treatment is not very common, or cannot usually be given that form of treatment (e.g. because typically his criminal record and type of offence are not thought serious enough by the courts to warrant a custodial sentence, or are too serious to let him be treated in the open).

From this point of view, a study of probation now being carried out by the Home Office Research Unit in England[22] seems especially promising, since it deals with an existing (and well-established) form of treatment now given to about 18 per cent of all persons convicted

209

of indictable offences in England. This project is investigating differences in outcome among different types of male probationers age 17 to 21, under different types of supervision. The hypothesis to be tested is that there is no particular form of supervision which is most suitable for all probationers. The treatment and offender typologies used are derived from social-psychological theory, and attempt to take into account both personal and social factors in the probation treatment relationship. Eight types of treatment are distinguished, according to the emphasis placed by the probation officer on individual or situational approaches to the offender, and the degree of 'support' and 'control' used. Thus, for example, 'Individual Control' supervision involves little home visiting by the probation officer, low support and high control; 'Situation Support' involves much home visiting, high support and low control. The main offender typology used attempts to distinguish probationers by reference to the main 'areas of difficulty' in their lives, taking into account both personal and environmental factors; eleven types in all have been identified, on the basis of terms frequently used by the probation officers taking part in the study in assessing their clients.

Typologies of treatment

In contrast to the plethora of offender typologies reported to date, there has been very little done to develop typologies of treatment. Though there have been many suggestions as to the best type of treatment for particular types of offenders, there have been few systematic attempts even at a theoretical level to classify treatments so as to reveal relevant similarities and differences in their constituent elements. (The study by Gibbons discussed in chapter 4 is a conspicuous exception.) Moreover, there has been very little research on the varieties of existing forms of treatment. The Home Office probation study and the SIPU project are the only studies to date to investigate this matter in any detail. As we shall see in the next chapter, some researchers have tried to draw broad distinctions between types of prison and reformatory according to formal institutional goals (viz, 'treatment' and 'control'). But a satisfactory typology of institutional treatment must obviously take into account many other factors as well, such as size and composition of the inmate population, training of staff and the nature of work, treatment and other elements in the institutional regime. Plainly it is not enough to consider only *deliberate* variations in treatment; descriptive research is needed which will bring out any differences in the experiences which prisoners may actually undergo, whether these are as a result of treatment policy or of other factors. This is likely to be very difficult to do.

Moreover, there is a special problem of reliability arising even with deliberate variations in treatment, such as the eight types of probation treatment identified in the Home Office study. Though probation officers may *intend* to rely on 'support' or 'control' in dealing with certain types of offender, and may have offenders allocated to them on this assumption, they may for various reasons *actually* follow a different type of approach; only continued research can show whether or not this is so. Still further complications may arise when two or more types of treatment are combined – for example, imprisonment and parole. Variations of the first type of treatment may be combined with variations of the second, and have different effects on different types of offenders. But since research on this subject is still in its infancy, it will clearly be some time before refinements of this type can be considered.

The value and limitations of research to date

It can be seen that the results of research to date are both meagre and vague; and they obviously furnish little basis for administrative or policy decisions. So far, not even the nature of our ignorance about interaction effects has been revealed by the handful of studies just reviewed.

In particular, no typology of offenders or treatments has yet been shown to be either valid or reliable; *a fortiori* no definite relationships have yet been established between any type of treatment and any type of offender. The offender typology most fully explored so far is that based on the theory of interpersonal maturity, which has been used in three projects apart from the Camp Elliott research of the Grants. It is interesting to note that the essentially descriptive typology derived by Jesness in the Fricot Ranch study (see pages 201–2) is in many respects similar to the I-level and sub-type classification, though of course Jesness's typology has not yet been independently validated. But the relations between interpersonal maturity and delinquency are not yet clear. According to Grant and Grant, low-maturity subjects, though not invariably delinquent, are much more likely to become involved in delinquency than high-maturity ones; and, as we have seen, the high-maturity offenders in the Camp Elliott study had the highest overall 'success rate'. In the Community Treatment Project, however, the high-maturity delinquents in both the experimental and control groups have been somewhat *less* successful in terms of subsequent parole revocation, though as already noted the differences between I-levels are not statistically significant for either group.

It should also be noted that no research has yet been carried out on the relations between types of offenders and alternative types of *sentences* (for example, imprisonment versus probation, or short-term versus long-term institutional sentences). Of course it may well be that even if interaction effects were found at this level, full use could not be made of them in practice by the courts. The prevention of recidivism is not and never can be the only objective of sentencing policy; the choice of sentence for any offender is necessarily limited by many considerations, of which the most obvious is the relative cost of the penal measures available. Nonetheless, the courts do have *some* freedom of choice in practice. If, for example, it could be shown that offenders of type X did well on probation but worse than expected when fined, and that the reverse was true for offenders of type Y, it might be possible for the courts to apply this knowledge, since the two types of non-custodial measures must often be feasible alternatives. Because the total number of offenders dealt with by the courts is much greater than the numbers placed on probation or sent to prison, the potential 'pay-off' of research on interaction at the sentencing stage is probably higher than that of research on different types of treatment within a single form of sentence. Of course, there are many methodological problems encountered in typological research at the sentencing level, the most serious of these being the inadequacy of records and the consequent difficulty of obtaining sufficient information about the offenders concerned. It is also very difficult, in practice, to allocate offenders randomly to different treatments at this stage. But on balance, these difficulties may be no greater than those encountered in typological research at later stages of the penal process.

So far as offender typologies are concerned, what is needed is what might be called 'basic typological research', which would show the relations *between* different sorts of typologies, and make it possible to compare them in scope and reliability. Samples of offenders – preferably drawn at random from those given different types of treatment – could be classified in eight or ten different ways, and the resulting groups compared in order to show empirically the relations between, say, interpersonal maturity and role-career, or self-image and rated 'amenability' to a certain type of treatment. (A pilot study of this kind has been carried out as part of the Community Treatment Project.) But until clearer operational criteria are provided for many of the typologies in the literature, this kind of research will be impossible.

We have noted that there are inherent limitations to the reduction of recidivism which can be accomplished through taking advantage of interaction effects. There are further practical limitations, for in many cases it would not be possible to take advantage of interaction effects even if these were shown to exist. As was said earlier, the prevention of recidivism is not the only objective of sentencing policy; justice, general prevention and comparative cost all limit the extent to which any type of offender can be sentenced to the type of treatment most likely to be effective for him. There are similar limits to the optimum allocation of offenders *within* any single type of treatment; in the case of penal institutions, for example, considerations of security must always play an important part.

It is also important to note that in the case of treatment which involves groups of offenders, the best *overall* result may be obtained by allocating some offenders to a type of treatment which is not the most effective for them. The research of Grant and Grant suggested that low-maturity subjects did best, under the predicted 'worst' supervision, in groups consisting solely of low-maturity subjects; but that high-maturity offenders did rather better, under the supervision rated 'best', in groups of *mixed* high and low-maturity offenders. Thus it may be that even if interaction effects are present, the maximum *overall* success rate will be something less than the theoretical maximum, i.e. the weighted sum of the highest success rates for each type of offender. Put another and crueller way, it may be necessary to 'write off' some offenders of one type, in order to make greater gains in reforming offenders of another type.

Given these limitations, it would seem reasonable to begin looking for interaction between types of treatment and types of offenders, both where the absolute numbers of offenders involved are greatest, and where there is the greatest potential scope for allocating offenders to the type of treatment found to be most effective for them. Unfortunately, as so often happens, these two criteria tend to point in opposite directions; the first to the sentencing stage of the penal process, the second to allocation of offenders within specific types of sentence. But a balance between them can surely be struck;

and at each level of the penal process there is probably some opportunity for research on interaction effects.

In the case of research on the comparative effectiveness of different sentences, a typological approach should surely become a standard part of research procedure: and descriptive typologies based mainly on social or sociological factors would seem especially promising, in view of the practical difficulties of obtaining detailed psychological information about offenders. In each case, of course, the offenders to concentrate on are the 'non-incorrigible recidivists'; these can at least be defined by exclusion of the 'once only' offender on the one hand and the hard-core persistent offender on the other. There is some scope, then, for research of this kind in connection with existing forms of treatment; and if a typology of offenders is shown to be invalid, in the sense of being unrelated to differences in outcome, it can be abandoned and other ones tried.

Thus despite all limitations, and the generally negative results obtained, the research done to date on interaction effects has certainly not been completely useless. These few studies are only a starting-point; they have brought to light many of the difficulties inherent in typological research, which later researchers may be able to avoid. It is important not to try to evaluate any type of penal treatment too soon after it has begun, and before it has worked out all the 'bugs' to which any innovation is prone; negative results, which may discourage further endeavour, may simply be due to the fact that the treatment in question has not yet really been put into practice. The same point may be made in trying to appraise research which attempts to evaluate treatment. After all, even negative results from typological research can be of some practical use – however disappointing they may be to idealists (if there are any left) in the fields of correctional administration and research.

8 The impact of imprisonment

At first sight it may seem somewhat beside the point even to try to measure the reformative effectiveness of prisons for adult offenders. In most prisons in England and the United States (and no doubt elsewhere) treatment and training programmes of any kind are at a minimum, and probably many people would still argue that the primary objectives of imprisonment should be deterrence, retribution, and the isolation from society of dangerous criminals. So far as official penal policy is concerned, in most countries the main aim in the case of prisons has been to keep offenders out of them: to use probation, the suspended sentence and other non-custodial measures wherever possible.

Up to a point, this policy seems justifiable, quite apart from its humanitarian attractions. As we saw in chapter 6, one of the main conclusions which can be drawn from research to date on the effectiveness of punishments and treatments is that many offenders now sent to prison could be dealt with 'in the open' without substantially increasing the risk of their reconviction. Of course, this is only true up to a point: for it must be remembered that whatever else it does, the prison does at least remove offenders from society, thus depriving them (as non-custodial measures do not) of the opportunity to commit further crimes against society at large. Imprisonment thus postpones reconvictions, even if it does not forever prevent them. Moreover, it is important to note that research to date has not shown imprisonment to be specially ineffective (in terms of subsequent recidivism); the most that can safely be said at the moment is that there does not seem to be much difference between custodial and non-custodial sentences, in terms of comparable offenders' after-conduct.

Because the prevention of recidivism is not the only objective of sentencing, it will never be possible to abolish imprisonment completely as a means of dealing with offenders. Like it or not, there will always be prisons, and there will always be a number of criminals who must be sent to prison. These criminals will generally be the most difficult to reform; but by the same token, they will generally be the ones whose reform (or deterrence) will be the most beneficial

215

to society. It is thus reasonable to try to discover exactly what impact, if any, the experience of imprisonment has on those who undergo it.

One way to do this is by 'follow-up' studies of the kind we have already discussed. But there is another way to assess the effectiveness of penal measures, which should ideally be coupled with the follow-up study: this is to study directly the *content* of the experience which offenders undergo in prison, and its impact on their attitudes, values, beliefs and capacities. For example, one might assess the offender's participation in individual or group counselling, and relate this to changes in his attitudes during the counselling period; this could conceivably show exactly which features of counselling had some effect on the offender, and which did not. Or again, it might be suggested that the acquisition of new work skills was a crucial factor in keeping offenders from recidivism after a prison sentence: studying the extent to which prisoners did in fact acquire new work skills, and then did or did not reform, could show whether or not this was so.

Research of this kind has been carried out in some of the studies of non-institutional treatment discussed in the last chapter – the Home Office probation research project, the Community Treatment Project, and the probation and parole research done by Lohman *et al* for example. Similar research was done by Glaser, in his large-scale investigation of the US federal prison and parole system.[1] But there have been very few other studies of imprisonment which have attempted to assess the impact of institutional treatment in any detail. One reason for this is that the methodological and practical problems of this kind of research in prisons are considerable; there are numerous difficulties about data collection (e.g. by observation or interview) in prison, and many variables in the institutional situation which are hard to control. For several other reasons as well, the work that has been done throws little light on the effectiveness of imprisonment in reducing recidivism, and for practical purposes nothing is yet known about this.

One reason why these studies have provided little information about the effectiveness of prisons in reducing recidivism is that they were not primarily aimed at doing so. Most of those who have carried out important research in prisons in recent years have been sociologists; with the notable exception of Glaser, they have been more interested in contributing to general sociology, and to the sociology of organisations, than to assessing the effectiveness of

216

penal systems. Some of the subjects with which they have been concerned have implications for other areas of criminology; but they are also important in their own right, and for the light which they help to shed on more general social phenomena. For example, Gresham Sykes has studied the maximum-security prison as one kind of totalitarian regime – 'a social system in which an attempt is made to create and maintain total or almost total social control'. In his book *The Society of Captives*,[2] published in 1958, Sykes examines the relations between inmates and custodial staff in a maximum security prison in New Jersey, and the difficulties which confront the custodians despite their apparently overwhelming position of power. He also sketches a theory to explain the riots which swept the New Jersey prison, and a number of other maximum-security institutions in the United States, in the early nineteen-fifties. Other researchers have examined such topics as the function of the system of communications in the prison; the relations between the prison and society; the consequences for institutional staff of trying to carry out simultaneously the objectives of 'treatment' and 'control'; and the relations between prisoners and prison staff, and their perceptions of each other.[3,4]

The topic which has received the most attention from researchers in this field, however, is the informal social organisation of the prison. It is this line of research with which we shall mainly be concerned in this chapter. The studies of this subject which have been carried out so far do not themselves show much about the effects of imprisonment on prisoners' after-conduct; but they do have an important bearing on this question. After summarising the most important research of this kind which has been carried out in recent years, we shall briefly indicate how insights gained from it might be used in future research aimed at measuring the impact of the experience of imprisonment on the offender.

The prison community

The main precursor of most modern research in prisons is Donald Clemmer's book *The Prison Community*,[5] originally published in 1940. Clemmer was a sociologist on the staff of the Menard (Illinois) State Penitentiary in the early 1930s. His book is a detailed description of that prison, which was (and probably still is) typical of many maximum-security prisons in the United States: in meticulous detail he presents a picture of the institution, its inmates and staff,

217

and the relations between them. From his work three related issues emerge which have preoccupied many subsequent researchers. The first of these is the nature of the informal social system of the prison – in particular, the norms and values of what has been called the 'inmate subculture'. The second concerns the origins of this sub-culture, and the factors which determine the form which it takes, in different kinds of institutions. The third concerns the effect of this social system on the individual inmate, and in particular his socialis-ation into the inmate community – a process which Clemmer called 'prisonization'.

The inmate social system By the expression 'informal social system' is meant the pattern of social relations – roles, norms, shared beliefs, values, lines of communication and co-operation, and so on – which may develop among the members of an organisation or continuing group, without being prescribed or defined by the formal rules of that organisation or group. In the case of imprisonment, as Sykes has put it, the act of custody means

… many individuals bound together for long intervals. Such aggregates enduring through time must inevitably give rise to a social system – not simply the social order decreed by the custodians, but also the social order which grows up more informally as men interact in meeting the problems posed by their particular environment. In attempting, then, to understand the meaning of imprisonment, we must see prison life as something more than a matter of walls and bars, of cells and keys. We must see the prison as a society within a society.

The principal feature of the inmate social system according to Clemmer, is the 'inmate code': an explicit (though unwritten) set of values and norms derived from them, which exists alongside the official rules of the institution.

The fundamental principle of the code may be stated thus: Inmates are to refrain from helping prison or government officials in matters of discipline, and should never give them information of any kind, and especially the kind which may work harm to a fellow prisoner. Supplementary to this, and following from it, is the value of loyalty among prisoners in their dealings with each other. This basic idea constitutes the prisoners' code.

The principal norms of the inmate code thus prohibit such things as 'ratting' (informing) on other inmates and contacts with prison staff ('never talk to a screw'). This value-system and the more or less elaborate set of norms based on it, backed by sanctions ranging from

218

ostracism to physical violence, is alleged to be found in most maximum-security prisons in the United States; according to Clemmer it was found there in the nineteenth century. As Goffman[6] and others have pointed out, there are many similarities between prisons and other 'total institutions' (that is, roughly, those institutions such as hospitals, boarding schools and monasteries, in which the participants live as well as work). But it is of interest to note that there is apparently no comparable code found among, for example, mental hospital patients.

Moreover, as would be expected, the content of the inmate culture appears to differ in different kinds of penal institution, and from one country to another. In studies of institutions for juvenile and young adult offenders in the United States, Grusky,[7] Berk[8] and Vinter et al.[9] found evidence that the values of the inmate social system (as reflected in the attitudes expressed by the inmates themselves, in a variety of tests) depended in part on the formal organisation and goals of the institutions. The inmates in institutions oriented toward treatment and reform were less 'anti-authority' in their outlook than those in institutions with a purely custodial or punitive regime. However, in none of these studies were the offenders randomly allocated to the different institutions; and the observed differences in their attitudes may have been due to the fact that the 'treatment-oriented' institutions contained less hardened criminals. Also since the offenders were relatively young – in Vinter's study they were mostly boys aged fourteen to sixteen – it is probable that the institutions were all relatively more 'treatment-oriented' than the typical American penitentiary or maximum-security prison, such as the New Jersey prison described by Sykes.

It also seems that the inmate solidarity and extreme opposition to authority which are said to be found in American maximum-security prisons are not so marked in prisons in some other countries. Cline,[10] Galtung[11] and Mathiesen[12] have found that this is so in the case of Scandinavian prisons. As Mathiesen has suggested, this may largely reflect cultural differences between the United States and the Scandinavian countries, in particular the relatively low degree of professionalisation of crime, and the weaker criminal subcultures existing in Scandinavia. On the other hand, Morris and Morris, in their description[13] of an English maximum-security prison (Pentonville), report the existence of an 'inmate code' and a number of inmate roles very similar to those found in comparable American prisons.

Clemmer was well aware that the inmate community, like almost any community, has a complex social structure: he distinguished three social classes among prisoners (which he called the élite, the middle class and the 'hoosier' class), and briefly sketched the relations between them. But the most important contribution in this area is undoubtedly that of Clarence Schrag, who first turned the attention of researchers to the different social roles in the inmate community, and to the dynamics of the interpersonal relationships which may result from them.

On the basis of participant observation at the Washington State Penitentiary, Schrag[14] identified five major social roles to which inmates tended to be allocated by other inmates. In the argot of the prison, these are the 'right guy', 'outlaw', 'square John', 'politician' and 'ding' roles. Briefly, the 'right guy' (later termed *anti-social* by Schrag) is oriented to crime and criminals and to the norms of the inmate community, in which he tends to be a leader. By contrast, the 'square John' or *pro-social* inmate has few if any previous criminal contacts; in prison he maintains strong contacts with his family and law-abiding friends, and takes as his standard of behaviour the rules of the prison administration. The 'politician' or *pseudo-social* prisoner shifts his frame of reference back and forth from staff to inmate norms, and shows great skill in manipulating both groups. The 'outlaw' or *asocial* inmate lacks the ability to identify with either the staff or other inmates; he is in 'perpetual anarchistic rebellion against both inmate and staff normative systems, and against affective involvements in general'.[15] Finally, the 'ding' role is occupied by a miscellaneous category of unstable and unpredictable inmates who tend to be shunned by other inmates – although this category has not been used much by Schrag or his associates in subsequent research.

Origins and maintenance of the inmate culture What is the origin of the inmate culture, and of the code which is its central feature? Two different explanations have been advanced. On the one hand, it has been argued – by Cressey and Irwin,[16] among others – that the values of the inmate social system are mainly those of a criminal subculture to which most prisoners belong before entering prison, and which they bring into the institution with them. On this view, prisoners' allegiance to the inmate code, and their opposition to the authority of the prison staff, merely reflect the anti-social values which led them to commit crimes in the first place.

220

Figure 8:1 Percentages of inmates thinking that most of their fellow inmates approved anti-staff behaviour (see page 223) in four types of Scandinavian penal institution.

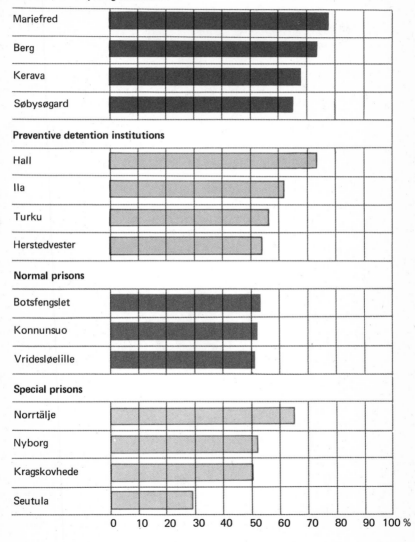

This theory is consistent with the evidence (to be discussed further on page 230) of differences in prison behaviour and attitudes among different types of offender, and with the cross-cultural differences mentioned earlier. It is important to note, however, that the inmate code, as it is usually described, does not really endorse *deviant* values. Instead, it stresses such things as loyalty, unselfishness and trustworthiness, as well as courage and self-sufficiency (being 'right'), which are approved by most social groups. The norms of the group to which loyalty, etc., are to be shown conflict, of course, with those of legitimate society; but this does not mean that the values of the inmate group are 'anti-social' in any other sense.

The second theory holds that certain features of imprisonment – especially in maximum-security prisons – are primarily responsible for the emergence and maintenance of the inmate code. Sykes,[17] Wheeler[18] and others have argued that the inmate code serves primarily to mitigate the pains of imprisonment – the deprivation of liberty, possessions, security, adult status and normal sexual relations – which prisoners experience. On this theory the maxims of the inmate code, which prescribe non-cooperation with prison staff and loyalty to inmate interests, have a cohesive function for the inmates. Sykes and Messinger[19] have claimed that:

As a population of prisoners moves towards a state of mutual antagonism, then, the many problems of prison life become more acute. On the other hand, *as a population of prisoners moves in the direction of solidarity, as demanded by the inmate code, the pains of imprisonment become less severe.* ... A cohesive inmate society provides the prisoner with a meaningful social group with which he can identify himself and which will support him in his struggles against his condemners.

In a somewhat similar vein, McCorkle and Korn[20] suggest that the major problems with which the inmate social system attempts to cope centre around the rejection of the prisoner by society: the code enables the prisoner to 'reject his rejectors' and thus avoid the devastating psychological effects of being an outcast, isolated from the free community. Thus the consensus among experienced observers is that the inmate social system, and the prisoners' acceptance of its norms and values, are at least in part a response to the experience of imprisonment; they are not merely manifestations of a criminal culture existing outside the prison. One empirical study aimed at settling this issue has been carried out in the United States, by the Tittles,[21] who investigated prisoners' acceptance of the inmate code by means of an attitude test, and related the results to the prisoners' previous careers, length of time served, and reported difficulty in adjusting to life in the institution (actually a secure hospital to which narcotic addicts were confined by court order). Though the results of this study are inconclusive – since the authors do not adequately control the possible effect of previous prison sentences – it does lend some support to the 'pains of imprisonment' theory of the inmate code, i.e. the view that it is a consequence of the conditions of imprisonment rather than merely a reflection of general anti-social attitudes among prisoners. There was some association between a high degree of acceptance of the inmate code, and a low degree of reported difficulty in adjusting to the regime of the institution.

However, somewhat different results were obtained by Cline,[22] in a study of fifteen Scandinavian penal institutions. Inmates in these institutions were given three hypothetical examples of behaviour indicating opposition to the staff and official rules of the institution, and were asked to estimate the percentage of their fellow-inmates who would approve of this behaviour. On the basis of responses, each institution was given an 'anti-staff social climate' score, consisting of the percentage of its inmates estimating that at least 75 per cent of their fellow-inmates approved of the 'anti-staff' behaviour in two or more of the three hypothetical examples. The results are shown in figure 8:1.

Further analysis showed that the institutions in which the inmates collectively had greater experience in crime tended to be the ones with the most severe anti-staff social climates – a finding which supports the 'direct importation' theory of the inmate culture. There was no support, however, for the 'pains of imprisonment' theory. The fifteen institutions were ranked according to the degree of social deprivation which their inmates were thought to experience (as measured by such things as restrictions on letters and visits, and permitted association between inmates); there was in fact a slight association between social deprivation and anti-staff climate, in the *opposite* direction from that predicted by the 'pains of imprisonment' theory. However, it may be that the measure of deprivation used in this study did not really reflect the pains of imprisonment most keenly felt by the inmates; it may also be that these are not in any case as severe, in either absolute or relative terms, as those suffered by inmates in most American penitentiaries.

To what extent does the inmate code actually control the behaviour of prison inmates? Most observers of American prisons report that inmates constantly pay lip service to the code's prescriptions: they *say* such things as 'never talk to a screw' and 'never rat on another con'. But do they actually observe these rules, and what happens if they do not? This question, like so many other questions about the experience of imprisonment, cannot now be answered by precise empirical evidence. But the consensus of experienced observers of prison life is that the inmate code is very often violated by prisoners, in a variety of ways. Clemmer, for example, described the social controls of the inmate community as 'only partially effective'; and while he claimed that 'a proportion' of the inmate population observed the precepts of the code, he gave many examples of violations of norms concerning informing, stealing from other inmates, and so on.

There are, no doubt, several reasons for this. One is probably the heterogeneous and constantly changing nature of the prison population. There are inevitably differences among the prisoners in age, social background, and degree of criminality; new inmates enter and old ones depart. While these factors may be minimised by sentencing policies or official allocation policies, they are seldom completely eliminated, so that complete consensus and co-operation among the prisoners is very unlikely. Another factor tending to discourage solidarity among prisoners is the presence of many individuals whose personalities are as disruptive in the prison community as in the free world. As Morris and Morris have pointed out, the prison

contains men who do not see that co-operation with other inmates might be to their advantage; men who are mentally unbalanced and incapable of any rational action; psychopathically greedy and selfish men; and men who are social outcasts in the outside world and retain that status in the inmate community. Behaviour among prisoners, far from representing a consistently cohesive reaction to the demands of the prison, oscillates about an uneasy internal equilibrium ... Thus at an ideological level 'all cons must stick together', but at the level of immediate reality solidarity depends upon the constellation of individual relationships.

Finally, there is the fact that there is a limited amount of close association and interaction among prisoners, in part because of official efforts to discourage it. In his study Clemmer classified the inmates of the Menard penitentiary according to the extent of their close association with other inmates. He found that 18 per cent were 'complete clique men', i.e. members of 'primary groups' of two or three men who were very close friends; 36 per cent were 'group men' who, while being friendly with a small group of other

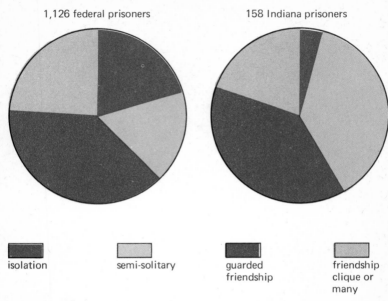

Figure 8:2 Patterns of friendship and isolation among two samples of American prisoners.

1,126 federal prisoners   158 Indiana prisoners

isolation   semi-solitary   guarded   friendship
                                          friendship   clique or
                                                           many

inmates, did not share close associations with any single group; 34 per cent were 'semi-solitary' men who were civil with other inmates, but never intimate with any of them; and three and a half per cent were 'complete solitary men' who kept entirely to themselves and shared nothing with other inmates. In his study of the US federal prisons Glaser found very similar results: 37 per cent of the inmates he interviewed stated that they tried to stay to themselves as much as possible, and the same proportion said they tried to know as many inmates as possible, but not be friendly with any of them (see figure 8:2). Relationships among prisoners are also governed by the physical constraints of prison life; men cannot usually choose their cells or cell-mates, and their friends may be distributed anywhere in the institution.

At first sight it seems paradoxical that prisoners should pay lip service to the solidarity implied by the maxims of the inmate code (such as 'never talk to a screw'), even though these norms are breached on many occasions. A possible explanation is that the inmates who do adhere most closely to the inmate code, and who are therefore the most pro-criminal and anti-staff in their orientation, are able to attain positions of high 'visibility' within the inmate social system, thereby giving a misleading impression to staff and other inmates alike of a culture which is uniformly anti-administration in its outlook. A sociometric study of prison inmates carried out by Schrag[23] showed that such men tended to be named by other inmates, to a disproportionate extent, as leaders; and as Cloward[24] found in a study of a military prison, inmates who in fact conform (or wish to conform) to socially acceptable values may nonetheless find it much easier to *say* that they agree with the anti-social norms and attitudes of leaders of the inmate community. Whatever the explanation, it is clear that prisoners' acceptance of the inmate code, and of the values implicit in the culture of the prison community, is far from complete; and that prisoners' behaviour often deviates from that prescribed by the code.

The concept of 'prisonization' How does the culture of the prison community impinge on the individual offender who is subjected to it? Basically, it seems clear that the new inmate must undergo a socialisation process just like that undergone by any new member of any group or culture: if he is not already familiar with them, he must learn at least some of the rules of the inmate community and he may also come to acquire many of the beliefs, attitudes and values of that community. Clemmer referred to this process as 'prisonization', which he defined as 'the taking on in greater or less degree of the folkways, mores, customs and general culture of the penitentiary.' Clemmer held that every man who enters prison becomes prisonised to some extent, owing to the existence of certain 'universal factors of prisonization':

Acceptance of an inferior rôle, accumulation of facts concerning the organisation of the prison, the development of somewhat new habits of eating, dressing, working, sleeping, the adoption of local language, the recognition that nothing is owed to the environment for the supplying of needs, and the eventual desire for a good job are aspects of prisonization which are operative for all inmates ... That is, even if no other factor of the prison culture touches the personality of an inmate of many years' residence, the influences of these universal factors are sufficient to make a man characteristic of the penal community and probably so disrupt his personality that a happy adjustment in any community becomes next to impossible.

In addition to these 'universal factors', Clemmer listed a number of other determinants of the extent to which a man became prisonised:

these included the length of his sentence, the stability of his pre-prison personality, his continuance of relationships with persons outside prison, his membership of 'primary groups', and his placement in work gangs and the cellhouse.

Clemmer also seems to have held two other ideas about the process of prisonisation, though he was not very explicit about either. First, he seems to have thought that prisonisation was a more or less linear process, so that the longer a prisoner's sentence, the more he would tend – *ceteris paribus* – to become prisonised. Secondly, though he did not simply identify prisonisation with an increased tendency toward recidivism, he seems to have thought that there was some relationship between them, and that men who became completely prisonised were much more likely to commit further offences after release from prison than men who did not. More recent research has cast doubt on both of these views; the first now seems pretty clearly incorrect, and the second is at least doubtful.

The first study to cast doubt on the idea that prisonisation is a linear process, increasing steadily with length of sentence, was carried out by Stanton Wheeler[18] at a reformatory in the western United States. Wheeler devised five hypothetical situations involving conflicts between inmates, or inmates and prison staff. Inmates were then asked to say whether they approved or disapproved of the behaviour of the inmates in each example. Wheeler then determined the proportion of inmates' responses to the questionnaire which conformed to official expectations of correct behaviour; and he analysed these responses according to the length of time the inmates had served, and the amount of time they had remaining to serve.

The first analysis strongly supported Clemmer's theory of prisonisation: the longer the inmate had been in the prison, the less likely he was to say that he approved of the officially 'correct' behaviour, and the more likely he was to assess the hypothetical situations in terms of the inmate code. But when time *left to be served* was taken into consideration, a very different picture emerged. Inmates in the early phase of their sentence (who had served less than six months) tended to conform to staff norms: whereas those in the middle phase (who had served six months or more, but had more than six months remaining to serve) were less likely to do so. But those in the late phase of their sentences (with less than six months to serve) appeared to shift back in the direction of conformity to staff norms, and, by implication, to accept the values of the inmate code *less* strongly

227

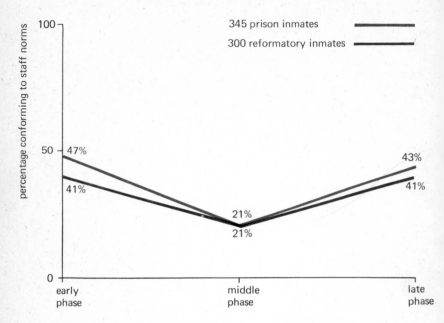

Figure 8:3 The 'U-shaped curve' of prisonisation.

percentage conforming to staff norms

100

345 prison inmates

300 reformatory inmates

50 — 47%

43%

41%

41%

21%

21%

0

early
phase

middle
phase

late
phase

than the middle-phase inmates. In other words, the pattern of conformity to staff norms appeared to be roughly U-shaped, as figure 8:3 (based on Wheeler's results) shows. This pattern was found to hold for recidivists as well as for first offenders, and for inmates having a high amount of contact with other inmates as well as for those having little such contact. Thus it appears that inmates tend to enter the prison with a relatively pro-social orientation, become progressively anti-social in their outlook into the middle phase of their sentences, but then undergo a further shift, back to conventional values, toward the end of their sentences. Very similar results have been found by a number of other researchers in penal institutions.

There are several conceivable explanations for this U-shaped pattern of attitude change, quite apart from the possibility – which cannot be completely ruled out – that prisoners may feel compelled to pretend to more 'pro-social' attitudes at the beginning and end of their sentences, than they actually feel. Perhaps the most plausible explanation is that suggested by Stratton:[25] namely that the prisoner's reference group (i.e. the group whose standard he tends to accept, whether or not he is a member of it) changes as he moves from one phase of his sentence to another. In the period immediately following his reception into prison, he still tends to look 'over the wall', and his attitudes still tend to be aligned with those of the legitimate community; in the middle of his sentence, when he is furthest away from the outside world, his reference group shifts to the inmate community, only to shift back again as he begins to think about and plan for his release from the prison. However this may be, it seems clear that the process of prisonisation is not a simple linear one, as Clemmer thought.

The experience of imprisonment and prisoners' after-conduct

But the finding that prisonisation is not a linear process, interesting and important as it is, leaves the more important question of the relation between prisonisation and recidivism completely unanswered. As we have noted, there is some reason to think that the values and norms of the inmate culture are a response to the experience of imprisonment, and are not merely a reflection of a general criminal subculture. Thus even if prisonisation – or, more precisely, the acquisition of attitudes opposed to the official norms of the prison – were a linear process, it would not necessarily lead to a 'deepening' of criminality, or an increased tendency to recidivism, as Clemmer seems to have thought. It may represent nothing more than a 'prison-specific', and thus purely transitory, adaptation – a sort of normative prison uniform; conceivably it may even be that for some prisoners this adaptation to the inmate community helps to prevent a deterioration in their ability to sustain relationships with others, and thus makes it less likely that they will relapse into crime after discharge.

What is needed, to investigate this question, is research which connects the prisoner's experiences inside the prison, with his conduct after discharge. No research of this kind has yet been done. But two studies, carried out by Garabedian[26] and Garrity[27] at a prison in the western United States, show how the subject might be investigated. Both of these studies make use of the prisoner typology developed by Schrag[14], according to which inmates are classified as 'right guys' (anti-social) 'square Johns' (pro-social), 'politicians'

229

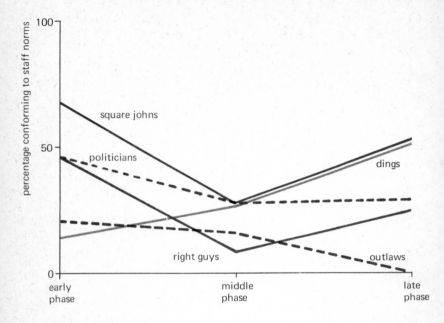

Figure 8:4 The 'U-shaped curve' of prisonisation for different prisoner types.

(pseudo-social), 'outlaws' (asocial), or 'dings' (see page 220).

Garabedian found that there were consistent differences between prison inmates of these types, not only in pre-prison factors (such as number of convictions and type of offence) but also in behaviour and experiences while in the institution such as participation in official training programmes and an inmate-sponsored 'therapy' group, use of leisure time, number of serious disciplinary charges, and reported contact with other prisoners. He also found that there were differences between inmates of the different types in their expressed conformity to staff norms. But it appeared (from evidence relating to a very small sample) that the U-shaped pattern of attitude change during sentence, found by Wheeler and others, was only displayed by the 'right guy' and 'square John' prisoners; the 'politicians', 'outlaws' and 'dings' apparently did not experience this shift away from, and then back to conventional values (see figure 8:4).

Garrity's research was concerned with the effects of different lengths of sentence on recidivism, and with the choice of an optimum

230

time for release on parole. He found that there were differences in the parole violation rates of both prison and reformatory inmates, classified according to the Schrag typology, according to the length of time served before parole. These differences – which are illustrated in figure 8:5 – were consistent with certain hypotheses which Garrity formulated, about the prisonisation of inmates of different types. For example, he hypothesised that the parole violation rates of the 'square John' inmates would be relatively low no matter how long the inmates' sentences, since they would not become prisonised; and that the failure rates of 'right guy' inmates would be higher than average after short sentences, but lower after longer sentences, since the longer sentences would tend to weaken these inmates' connections with criminal subcultures outside the prison.

At first sight, these two studies appear to link together the prison experiences and after-conduct of inmates of different types, so as to show something about the effects of the inmate social system on recidivism. Unfortunately, however, they do not, for two related reasons. The first is that Garabedian and Garrity used very different criteria for classifying prisoners according to the Schrag typology. Garabedian used the prisoners' responses to an attitude test to define the five types; whereas Garrity used a number of factors relating to the prisoners' social and criminal histories before beginning their sentences. Though Garabedian did investigate the pre-prison careers of the offenders in his sample, it is far from clear that the prisoners identified as 'square Johns', 'right guys', and so forth by his criteria would have been classified in the same way by Garrity's criteria.

Secondly, neither study was really designed to investigate the relations between different positions in the inmate social system, and attitude change or after-conduct. The argot expressions 'right guy', 'square John', 'politician' and 'outlaw' supposedly refer to *inmate social roles* – that is, roughly speaking, to patterns of behaviour which inmates are expected (in the sense of required) *by other inmates* to display. The methodology used by Schrag, in the original study in which these roles were identified, was consistent with this concept of role: 'politicians', 'outlaws' and so forth were identified on the basis of assessments made by a group of inmate 'judges'. Schrag then examined the records of the inmates thus identified, and found that there were, as a matter of fact, some rather vague correlations between these role-classifications and certain background variables: for instance, the 'right guy' tended to come from an urban slum,

231

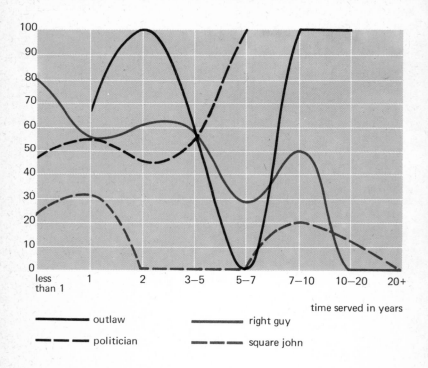

Figure 8:5 Parole violation rates of penitentiary inmates classified according to Schrag's typology, after sentences of different lengths.

and belong to a delinquent gang. But these correlations were not particularly strong ones, and Schrag's sample was a small one. In fact, there has never been an adequate investigation of the empirical relations between pre-prison factors (such as criminal career) and inmate social roles. Despite this, Garrity used mainly pre-prison factors to *classify* the prisoners in his study as 'right guys', 'square Johns', etc. He did not investigate the prisoners' social roles in the inmate community. A similar criticism applies to Garabedian's study. While he did investigate prisoners' behaviour, and changes in their attitudes, during their sentences, he also used their (expressed) attitudes to *classify* them as 'right guys', 'square Johns' and so on; this tells us nothing about the roles they may actually have occupied in the inmate community, or about the effects which those role relationships may have had on their attitudes.

There are many other theoretical and practical problems raised by this line of research. For example, how far do individuals typically accept the roles to which they are allocated by other inmates? What difference does it make to their attitudes and behaviour if they do not? If a man with the background attributes of the typical 'right guy' is mistakenly regarded by other inmates as an 'outlaw', how does he tend to react – and what are the consequences of this? Do inmates ever change social roles while in prison – if so, how, and what are the consequences of this? It is likely that the concepts 'right guy', 'square John', and so on, refer to 'ideal types'; Glaser and Stratton[28] found that while prisoners could classify some of their fellow-inmates according to Schrag's definitions, they inevitably disagreed if asked to classify all of them in this way. What, then, are the effects of the inmate social system on those prisoners who do not fall clearly into one of the types described by Schrag? At a practical level, it is obviously very difficult for a researcher to observe the process of role-allocation and its effects; indeed, it is very difficult for a researcher directly to observe any kind of interaction among inmates, or between inmates and staff, because the mere fact of his presence is likely to distort the processes which he wishes to observe. Of course, inmates can be interviewed about their experiences in prison; but it is likely to be difficult to decide how far the picture of the inmate social system which emerges from these interviews is an accurate one.

Nevertheless, the research summarised above has focused attention on a highly important factor in the institutional treatment of offenders, which had not previously received enough attention: namely, the impact on the offender of enforced relationships with other inmates during his sentence. Traditionally, it has been assumed that these relationships could only have an adverse effect on the reform or rehabilitation of the offender: the more criminal prisoners could only 'contaminate' the less criminal. But the work of Garabedian, Garrity and others suggests that this hypothesis is not necessarily correct; in fact, just the opposite may happen in some cases. For example, Sykes[2] has pointed out that for many inmates one of the 'pains' of imprisonment is the enforced association with other prisoners, who may be aggressive, violent and dangerous. It is at least conceivable that a non-violent thief or confidence trickster, being exposed in prison to the ruthless or psychopathic violence of a prisoner of the 'outlaw' type, may thereby become more law-abiding: he may think '*he* is a criminal, and *I* am not like that'. In recent years a number of writers have suggested that inmate groups can be deliberately used as a part of the 'treatment' process: group counselling, and other forms of so-called 'milieu therapy', are now in use in many penal institutions. But quite apart from these attempts to use – or manipulate – relationships between inmates, the impact of the inmate social system, and of informal contacts between prisoners, is clearly something which should be taken into account in future studies of the effectiveness of imprisonment.

It must be emphasised, however, that the first task for researchers in this field is to discover whether or not the experience of imprisonment makes any difference at all to the after-conduct of offenders who are subjected to it. Is the reconviction rate of any type of ex-prisoner significantly lower (or higher) than would be expected, given his social background, personality and criminal career before entering the prison? If not – if the prison has no lasting effect on the attitudes, values and behaviour of its inmates – then there is obviously no point in trying to discover which features of the experience of imprisonment are effective and which are not. Of course, even if follow-up studies do show that there are significant increases or reductions in the recidivism rates of ex-prisoners, when their base expectancies are taken into account, it must still be shown that these changes are due to something about the offender's experience while inside the institution, and not to events which take place after he is released – such as difficulties in finding work, or continued rejection by law-abiding members of society. In other words, a very great deal of difficult empirical research must still be done before criminologists can even begin to investigate the impact of the inmate social system on the criminality of prisoners.

234

Notes and references

1 How much hidden crime?

1 For example, D.J.West, *The young offender*, Harmondsworth: Penguin Books, (1967), E.Sutherland and D.Cressey, *Principles of criminology*, 7th ed, Chicago: Lippincott Co., (1966). Textbooks in all countries normally begin with their own national statistics. For an international comparison see K.O.Christiansen, *Report on the post-war trends of crime in selected European countries*, a supporting document submitted to the United States President's Commission on Law Enforcement and Administration of Justice, (1967). For a discussion of the difficulties involved in such comparisons see M.Ancel, Observations on the international comparison of criminal statistics, *Int. J. of Criminal Policy*, **1**, (1952), 41-8.

2 I.Anttila, The criminological significance of unregistered criminality, *Excerpta Criminologica*, **4**, (1964), 411-14.

3 R.A.Dentler, L.J.Monroe, B.Zamoff and R.Zamoff, *Five scales of juvenile misconduct*, The Center for Urban Education and Teachers College, Columbia University, (1966), Mimeo.

4 For example, H.Becker, *Outsiders*, Glencoe Ill.: The Free Press, (1963), H.Becker, ed., *The other side*, Glencoe Ill.: The Free Press, (1964).

5 T.Sellin and M.E.Wolfgang, *The measurement of delinquency*, New York: Wiley & Sons, (1964). See also L.T.Wilkins, New thinking in criminal statistics, *J. Crim. Law, Criminol. & Police Sci.*, **56**, (1965), 277-84.

6 L.Radzinowicz, The criminal in society, *J. Royal Soc. Arts*, **112**, (1964), 916-29. For estimates for Germany, see Bernard Wenner, *Die Latenz der Straftaten*, Schriftenreihe des Bundeskriminalamtes. Herausgeber: Bundeskriminalamt, Wiesbaden, (1957), **1**.

7 H.Jones, *Crime in a changing society*, Penguin Books, (1965), 18.

8 These figures, and those of Peijster are quoted in Sellin and Wolfgang, *op. cit.*, 37-9.

9 L.Radzinowicz, ed., *Sexual Offences*, London: Macmillan, (1959), 517-20.

10 See B.M.Dickens, *Abortion and the law*, London: Macgibbon and Kee, (1966). For other countries see, P.H.Gebhard, W.B.Pomeroy, C.E. Martin and C.V.Christenson, *Pregnancy, birth and abortion*. London: Heinemann, (1959), 215-47.

11 T.Sellin, *Research memorandum on crime in the depression*, Social Science Research Council, Bulletin 27: New York, (1937).

12 M.O.Cameron, *The booster and the snitch*, Glencoe, Ill.: The Free Press, (1964).

13 T. C. N. Gibbens and J. Prince, *Shoplifting*, London: ISTD, (1962).

14 A. J. Reiss, Jr., *Studies in crime and law enforcement in major metropolitan areas, Field Surveys III*, vol. 1, (The President's Commission on Law Enforcement and Administration of Justice), (1967), 84-102.

15 K. Elmhorn, Study on self-reported delinquency among school children in Stockholm. In K. O. Christiansen (ed.), *Scandinavian Studies in Criminology*, 1, London: Tavistock, (1965), 117-46.

16 M. L. Erickson and L. M. Empey, Court records, undetected delinquency and decision-making, *J. Crim. Law, Criminol. & Pol. Sci.*, **54**, (1963), 456-69. See also L. T. Empey and M. L. Erickson, Hidden delinquency and social status, *Social Forces*, **44**, (1966), 546-54.

17 F. J. Murphy, M. M. Shirley and H. L. Witmer, The incidence of hidden delinquency, *Amer. J. of Orthopsychiatry*, **16**, (1946), 686-96.

18 M. Gold, Undetected delinquent behaviour, *J. Research in Crime & Delinq.*, **3**, (1966), 27-46.

19 N. Christie, J. Andenaes and S. Skirbekk, A study of self-reported crime. In K. O. Christiansen, ed., *Scandinavian Studies in Criminology*, 1, (1965) 86-116.

20 These reports are published as *Field Surveys I, Field Surveys II, Field Surveys III*, vol. 1.

21 J. P. Martin, *Offenders as employees*, London: Macmillan, (1962), 114-19. There have been a number of German unpublished dissertations on 'the organisational containment of crimes committed by workers and public servants'. See, for example, Dieter Goos, *Die Kriminalität in Betrieben der Elektroindustrie in den Jahren 1955–1960* (Diss. Bonn), (1963). Quoted in F. H. McClintock, *Criminological and penological aspects of the dark figure of crime and criminality,* (1969), Sixth European Conference of Directors of Criminological Research Institutes. Council of Europe, Strasbourg. For a general essay on social toleration, see T. Morris, The social toleration of crime. In H. J. Klare, ed., *Changing concepts of crime and its treatment*, London: Pergamon Press, (1966).

22 B. M. Dickens, *op. cit.*, (1966).

23 M. E. Wolfgang, *Crimes of violence*, a supporting document submitted to the United States President's Commission on Law Enforcement and Administration of Justice, (1967), 33.

24 L. W. Shannon, Types and patterns of delinquency referral in a middle-sized city, *Brit. J. Criminol.*, **4**, (1963), 24-36.

25 F. H. McClintock, *Crimes of violence*, London: Macmillan, (1963), 66.

26 See J. Goldstein, Police discretion not to invoke the criminal process: low visibility decisions in the administration of justice, *Yale Law J.*, **69**, (1960), 543-94.

27 W. R. La Fave, *Arrest*, Boston: Little, Brown & Co., (1965). *Also*, The police and non-enforcement of the law, *Wisconsin Law Review*, Jan. 1962, 104-37.

28 D. J. Newman, *Conviction*, Boston: Little, Brown & Co., (1966), 155-9.

29 F. H. McClintock and E. Gibson, *Robbery in London,* London: Macmillan, (1961), 5.

30 A. D. Biderman and A. J. Reiss, On exploring the dark figure of crime, *Annals of the Amer. Acad. of Pol. & Soc. Sci.,* **374,** (1967), 1-15.

31 J. H. Skolnick, *Justice without trial,* John Wiley & Sons, (1966), esp. pp. 164-81.

32 In *Crimes of violence, op. cit.,* 73.

33 D. M. Downes, *The delinquent solution;* London: Routledge & Kegan Paul, (1966), 215.

34 *Op. cit.* 68.

35 A. D. Biderman, Social indicators and goals. In R. A. Bauer, ed., *Social Indicators,* Cambridge, Mass.: The MIT Press, (1966), 115. See 111-29.

36 J. I. Kitsuse and A. V. Cicourel, A note on the use of official statistics, *Social Problems,* **11,** (1963), 131-8.

2 Official and hidden delinquents

1 A. K. Cohen, *Delinquent boys: the culture of the gang,* Glencoe Ill.: The Free Press, (1955), 170-1.

2 J. S. Wallerstein and C. L. Wyle, Our lawabiding lawbreakers, *National Probation,* (1947), March-April, 107-12.

3 For example, T. P. Monohan, on the incidence of delinquency, *Social Forces,* **39,** (1960), 66-72; J. C. Ball and A. Simpson, The extent of recidivism among juvenile delinquents in a metropolitan area, *J. Res. in Crime & Delinq.,* **2,** (1965), 77-84. Ronald Christensen projected the percentage of the United States population with criminal arrest and conviction records. He estimated that about 28 per cent would be arrested by 18, and about half of these convicted. *See* President's Commission, *Task Force Report on Science and Technology,* Washington, D.C.: U.S. Government Printing Office, (1967), 216. A. Little, The 'prevalence' of recorded delinquency and recidivism in England and Wales, *Amer. Soc. Rev.,* **30,** (1965), 260-3; J. W. B. Douglas, *et al.,* Delinquency and social class, *Brit. J. Criminol.,* **6,** (1966), 294-320; F. H. McClintock and N. H. Avison, *Crime in England and Wales,* London: Heinemann, (1968), 190-4 (note the foreign bibliography on p. 190).

4 R. A. Dentler and L. J. Monroe, Social correlates of early adolescent theft, *Amer. Sociol. Review,* **26,** (1961), 733-43.

5 L. T. Empey and M. L. Erickson, Hidden delinquency and social status, *Social Forces,* **44,** (1966), 546-54. See also M. L. Erickson and L. T. Empey, Court records, undetected delinquency and decision making, *J. Crim. Law, Criminol. & Pol. Sci.,* **54,** (1963), 456-69.

6 I. Anttila and R. Jaakkola, *Unrecorded criminality in Finland,* Helsinki: Kriminologinen Tutkimuslaitos, (1966).

7 K. Elmhorn, Study in self-reported delinquency among school children in Stockholm. In K. O. Christiansen, ed., *Scandinavian Studies in Criminology* **1,** London: Tavistock, (1965), 117-46.

237

8 H.D.Willcock, *Deterrents and incentives to crime among youths aged 15 to 21 years*. Mimeo. (1966), Report and Tables prepared by the U.K. Government Social Survey.

9 W.A.Belson, *The extent of stealing by London boys and some of its origins*, reprint series of the Survey Research Centre, London School of Economics, No. 39 (1969), and *Advancement of Science*, **25,** No. 124 (Dec. 1968).

10 W.L.Slocum and C.L.Stone, Family culture patterns and delinquent-type behaviour, *Marriage and Family living*, **25,** (1963), 202-8.

11 J.F.Short, Jr. and F.I.Nye, Extent of unrecorded juvenile delinquency, *J. Crim. Law, Criminol. & Police Sci.*, **49,** (1958), 296-302.

12 R.Akers, Socio-economic status and delinquent behaviour: a retest, *J. Research in Crime & Delinq.*, **1,** (1964), 38-46.

13 N.Christie, J.Andenaes and S.Skirbekk, A study of self-reported crime. In K.O.Christiansen, ed., *Scandinavian Studies in Criminology*, **1,** London: Tavistock, (1965), 86-116.

14 K.Elmhorn, *op. cit*. In an institutional population studied in the USA girls were as frequently delinquent as boys and as versatile in their acts. This finding is probably due to the fact that girls are less frequently sent to institutions and only then when they are incorrigible. See Shirley Clarke, Similarities in components of female and male delinquency: implications for sex-role theory. In, W.C.Reckless and C.L.Newman, eds., *Interdisciplinary problems in criminology*, Columbus Ohio: American Society of Criminology, (1964), 217.

15 M.Gold, Undetected delinquent behaviour, *J. Research in Crime & Delinq.*, **3,** (1966), 27-46.

16 J.W.B.Douglas, *et. al., op. cit.*

17 A.Porterfield, *Youth in trouble*, Austin, Texas: New Pottisnam Foundation, (1946).

18 E.W.Vaz, Self-reported delinquency and socio-economic status, *Canadian J. of Corrections*, **8,** (1966), 20-7.

19 H.L.Voss, Socio-economic status and reported delinquent behaviour, *Social Problems*, **13,** (1966), 314-24.

20 W.R.Arnold, Continuities in research: scaling delinquent behaviour, *Social Problems*, **13,** (1965), 59-66.

21 L.M.Empey and M.L.Erickson, *op. cit.*

22 A.J.Reiss and A.L.Rhodes, The distribution of juvenile delinquency in the social class structure, *Amer. Soc. Rev.*, **26,** (1961), 720-32.

23 H.B.Gibson, Self-reported delinquency among schoolboys, and their attitudes to the police, *Brit. J. Social & Clinical Psychol.*, **6,** (1967), 168-73.

24 D.H.Hargreaves, *Social relations in a secondary school*, London: Routledge & Kegan Paul, (1967), 108-10.

25 F.H.McClintock and E.Gibson, *Robbery in London*, London: Macmillan, (1961), 89.

26 J.H.Skolnick, *Justice without trial*, New York: Wiley & Sons, (1966), ch. 6.

27 Reported in: D.Glaser, National goals and indicators for the reduction

of crime and delinquency, *Annals of the Amer. Acad. of Pol. & Soc. Sci.*, **371,** (1967), 104-26. See C. Kirkpatrick and E. Kanin, Male sex aggression on a University campus, *Amer. Soc. Rev.*, **22,** (1957), 52-8.

28 N. Christie *et al., op. cit.* See also N. Christie, *Hidden delinquency: some Scandinavian experiences,* Univ. of Cambridge, Institute of Criminology. Paper to Third National Conference on Research and Teaching in Criminology, (1968). Christie says: 'This all leads us to the point where it has to be admitted that our present studies on self-reported crime have the same principal weaknesses as the official crime statistics. We have exchanged the official system of registration for some social scientists' system of registration.'

29 M. Gold, *op. cit.,* 30.

30 See R. A. Dentler's remarks in R. H. Hardt and G. E. Bodine, *Development of self-report instruments in delinquency research,* Syracuse University: Youth Development Center, (1965), 18.

31 H. Forssman and C. F. Gentz, Kriminalitets-förekomsten hos presumtivt ostraffade. En enkätundersökning. *Nordisk Tidsskrift for Kriminalvidenskab,* **50,** (1962), 318-24. Quoted in N. Christie *et al., op. cit.,* 94. Using a completely different technique (card-sorting) W. A. Belson tested respondents again after an interval of one week and found an 88 per cent consistency in the ways the cards were sorted into the YES and NEVER boxes. See W. A. Belson, G. L. Millerson and P. J. Didcott, *The development of a procedure for eliciting information from boys about the nature and extent of their stealing.* London School of Economics: Survey Research Centre, (no date). Belson and his associates have developed the card-sorting plus interviewing technique furthest. The interviewer sits on one side of a screen and passes cards beneath it to the respondent who sorts them according to whether he admits the offences on the cards or not. The process has an elaborate system of checks and probes from the interviewer. McClintock has described the method as 'strongly resembling an ecclesiastical confessional'. See, F. H. McClintock, *Criminological and penological aspects of the dark figure of crime and criminality,* Strasbourg: Council of Europe, Sixth European Conference of Directors of Criminological Research Institutes, (1968).

32 R. A. Dentler, *Notes on the self-report technique in the study of juvenile misconduct,* (1963). Mimeo. On validity in general, *see* R. H. Hardt and G. E. Bodine, *op. cit.,* 19-25.

33 J. P. Clark and L. L. Tifft, Polygraph and interview validation of self-reported deviant behaviour, *Amer. Soc. Rev.,* **31,** (1966), 516-23.

34 J. S. Coleman, *The adolescent society,* Glencoe, Ill.: The Free Press, (1961), 16-17.

35 T. Sellin and M. E. Wolfgang, *The measurement of delinquency,* New York: Wiley & Sons, (1964). *See also* T. Sellin and M. E. Wolfgang, *Constructing an index of delinquency – a manual,* Philadelphia: Center of Criminological Research, Univ. of Pennsylvania, (1963).

36 R.A. Dentler, L.J. Monroe, B. Zamoff and R. Zamoff, *Five scales of juvenile misconduct,* The Center for Urban and Teachers Colleges, Columbia University. Mimeo. (1966).

37 W.R. La Fave, The police and non-enforcement of the law, Part 2, *Wisconsin Law Review,* (1962), 206, n. 113. See also W.R. La Fave *Arrest.* Boston: Little, Brown and Co., (1965), 139.

38 R.M. Terry, The screening of juvenile offenders, *J. Crim. Law, Criminol. & Police Sci.,* **58,** (1967), 173-81.

39 N. Goldman, *The differential selection of juvenile offenders for court appearance,* National Council on Crime and Delinquency, (1963).

40 J.Q. Wilson, The police and the delinquent in two cities. In S. Wheeler ed., *Controlling delinquents,* New York: Wiley & Sons, (1968), 9-30.

   See also J.Q. Wilson, *Varieties of police behaviour,* Cambridge Mass: Harvard Univ. Press, (1968), 83-139.

   For a Scandinavian study of police attitudes, see D. R. Cressey and E. Elgessem, The police and the administration of justice. In N. Christie, ed., *Scandinavian Studies in Criminology,* **2,** London: Tavistock, (1968), 53-72.

41 F.H. McClintock and N.H. Avison, *op. cit.,* 155-62.

42 Canada, Minister of Justice and Attorney General, *Juvenile delinquency in Canada,* The Report of the Department of Justice Committee on Juvenile Delinquency. Ottawa, (1965), 111.

43 H.L. Voss, Ethnic differentials in delinquency in Honolulu, *J. Crim., Law, Criminol. & Police Sci.,* **54,** (1963), 322.

44 W.R. La Fave, *op. cit.,* 206.

45 I. Piliavin and S. Briar, Police encounters with juveniles, *Amer. J. Sociol.,* **70,** (1964), 206-14.

46 W.R. La Fave, *op. cit.,* 207, n. 114.

47 M.O. Cameron, *The booster and the snitch,* Glencoe, Ill.: The Free Press, (1964).

48 J.H. Skolnick, *op. cit.,* 80-6.

49 J.D. Lohman and G.E. Misner, *The police and the community,* President's Commission on Law Enforcement and Administration of Justice, (1967), Field Survey IV, vol 1., 89, and 60-130; vol 2, 133-207. *See also* J.H. Skolnick, *The police and the urban ghetto,* Research contributions of the American Bar Foundation, No. 3, Chicago, Ill.: ABF, (1968), 3-9.

50 C. Werthman and I. Piliavin, Gang members and the police, In D. Bordua, ed., *The police: six sociological essays,* New York: Wiley & Sons, (1967), 72.

   This argument has been taken furthest by Aaron Cicourel who holds that 'the officers' preconstituted typifications and stock of knowledge at hand leads him to prejudice much of what he encounters' and 'official statistics reflect socially organized activities divorced from the sociological theories used retrospectively for explaining the same statistics'. See A. Cicourel, *The social organisation of juvenile justice,* New York: Wiley &

Sons, (1968), 67 and 37.
51 R.M.Terry, Discrimination in the handling of juvenile offenders by social-control agencies, *J. Research in Crime and Delinq.*, **4**, (1967), 218-30.

3 Subcultural and gang delinquency

1 J.F.Short, Jr., On gang delinquency and the nature of subcultures, in J.F.Short, Jr., ed., *Gang delinquency and delinquent subcultures*, New York: Harper and Row, (1968), 1–16.
2 *Ibid.*, 12.
3 F.W.Thrasher, *The gang*, Chicago: Univ. Press, (1960 reprint).
4 T.P.Morris, *The criminal area*, London: Routledge & Kegan Paul, (1958).
5 A.P.Jephcott and M.P.Carter, *The social background of delinquency*, Univ. Nottingham, (1954). Mimeo.
6 W.B.Miller, Lower class culture as a generating milieu of gang delinquency, *J. of Social Issues*, **14**, (1958), 5-19.
7 A.K.Cohen, *Delinquent boys: the culture of the gang*, Glencoe, Ill.: The Free Press, (1955).
8 R.A.Cloward and L.E.Ohlin, *Delinquency and opportunity*, London: Routledge & Kegan Paul, (1961).
9 J.M.Yinger, Contraculture and subculture, *Amer. Soc. Rev.*, **25**, (1960), 625-35.
10 A.K.Cohen, *op. cit.*, 31.
11 R.K.Merton, *Social theory and social structure*, Glencoe, Ill.: The Free Press, (1957), 131-94. See also R.K.Merton, Anomie, anomia, and social interaction: contexts of deviant behaviour. In M.B.Clinard, ed., *Anomie and deviant behaviour*, New York: The Free Press, (1964), 213-43.
12 R.A.Cloward and L.E.Ohlin, *op. cit.*, 7.
13 A.K.Cohen and J.F.Short, Jr., Research in delinquent subcultures, *J. of Social Issues*, **14**, (1968), 20-37.
14 D.Matza, *Delinquency and drift*, New York: Wiley & Sons, (1964).
15 G.M.Sykes and D.Matza, Techniques of neutralisation: a theory of delinquency, *Amer. Soc. Rev.*, **22**, (1957), 664-70.
16 D.Matza and G.M.Sykes, Juvenile delinquency and subterranean values, *Amer. Soc. Rev.*, **26**, (1961), 712-19.
17 A.K.Cohen, *op. cit.*, 173-4.
18 The work of Shaw and McKay, the Gluecks and others are all reviewed in: K.Sveri, Group activity. In K.O.Christiansen, ed., *Scandinavian Studies in Criminology*, **1**, London: Tavistock, (1965), 173-85. For a general review of the literature on groups and gangs, see, G.Geis, *Juvenile gangs*, President's Committee on Juvenile Delinquency and Youth Crime, (1965).
19 W.B.Miller, Theft behaviour in city gangs. In M.Klein, ed., *Juvenile gangs in context*, New Jersey: Prentice Hall, (1967), 25-37.
20 L.Yablonsky, *The violent gang*, New York: Macmillan, (1962), quotation from p. 7.

21 J. F. Short, Jr., and F. L. Strodtbeck, *Group process and gang delinquency*, Chicago: Univ. Press, (1965).

22 T. M. Gannon, Emergence of the defensive gang, *Federal Probation, 30*, No. 4, (1966), 44-8.

23 M. W. Klein and L. Y. Crawford, Groups, gangs and cohesiveness, *J. Research in Crime & Delinq., 4*, (1967), 63-75.

24 L. B. de Fleur, Delinquent gangs in cross-cultural perspective: the case of Cordoba, *J. Research in Crime and Delinq., 4*, (1967), 132-41.

25 J. Monod, Juvenile gangs in Paris: towards a structural analysis, *J. Research in Crime & Delinq., 4*, (1967), 142–65.

26 L. Yablonsky, *op. cit.*, 107.

27 L. R. Jansyn, Jr., Solidarity and delinquency in a street corner group, *Amer. Soc. Rev., 31*, (1966), 600-14.

28 P. D. Scott, Gangs and delinquent groups in London, *Brit. J. Delinq., 7*, (1956), 8-21.

29 D. M. Downes, *The delinquent solution*, London: Routledge & Kegan Paul, (1966), 195-254 (quotation, 199).

30 A large gang of sixty members has also been found in Paris, but this seems to have consisted of a large number of loosely-joined cliques of different ages pursuing different types of delinquent activity. E. W. Vaz., Juvenile gang delinquency in Paris, *Social Problems, 10*, (1962), 23-31.

31 J. Monod, *op. cit.*

32 I. Spergel, *Racketville, slumtown, haulberg*, Chicago: Univ. Press, (1964). See also I. Spergel, *Street gang work*, Reading, Mass.: Addison-Wesley Publ. Co., (1966).

33 I. Chein, *Narcotics, delinquency and social policy*, London: Tavistock (1964), 177-92.

34 J. F. Short, Jr. and F. L. Strodtbeck, *op. cit.*, 88-89.

35 W. B. Miller, Violent crimes in city gangs, *Annals of the Amer. Acad. of Pol. & Soc. Sci., 364*, (1966), 96-112. See also W. B. Miller, H. Geertz and H. S. G. Cutter, Aggression in a boys' street corner group. In J. F. Short, jr., ed., *op. cit.*, 52-78.

36 G. T. Robin, Gang member delinquency: its extent, sequence and typology. *J. Crim. Law, Criminol. & Pol. Sci., 55*, (1964), 55-69. See also G. T. Robin, Gang member delinquency in Philadelphia. In M. Klein, ed., *op. cit.*, 15-24.

37 M. Sherif and C. W. Sherif, Group processes and collective interaction in delinquent activities, *J. Research in Crime & Delinq., 4*, (1967), 43-62.

38 J. F. Short, Jr., and F. L. Strodtbeck, Why gangs fight. In J. F. Short, Jr., ed., *op. cit.*, 248.

39 C. Werthman and I. Piliavin, Gang members and the police. In D. Bordua, ed., *The police: six sociological essays*, New York: Wiley & Sons, (1967), 56-98. Also J. D. Lohman and G. E. Misner, *The police and the community*, Field Surveys IV, vol 1, 108-19, vol 2, 137-55. The President's Commission, (1967).

40 L.T.Wilkins, *Social deviance,* London: Tavistock, (1964), 45-104.

41 E.M.Lemert, *Human deviance, social problems, and social control,* New Jersey: Prentice Hall, (1967), 40-64.

42 J.F.Short, Jr., Gang delinquency and anomie. In M.B.Clinard, ed., *Anomie and deviant behaviour,* Glencoe, Ill.: The Free Press, (1964).

43 H.Schwendinger and J.Schwendinger, Delinquent stereotypes of probable victims. In M.Klein, ed., *op. cit.,* 91-105.

44 M.Klein, *Judgmental factors in specification of the structure of natural groups,* Univ. Southern California: Youth Studies Center, (1965). Mimeo.

45 N.L.Gerrard, The core member of the gang, *Brit. J. Crim.,* **4,** (1964), 361.

46 E.R.Rice and R.B.Christensen, *The juvenile gang: its structure, function and treatment as perceived by the gang leader,* Los Angeles County Probation Department, Research Office, Report No. 24 (undated).

47 B.Spiller, Delinquency and middle class goals, *J. Crim. Law, Criminol. & Police Sci.,* **56,** (1965), 463-78. 'All the behaviour categories, such as drinking, vandalism and fighting etc., were classified as to whether they were essentially lower class, middle class or culturally neutral (adolescent) … Lower class adolescent behaviour is characterised by free expression of feelings with intense loyalty to a corporate group (specifically to those displaying aggressive masculinity), and pronounced suspicion of outsiders, especially authority figures, resulting in refinement of conning techniques, and use-abuse and discard of property. Middle class adolescent behaviour is characterised by an acceptance of law-supportive institutions, a tendency to defer gratification, and an orientation to achievement by directed work effort, which result in a tendency to atomistic behaviour. Adolescent, or culturally neutral, behaviour is defined as pleasure-oriented behaviour such as sports, club activities, outings, dancing, dating, and the like.' (466). *See also,* M. Gold, *Status forces in delinquent boys,* Univ. of Mchigan: Institute of Social Research.

48 M.Sherif and C.Sherif., *op. cit.,* 59.

49 J.F.Short, Jr., In M.B.Clinard, ed., *op. cit. See also* R.R.Rivera and J.F.Short, Jr., Occupational goals: a comparative analysis, In M.W. Klein, ed., *op. cit.,* 70-90.

50 J.P.Clark and E.P.Wenninger, Goal orientations and illegal behaviour among juveniles, *Social Forces,* **42,** (1963), 49-59. See also J.R.Landis and F.R.Scarpitti, Perceptions regarding value orientations and legitimate opportunity: delinquents and non-delinquents, *Social Forces,* **44,** (1965), 83-91.

51 D.H.Hargreaves, *Social relations in a secondary school,* London: Routledge and Kegan Paul, (1967). *See also* D.E.Elliott, Delinquency, school attendance and drop out, *Social Problems,* **13,** (1966), 307-14.

52 B.Sugarman, Involvement in youth culture, academic achievement and conformity in school: an empirical study of London schoolboys, *Brit. J. Sociol.,* **18,** (1967), 151-64.

53 A.K.Cohen and J.F.Short, Jr., *op. cit.,* 28.

54 H.L. Myerhoff and B.G. Myerhoff, Field observations of middle class 'Gangs', *Social Forces*, **42**, (1964), 328-35.
55 E.W. Vaz, Juvenile delinquency in the middle class culture. In E.W. Vaz, ed., *Middle class juvenile delinquency*, New York: Harper and Row, (1967), 131-47. Also R.L. Chilton, Middle class delinquency and specific offense analysis. In E.W. Vaz, ed., *op. cit.*, 91-101.

4 The classification of crimes and criminals

 1 S. and E.T. Glueck, *Unraveling juvenile delinquency*, Cambridge, Mass.: Harvard Univ. Press, (1950).
 2 E. Lemert, An isolation and closure theory of naive check forgery, *Journal of Crim. Law, Criminol. & Pol. Sci.*, **44**, (1953), 296-307; *Also*, The behaviour of the systematic check forger, *Social Problems*, **6**, 141-9.
 3 E.H. Sutherland, *The professional thief*, Chicago: Univ. of Chicago Press, (1937).
 4 E.H. Sutherland, *White-collar crime*, New York: Dryden Press, (1950).
 5 D.R. Cressey, *Other people's money*, Glencoe, Ill.: The Free Press, (1953).
 6 W.W. Wattenberg, and J. Balistrieri, Automobile theft: a 'favoured group' delinquency, *Amer. J. of Sociology*, **57**, (1952), 575-9.
 7 M.B. Clinard and A.L. Wade, Toward the delineation of vandalism as a sub-type of juvenile delinquency, *Journal of Crim. Law, Criminol. & Pol. Sci.*, **48**, (1958), 493.
 8 C.E. Sullivan, D.J. Grant and M.Q. Grant, The development of interpersonal maturity: applications to delinquency, *Psychiatry*, **20**, (1957), 373-85.
 9 A.R. Lindesmith and H.W. Dunham, Some principles of criminal typology, *Social Forces*, **19**, (1941), 307-14.
10 H. Mayhew, *London labour and the London poor: Part IV: Those who will not work*, London, (1961).
11 J. Rich, Types of stealing, *Lancet*, ii, (1956), 496.
12 W.T. Williams and M.J. Lambert, Multivariate methods in plant ecology, *Journal of Ecology*, **47**, (1959), 83.
13 L.T. Wilkins and P. MacNaughton-Smith, New prediction and classification methods in criminology, *J. of Res. in Crime and Delinq.*, **1**, (1964), 19.
14 R.T. Lange, N.S. Stenhouse, and C.E. Offler, Experimental appraisal of certain procedures for the classification of data, *Australian J. of Biological Sci.*, **18**, (1965), 1189-205.
15 N. Goodman and J. Price, *Studies of female offenders*, Home Office Research Unit, Report No. 11, London: H.M.S.O., (1967).
16 P. MacNaughton-Smith, *Some statistical and other numerical techniques for classifying individuals*, Home Office Research Unit Report No. 6, London: H.M.S.O., (1966).
17 L. Hewitt and R.L. Jenkins, *Fundamental patterns of maladjustment: the dynamics of their origin*, Springfield, Ill.: State Printer, (1944).
18 E. Field, *Types of delinquency and home background. A validation study of*

Hewitt and Jenkins' hypothesis, Home Office Research Unit Report No. 10, London: H.M.S.O., (1967).

19 K. Friedlander, *The psycho-analytical approach to juvenile delinquency*, London: Routledge, (1947).

20 M. Argyle, A new approach to the classification of delinquents, with implications for treatment. In *Inquiries concerning types of treatment for types of offender*, California Department of Corrections, Monograph No. 4, (1961).

21 D. Gibbons, *Changing the lawbreaker*, Englewood Cliffs, New Jersey: Prentice-Hall, (1965). The quoted passage is on p. 40.

22 M. B. Clinard and E. T. Quinney, *Criminal behaviour systems: a typology*, New York: Holt, Rinehart and Winston, (1967).

23 J. Roebuck, *Criminal typology*, Springfield, Ill.: Chas. C. Thomas, (1965).

24 F. H. McClintock and E. Gibson, *Robbery in London*, London: Macmillan, (1961).

25 *Op. cit.*, note 21 above.

26 President's Commission: Task Force Report on Science and Technology, Washington: U.S. Govt. Printing Office, (1966).

27 Federal Bureau of Investigation, *Uniform Crime Reports*, Washington, D.C.: U.S. Govt. Printing Office, (1967).

28 R. A. Peterson, D. J. Pittman and P. O'Neal, Stabilities in deviance: A study of assaultive and non-assaultive offenders, *Journal of Crim. Law, Criminol. & Pol. Sci.*, **53**, (1962), 44-8.

29 G. Robin, Gang member typology: its extent, sequence and typology, *J. Crim. Law, Criminol. & Pol. Sci.*, **55**, (1963), 59.

30 L. Radzinowicz (ed.), *Sexual offences*, A report of the Cambridge Department of Criminal Science, London: Macmillan, (1957).

31 F. H. McClintock, *Crimes of violence*, London: Macmillan, (1961).

32 T. B. Hadden, *The development and administration of the English law of criminal fraud*, Unpublished Ph.D. thesis, University of Cambridge, (1967).

33 D. Glaser, *The effectiveness of a prison and parole system*, Indianapolis: Bobbs-Merrill, (1964), pp. 465-96.

34 N. Polsky, *Hustlers, beats and others*, Chicago: Aldine Press, (1967).

5 Understanding the sentencing process

1 D. A. Thomas, Sentencing – the basic principles, *Crim. Law Review*, (1967), 455-65, 503-25. *Also,* Theories of punishment in the Court of Criminal Appeal, *Modern Law Review*, **27**, 546-67, and, *Sentencing policy*, Cambridge Studies in Criminology, London: Heinemann, 1970.

2 United Nations, *Measures to combat recidivism (with particular reference to adverse conditions of detention pending trial and inequality in the administration of justice)*. Working paper prepared by the Secretariat, 3rd U.N. Congress on the Prevention of Crime and the Treatment of Offenders,

Stockholm, (1965).

3 L. W. Youngdahl, Remarks opening the sentencing Institute program, *Institute for sentencing for United States District Judges*, Denver, Colorado, (1964), *35. Federal Rules Decisions*, 389-90.

4 M. Grünhut, *Juvenile offenders before the courts*, Oxford: The Clarendon Press, (1956), 53-84.

5 K. W. Patchett and J. D. McClean, Decision making in juvenile cases, *Crim. Law Review*, (1965), 699-710.

6 F. J. Gaudet, The sentencing behaviour of the judge. In V. C. Branham and S. B. Kutash, eds., *Encyclopaedia of Criminology*, New York: Philosophical Library, (1949), 449-61.

7 E. Green, *Judicial attitudes in sentencing*, London: Macmillan, (1961), 16-19.

8 S. Shoham, Sentencing policy of criminal courts in Israel, *J. Crim. Law, Criminol. & Pol. Sci.*, **50**, (1959), 327-37. Shoham has informed us (in a personal communication) that the eight judges each received the following number of cases: 65, 90, 52, 34, 30, 33, 103, 159. Such small numbers make it likely that there were some differences between the case-loads of different judges, although Professor Shoham states that the cases 'were randomly allocated and we have tested their randomisation'.

9 E. Green, *op. cit.*, 69.

10 H. Mannheim, J. Spencer and G. Lynch, Magisterial policy in the London juvenile courts, *Brit. J. Delinq.*, **8**, (1957), 13-33, 119-38.

11 R. G. Hood, *Sentencing in magistrates' courts*, London: Stevens, (1962). For a critique of this study, see R. F. Sparks, Sentencing by magistrates: some facts of life. In P. Halmos, ed., *Sociological studies in the British penal services*, Keele: The Sociological Review Monograph, No. 9, 71-86.

12 J. E. Hall Williams, Sentencing in transition. In T. Grygier, *et. al.*, eds., *Criminology in transition*, London: Tavistock, (1965), 23-42.

13 E. Green, *op. cit.*, 102.

14 E. N. Levi, *An introduction to legal reasoning*, Chicago: Univ. of Chicago Press, (1949).

15 H. L. A. Hart, *The concept of law*, Oxford: The Clarendon Press, (1961), chap. VII. Also, Definition and theory in jurisprudence, *Proceedings of the Aristotelian Society*, Supplem. vol. 29, (1955), 258-64.

16 J. Hogarth, Sentencing research – some problems of design, *Brit. J. Criminol.*, **7**, (1967), 84-93.

17 C. Winick, I. Gerver and A. Blumberg, The psychology of judges. In H. Toch, ed., *Legal and criminal psychology*, New York: Holt, Rinehart and Winston, (1961), 121-45.

18 A. S. Blumberg, *Criminal justice*, Chicago: Quadrangle Books, (1967), 117 *et seq*. *See also*, A. B. Smith and A. S. Blumberg, The problem of objectivity in judicial decision-making, *Social Forces*, **46**, (1967), 96-105.

19 S. S. Nagel, Off the bench judicial attitudes. In G. Schubert, ed., *Judicial decision-making*, Glencoe, Ill.: The Free Press, (1963). See also, Judicial

backgrounds and criminal cases, *J. Crim. Law, Criminol. & Pol. Sci.,* **53,** (1962), 333-9. See also, S.C.Versele, Un sondage psychologique des équipes de probation, *Revue de Droit Pénal et de Criminologie (Belge),* **47,** (1967), 544-83.

20 S.Wheeler, *et al.,* Agents of delinquency control: a comparative analysis. In S.Wheeler, ed., *Controlling delinquents,* New York: Wiley & Sons, (1968), 31-60.

21 R.G.Hood, *Research on the sentencing of motoring offenders in magistrates' courts,* Cambridge: 2nd National Conference on Research and Teaching in Criminology, (1966), Mimeo.

22 L.T.Wilkins and A.Chandler, Confidence and competence in decision-making, *Brit. J. Criminol.,* **5,** (1965), 22-35.

23 R.M.Carter, The pre-sentence report and the decision-making process, *J. Research in Crime & Delinq.,* **4,** (1967), 203-11.

24 A.Blumberg, *op. cit.,* The first quotation is taken from pp. 67 and 160. The second is taken from 124-5 and 137.

25 R.M.Carter and L.T.Wilkins, Some factors in sentencing policy, *J. Crim. Law, Criminol. & Pol. Sci.,* **58,** (1967), 503-11.

6 Assessing the effectiveness of punishments and treatments

1 J.Andenaes, General prevention – illusion or reality? *J. of Crim. Law, Criminol. & Pol. Sci.,* **43,** (1952), 176-98. See also, The general preventive effects of punishment, *Univ. of Pennsylvania Law Review,* **114,** (1963), 949-83.

2 E.Durkheim, *De la division du travail social,* Paris: Alcan, (1893), 109; the phrase used is *'les consciences honnêtes'.*

3 D.Glaser, *The effectiveness of a prison and parole system,* Indianapolis, Indiana: Bobbs-Merrill, (1964), chap. IV.

4 T.Sellin and M.Wolfgang, *The measurement of delinquency,* New York: John Wiley & Sons, (1964).

5 P.Scott, Approved school success rates, *British J. of Criminology,* **4,** (1964), 525.

6 F.H.McClintock and E.Gibson, *Robbery in London,* London: Macmillan, (1961).

7 Cambridge Department of Criminal Science, *The results of probation,* London: Macmillan, (1958).

8 F.H.McClintock, *Attendance Centres,* London: Macmillan, (1961).

9 W.H.Hammond and E.Chayen, *Persistent criminals,* Home Office Research Unit Report No. 3, London: H.M.S.O. (1963).

10 C.F.Jesness, *The Fricot Ranch study,* Research Report No.47, State of California, Department of the Youth Authority, (1965).

11 H.Mannheim and L.T.Wilkins, *Prediction methods in relation to Borstal Training,* London: H.M.S.O., (1955).

12 F.H.McClintock, *Crimes of violence,* London: Macmillan, (1963).

13 President's Commission on Law Enforcement and Administration of

Justice, Task Force Report on Science and Technology, Washington: U.S.Govt. Printing Office, (1966), 60.

14 J.Havel and E.Sulka, *Special intensive parole unit*, Research Report No.3, Research Division, California Department of Corrections, Sacramento, (1962).

15 L.T.Wilkins, A small comparative study of the results of probation, *Brit. J. of Delinq.*, **8,** (1958), 201-9.

16 H. Mannheim and L.T.Wilkins, *op. cit.,* note 11 above.

17 T.C.N.Gibbens, D.Stafford-Clark, D.A.Pond, A follow-up study of criminal psychopaths, *Brit. J. of Delinq.*, **6,** (1956), 126-36. See also the same authors' paper, A follow-up study of criminal psychopaths, *Journal of Mental Science*, **105,** (1959), 108.

18 T.C.N.Gibbens, *Psychiatric studies of Borstal lads,* London: Oxford Univ. Press, (1963), chap.

19 R.G.Hood, *Homeless Borstal boys,* London: G. Bell & Sons, (1966).

20 D.Glaser, *op. cit.,* note 3 above, pp. 292-301.

21 P.MacNaughton-Smith, *Some statistical and other numerical methods for classifying individuals,* Home Office Research Unit Report No. 6, (1966), London: H.M.S.O.

22 D.V.Babst and J.W.Mannering, Probation vs. imprisonment for similar types of offenders – a comparison by subsequent violations, *J. of Res. in Crime and Delinq.*, **2,** (1965), 60.

23 J.B.Martin, The Saginaw project, *Crime and Delinquency,* **6,** (1960), 357.

24 *The sentence of the court. A handbook for sentencers,* London: H.M.S.O., (1969). Instead of constructing a prediction table, however, Hammond simply divided up his sample into sub-groups, using combinations of a few factors – such as age, current offence, number of previous convictions, and age at first conviction – which were known to be associated with reconviction in the sample as a whole. He then found the average reconviction rate for each of these sub-groups, and used these averages to compute 'expected' reconviction rates for the offenders in his sample who had been fined, discharged, put on probation, etc. He then compared these 'expected' rates with the actual reconviction rates for the different measures, to obtain an indication of the comparative effectiveness of these measures.

25 *See* the California Board of Corrections Probation Study, Final Report: Sacramento,(1965), 90-6.

26 G.F.Davis, A study of adult probation violation rates by means of the cohort approach, *J. of Crim. Law, Criminol. & Pol. Sci.,* **55,** (1964), 70.

27 F.H.McClintock, *op. cit.,* note 12 above.

28 J.D.Lohman, A.Wahl, and R.M.Carter, *The San Francisco project, Research Report No. 11: the intensive supervision caseload,* Berkeley, California: School of Criminology, Univ. of California, (1967).

29 G.Benson, Prediction methods and young prisoners, *Brit. J. of Delinq.*, **9,** (1959), 192-9.

30 C. Banks, Reconviction of young offenders. In G. W. Keeton and E. N. Schwarzenberger, eds., *Current Legal Problems*, **17**, (1964), 61.

31 H. A. Weeks, *Youthful offenders at Highfields,* Ann Arbor, Michigan: Univ. of Michigan Press, (1958).

32 B. M. Johnson, *An analysis of parole performance and of judgments of supervision in the parole research project,* Research Report No. 32, California Youth and Adult Corrections Agency. Sacramento, California, (1962).

33 P. F. C. Mueller, *Advanced release to parole.* Research Report No. 20, Research Division, California Department of Corrections, Sacramento, California, (1965).

34 E. Reimer and M. Warren, *Special intensive parole unit, Phase II: thirty-man caseload study,* California Department of Corrections, Division of Adult Paroles: Sacramento, (1958). See also the report for Phase I of this project, (1956).

35 K. Berntsen and K. O. Christiansen, A resocialisation experiment with short-term offenders, in K. O. Christiansen, *et al.,* eds., *Scandinavian Studies in Criminology, 1,* London: Tavistock, (1965), 35-54.

36 J. Havel and E. Sulka, *op. cit.,* note 14 above.

37 W. C. Bailey, Correctional outcome: an evaluation of 100 reports, *J. of Crim. Law, Criminol. & Pol. Sci.,* **57,** (1966), 153.

7 Interaction between type of treatment and type of offender

1 J. D. Grant and M. Q. Grant, A group dynamics approach to the treatment of nonconformists in the navy, *Annals of the Amer. Acad. of Political & Social Sci.,* **322,** (1959), 126.

2 C. E. Sullivan, J. D. Grant and M. Q. Grant, The development of interpersonal maturity: applications to delinquency, *Psychiatry,* **20,** (1957), 373.

3 D. Glaser, *The effectiveness of a prison and parole system,* Indianapolis, Indiana: Bobbs-Merrill, (1964).

4 L. T. Wilkins, Research methods in criminology: a critical note, *International Review of Criminal Policy,* **23,** (1965), 47.

5 D. M. Gottfredson and K. B. Ballard, *Interpersonal maturity measurement by the California personality inventory,* Report No. 1, Institute for the Study of Crime and Delinquency, Vacaville, California, (1963).

6 M. Q. Grant, Interactions between kinds of treatments and kinds of delinquents. A current trend in correctional research. In *Inquiries concerning kinds of treatment for kinds of delinquents,* California Board of Corrections, Monograph No. 2. Sacramento, California, (1961), 5.

7 S. Adams, Interaction between individual interview therapy and treatment amenability in older youth authority wards. In *Inquiries concerning kinds of treatment for kinds of delinquents, op. cit.,* note 6 above, (1961).

8 C. F. Jesness, *The Fricot Ranch study,* Research Report No. 47, California Youth Authority, Sacramento, California, (1965).

9 J. Havel, *SIPU-Phase 4: the parole outcome study*, Research Report No. 13, California Department of Corrections, Sacramento, California, (1965).

10 M. Q. Warren, Recent findings in the community treatment project. In *Correction in the community: alternatives to incarceration*, California Board of Corrections, Monograph No. 4, Sacramento, California, (1964), 40.

11 T. B. Palmer, *et al., Community treatment project: Research Report No. 9*, State of California Youth and Adult Correction Authority. Sacramento, California, (1969).

12 M. Q. Warren, T. B. Palmer, V. Neto and J. K. Turner, *Community treatment project: Research Report No. 7*. California Youth and Adult Correction Authority, Sacramento, California, (1966).

13 J. P. Conrad, *Crime and its correction*, London: Tavistock, (1965).

14 *Op. cit.*, note 5 above.

15 D. M. Gottfredson and K. B. Ballard, Jr., *op. cit.*, note 5 above.

16 R. F. Beverley, *The BGOS: an attempt at the objective measurement of levels of interpersonal maturity*, Research Report No. 40, California Department of the Youth Authority, Sacramento, California, (1965).

17 C. F. Jesness, *Redevelopment and revalidation of the Jesness Inventory*, Research report No. 35, California Youth Authority, Sacramento, California, (1963).

18 M. Davies, *The use of the Jesness inventory on a sample of British probationers*, Home Office Research Unit, Report No. 12, London: H.M.S.O., (1967). *See also* J. Mott, *The Jesness inventory: application to approved schoolboys*, Home Office Research Unit Report No. 13, London: H.M.S.O., (1969).

19 M. Q. Warren, T. B. Palmer, and J. K. Turner, *Community treatment project: Research Report No. 5*, California Youth and Adult Corrections Authority, Sacramento, California, (1964), 5. The authors add that some school systems, at first helpful to project agents, later grew to feel 'haunted' by them, and began to view their efforts in a negative light, (*loc. cit.*).

20 L. T. Empey, M. L. Erickson and Max C. Scott, *The Provo Experiment in Delinquency Rehabilitation*, 5th annual progress report (1963-4); same, The Provo experiment: evolution of a community program, in *Correction in the community*, State Board of Corrections: Sacramento, California, (1964), pp. 29-38. For an earlier description of this project see L. T. Empey and J. Rabow, The Provo experiment in delinquency rehabilitation, *American Sociological Review*, **26,** (1961), 679-96.

21 M. Q. Warren and T. B. Palmer, *op. cit.*, note 19 above.

22 For a description of this project see S. Folkard, *Probation research: a preliminary report*. Home Office Research Unit Report No. 7, London: H.M.S.O., (1966).

8 The impact of imprisonment

1 D. Glaser, *The effectiveness of a prison and parole system*, Indianapolis, Indiana: Bobbs-Merrill, (1963).

2 G. M. Sykes, *The society of captives*, Princeton, N.J.: Princeton Univ. Press, (1958).

3 D. R. Cressey, ed., *The prison: studies in institutional organization and change*, New York: Holt, Rinehart & Winston, (1961).

4 G. A. Grosser, ed., *Theoretical studies in the social organization of the prison*, New York: Social Science Research Council, (1960).

5 D. Clemmer, *The prison community*, Boston: Christopher Publishing Co. (1940).

6 E. Goffman, On the characteristics of total institutions, Chap. 1, in Cressey, ed. *The prison, op. cit.*, note 3 above.

7 O. Grusky, Organizational goals and the behaviour of informal leaders, *Amer. J. of Sociology*, **65**, (1959), 59.

8 B. B. Berk, Organizational goals and inmate organization, *Amer. J. of Sociology*, **71**, (1966), 522.

9 D. Street, R. Vinter and C. Perrow, *Organization for treatment*, New York: The Free Press, (1966).

10 H. Cline, in collaboration with S. Wheeler, The determinants of normative patterns in penal institutions. In N. Christie, ed., *Scandinavian Studies in Criminology*, **2**, London, Tavistock, (1968), 173.

11 J. Galtung, The social function of a prison, *Social Problems*, **6**, (1958), 127, 133.

12 T. Mathiesen, *The defences of the weak*, London: Tavistock, (1965).

13 T. Morris and P. Morris, *Pentonville*, London: Routledge, (1963).

14 C. Schrag, *Social types in a prison community*, unpublished M. A. thesis, Univ. of Washington. See also, C. Schrag, A preliminary criminal typology, *Pacific Sociological Review*, **4**, (1961), 12.

15 C. Schrag, Some foundations for a theory of corrections. In Cressey, ed., *The prison, op. cit.*, note 3 above.

16 J. Irwin and D. R. Cressey, Thieves, convicts and the inmate culture, *Social Problems*, **10**, (1962), 142.

17 G. Sykes, *op. cit.*, note 2 above.

18 S. Wheeler, Socialization in correctional communities, *Amer. Sociological Review*, **26**, (1961), 697.

19 G. Sykes and S. L. Messinger, The inmate social system. In Grosser, ed., *op. cit.*, note 4 above.

20 L. W. McCorkle and R. Korn, Resocialization within walls, *Annals of the Amer. Acad. of Political and Social Sci.*, **293**, (1954), 88.

21 C. R. Tittle and D. P. Tittle, Social organization of prisoners: an empirical test, *Social Forces*, **43**, (1964), 216.

22 H. Cline, in collaboration with S. Wheeler, *op. cit.*, note 10 above.

23 C. Schrag, Leadership among prison inmates, *Amer. Sociological Review*, **19**, (1954), 37.

24 R.A.Cloward. In H.L.Witmer, and R.Kotinsky, *New perspectives for research on juvenile delinquency*, Washington, D.C.: U.S.Govt Printing Office, (1955), 80-91.

25 J.G.Stratton, *The measurement of inmate change during imprisonment*, unpublished Ph.D. dissertation, Univ. of Illinois, (1963).

26 P.G.Garabedian, *Western penitentiary: a study in social organization.* Unpublished Ph.D. dissertation, Univ. of Washington, (1959). *See also*, Social roles in a correctional community, *J. of Crim. Law, Criminol. & Pol. Sci.*, **55**, (1964), 338; Social roles and the processes of socialization in the prison, *Social Problems,* **11**, (1963), 139.

27 D.G.Garrity, *The effects of length of incarceration upon parole adjustment and the estimation of optimum sentence,* unpublished Ph.D. dissertation, Univ. of Washington, (1958). *See also* D.L.Garrity, The prison as a rehabilitation agency. In Cressey, ed., *The prison, op. cit.* note 3 above.

28 D.Glaser and J.Stratton, Measuring inmate change in prison. In Cressey, ed., *The prison, op. cit.* note 3 above.

Acknowledgments for figures and tables

Figures and tables on the pages listed below were taken or adapted from the following sources (full references will be found in the Notes and references for each chapter):

16, 17 Sellin & Wolfgang (1964); 20, 21 Field Surveys III, vol. 1 (1967); 22, Elmhorn (1965); 24, 62 Erickson & Empey (1963); 26, 29 (top), 33, 35, 36 Field Surveys II (1967); 27, 40 *The Challenge of Crime in a Free Society*, Report of the President's Commision ... (1967); 29 (bottom) Field Surveys III, vol. 1; 41 McClintock & Gibson (1961); 44 Christiansen (1967); 48 Wallerstein & Wyle (1947); 49 Anttila & Jaakkola (1966); 50 Belson (1969); 52 Elmhorn (1965) and Gold (1966); 53 Short & Nye (1958); 56 Gold; 57 Douglas *et al.* (1966); 59 Hargreaves (1967); 60 Christie *et al.* (1965) and Anttila & Jaakkola; 72 Terry (1967); 73 McClintock & Avison (1968); 75 Goldman (1963); 88 (top) Downes (1966); 88 (bottom) Sveri (1965); 91 Yablonsky (1962); 92, 93, 94 Klein & Crawford (1967); 118 Rich (1956); 122 Goodman & Price (1967); 123 Hewitt & Jenkins (1944); 127 Clinard & Quinney (1967); 130 Roebuck (1965); 133 Gibbons (1965); 144, 148 Shoham (1959); 145 Gaudet (1949); 147, 149, 150 Green (1961); 153 Hood (1962); 162 Wheeler *et al.* (1968); 165 Carter (1967); 180 Havel & Sulka (1962); 183, 184 Mannheim & Wilkins (1955); 187 Wilkins (1958); 188 *The sentence of the court*, HMSO (1969); 198 Grant & Grant (1959); 200 Adams (1961); 204 Palmer (1969); 206 A.E. Bottoms & F.H.McClintock, *Research into Institutional Treatment of Young Offenders*, 3rd National Conference, Cambridge (1968), mimeo. & forthcoming book; 221 Cline & Wheeler (1968); 225 Clemmer (1940) & Glaser (1963); 228 Wheeler (1961); 230 Garabedian (1963); 232 Garrity (1958).

Index of Sources

(Numbers in italics refer to entries in the Notes and references)

254

Subject index

256